Leading the
TEACHER
INDUCTION
and
MENTORING
PROGRAM second edition

Leading the
TEACHER
INDUCTION
and
MENTORING
PROGRAM second edition

— Barry W. Sweeny —

A Joint Publication

CORWIN PRESS
A SAGE Publications Company
Thousand Oaks, CA 91320

NATIONAL ASSOCIATION
OF SECONDARY SCHOOL
PRINCIPALS
promoting excellence in middle and high school leadership

For information:

Corwin Press
A Sage Publications Company
2455 Teller Road
Thousand Oaks, California 91320
www.corwinpress.com

Sage Publications Ltd.
1 Oliver's Yard
55 City Road
London EC1Y 1SP
United Kingdom

Sage Publications India Pvt. Ltd.
B 1/I 1 Mohan Cooperative Industrial Area
Mathura Road, New Delhi 110 044
India

Sage Publications Asia-Pacific Pte. Ltd.
33 Pekin Street #02-01
Far East Square
Singapore 048763

Printed in the United States of America

Library of Congress Cataloging-in-Publication Data

Sweeny, Barry W.
Leading the teacher induction and mentoring program/Barry W. Sweeny.—2nd ed.
    p. cm.
Includes bibliographical references and index.
ISBN 978-1-4129-4460-1 (cloth)
ISBN 978-1-4129-4461-8 (pbk.)
    1. Teacher orientation—United States. 2. Mentoring in education—United States.
3. First-year teachers—Supervision of—United States. I. Title.

LB1731.4.S88 2008
371.102—dc22   2007014593

This book is printed on acid-free paper.

07 08 09 10 11 12 10 9 8 7 6 5 4 3 2 1

Acquisitions Editor:	Cathy Hernandez
Editorial Assistants:	Megan Bedell, Charline Wu
Production Editor:	Denise Santoyo
Copy Editor:	Susan Jarvis
Proofreader:	Dennis W. Webb
Typesetter:	C&M Digitals (P) Ltd.
Indexers:	Nara Wood and Kathleen Paparchontis
Cover Designer:	Scott Van Atta

Contents

List of Figures

Preface

What I stated in the first edition of this book is still true today: most of what has been written in this field has focused on helping the mentor and the new teacher. Very little has been written to guide the leaders of teacher mentoring and induction programs. The first edition was one of the few resources for leaders of programs. However, so much has changed in education since 2001 that this second edition must be more than a revision. With this in mind, I have greatly expanded the book to share all of the step-by-step, practical strategies that I have developed as a consultant and trainer. Program leaders will find a wealth of resources in this new edition.

In the past, most educational leaders who developed or led a mentoring and induction program did so out of a laudable desire to better support the initial success of novice teachers. Doing so is not only the right thing; research indicates that ensuring that success is an important means for attracting and retaining novice teachers (Fideler & Haselkorn, 1999), which provides significant cost savings.

If you want to develop a teacher induction and mentoring program to better support new teachers during their initial months and to improve their retention, you can count on this book to help you accomplish those goals. However, I suspect that the percentage of readers for whom these are their *only* goals is much smaller in 2006 than it was in 2001. Accountability pressures have necessitated that every mentoring and induction program must also clearly contribute to the goals of improving teaching and student achievement. This book is designed to serve exactly that purpose.

> Accountability pressures have necessitated that every mentoring and induction program must also clearly contribute to the goals of improving teaching and student achievement. This book is designed to serve exactly that purpose.

In this age of accountability, your work as an educator has likely become more challenging. One wonders whether policy makers have forgotten—or perhaps never knew—what every educator knows is true. Professional development to improve the learning and skills of educators is the *prerequisite* for improving students' learning and achievement. Sadly, some schools have been pressured to stop school improvement efforts and focus solely on instruction to improve test scores. From my personal perspective, this is a change for the worse! Effectively addressing these challenges is exactly why it is time for a new edition of this book to be published.

WHAT YOU WILL FIND IN THIS BOOK AND HOW IT IS ORGANIZED

The Introduction starts by setting out the fundamental premise on which this book is based. Next, "Mentoring Questions Leaders Want Answered" are presented. Both of these sections should be read to determine whether or not this book will effectively meet your needs. Finally, a section titled "Defining Mentoring, Induction, and Peer Coaching" will ensure that you grow beyond your current assumptions and understand all that is provided in the remainder of the book's discussion.

Chapter 1, "Getting Off to the Right Start," provides the background and conceptual basis for the rest of the book. Whether you need to design and implement a *new* program, or your intention is to learn how to improve an already *existing* program, you'll be excited by what you learn in this chapter.

Chapter 2 lays out the overall program design *process.*

Chapter 3 shows you how to design and develop an *induction program* so it functions as a high impact novice teacher support system.

Chapter 4 provides strategies for addressing a major challenge in developing induction programs—finding or making the *time* available for effective mentoring.

Chapter 5 leads you through the steps of designing the *mentoring program* so mentors have the support they need to achieve high levels of effectiveness. This chapter is packed with information about mentor recruitment, selection, and matching. In addition, dealing with mentoring mismatches and incentives for mentoring are given in-depth treatment.

Implementing the ideas in Chapters 1 through 5 will position you to lead the design and implementation of a powerful "high impact" mentoring and induction program. Then all the structures but one will be in place for your program to achieve its goals.

Chapter 6 is a comprehensive and practical activity-by-activity guide to powerful *mentor training.* I have provided a detailed model based on my own work to show how you too can design and deliver a high impact mentor training. As a result, your mentors will learn the skills and insights they need to effectively contribute to the program goals. Also, you will learn about Mentoring of Mentors, and how to plan and provide the high quality follow-up support that mentors *must have* to facilitate improved novice teacher performance.

In Chapter 7, you'll learn how to ensure that people do not perceive induction as one more thing to do, but instead see mentoring and induction as integral to the district's improvement process. The research shared in this chapter will help you gain crucial early support from decision makers. You will also learn how to design and lead an effective and practical program evaluation process that will improve and demonstrate your program's impact.

Finally, there are also three Resources sections to provide further assistance.

If you are responsible for increasing and demonstrating results created by your induction and mentoring program, this book is the closest thing to a "bible" you will find. It is written for induction and mentoring program leaders, not only as an immediate help and inspiration on your first reading, but as a resource to which you can return time after time and continue to find more help and inspiration.

Acknowledgments

My journey of rewriting the original *Leading the Teacher Induction and Mentoring Program* book to create a second, updated and expanded version started just after learning that Corwin Press had purchased the copyright for that book from the original publisher. Every step of this process with Corwin has been a great experience. What professionals! I am so grateful for the friendly, flexible, yet clear process it has been and for the wonderful people at Corwin with whom I have worked.

Chief among these great folks is my Acquisitions Editor, Cathy Hernandez, whose thoughtful, appreciative yet challenging assistance has been very helpful. She was the "face" of Corwin Press, working with and guiding me through some tough phases. Her Editorial Assistant, Charline Wu, has been so helpful as well, keeping close watch over many details of the process. Susan Jarvis, my copy editor, was a wonderful encourager and so helpful.

Reviewers are a special part of the process of writing. Mary Hasl is the Mentor Program Coordinator in Poudre School District, Fort Collins, Colorado. She bought and devoured the first edition and some of her amazing experiences thereafter are within these pages. She is a true mentor of mentors and she graciously agreed to review my revised manuscript.

I am grateful to the group of "blind" reviewers of the first edition who have helped me see the original work through their eyes and to do an even better job this second time. Thanks also to others who reviewed the manuscript for this revision, including my brother, Mark Sweeny. Not only were their reviews helpful in perfecting the book, but they were affirming. These good colleagues in the journey are such a blessing!

Thanks also to those who gave me permission to quote their writing, show their examples, and use materials from their websites. Educators are wonderful! All this additional material helped bring the text to life and made it even more practical and visually appealing.

Thanks must be offered for my terrific wife, Marilyn. During the entire process, she graciously handled so many other of our life's details so I could "keep writing." I love you, sweetheart! Finally, I give my thanks to my Creator God who gives me joyous and satisfying work to do each day, opportunities to serve others, the mind, skill and strength to do it all, an amazingly beautiful world in which to live, and a terrific, loving family. Amen.

PUBLISHER'S ACKNOWLEDGMENTS

Corwin Press gratefully acknowledges the contributions of the following reviewers:

Carol A. Bartell, Dean of the College of Education and Integrative Studies
California State Polytechnic University, Pomona, CA

Jason Fulmer, Induction Teacher Coach
Aiken County School District, Aiken, SC

Janice L. Hall, Associate Professor of Secondary Education
    and Director of Field Experiences
Utah State University, Logan, UT

Lori Helman, Assistant Professor of Curriculum and Instruction
University of Minnesota, Minneapolis, MN

Lisa Scherff, Assistant Professor of Secondary English Education
University of Alabama,Tuscaloosa, AL

Jay Scribner, Associate Professor of Educational Leadership and Policy Analysis
University of Missouri-Columbia, Columbus, MO

Vicki Seeger, Literacy Coach
Seaman Unified School District #345, Topeka, KS

Anne Smith, Education Research Analyst
U.S. Department of Education, Washington, DC

Brigitte Tennis, Head Teacher
Stella Schola Middle School, Redmond, WA

About the Author

 **Barry W. Sweeny** is President of Best Practice Resources, Inc., an independent educational consulting firm in Wheaton, Illinois. He has been a consultant, facilitator, trainer, and author since 1987, and a presenter and keynoter at dozens of conferences. Sweeny has trained thousands of mentors and administrators and helped develop or improve hundreds of programs in school districts, professional associations and collaboratives, universities, regional agencies, community and governmental agencies, and businesses all over the world. He is probably best known for his extensive list of mentor training and induction program publications, his mentoring website at www.teachermentors.com, and his role in founding the ASCD Mentoring Leadership and Resource Network in 1991, an international network at www.mentors.net. He is also a Director Emeritus of the International Mentoring Association.

Sweeny has also worked in school improvement, peer coaching, staff development, and performance-based teaching, learning, and assessment. Previously, he was an award-winning classroom teacher for twenty-two years, district staff developer and mentor program coordinator, and then the Manager of School and Program Development at two different Regional Offices of Education in Illinois. He was a president of the Illinois Staff Development Council and has served on or led six national and state-level commissions on teacher mentoring and induction.

Sweeny's specialty is development of teacher mentoring and induction programs and practices which result in high quality instruction and increased student learning. His "High Impact" model of induction and mentoring is known all over the world for accomplishing all the typical goals for supporting and guiding new teachers into the profession *and* for creating programs that help districts accomplish their strategic initiatives. "High Impact Mentoring and Induction" is the only program of its kind in North America. Barry Sweeny can be reached at sweenyb@sbcglobal.net.

Introduction

Until recently, mentor program designers have relied on common sense to guide their planning. After all, we have all been new teachers and know what they need. That may have been the case previously, but it is no longer so today. The increased accountability alone demands new approaches. The design of mentoring and induction programs is not so straightforward because *delivering results* is the major priority. *Only a highly effective program will do.* Just as teaching has become more complex and challenging, development of a high-impact program is neither as simple nor as intuitive as it once was. This book will help you successfully navigate these complexities and develop a mentoring and induction program that meets these challenges and delivers your desired results.

MENTORING QUESTIONS LEADERS WANT ANSWERED

This book will focus on answering leaders' most frequently asked questions regarding how to use mentoring and induction to help novice teachers *and* improve teacher and student performance. That is the purpose we all serve, and it is what we mean when we use that word "effective." Among their many questions are:

- What, besides mentoring, are the components of an effective induction program?
- How can I develop my school's induction and mentoring program so it will have a positive impact on student learning and achievement?
- What is the appropriate role of administrators in a mentoring program?
- How can mentoring support teachers and school districts in meeting new requirements for initial teacher certification?
- How can I locate the resources needed to support an effective induction program?
- How can I gain support for my program from decision makers?
- What kinds of leadership are needed in an induction program?
- What are the best options for training mentors and for providing incentives, support, and recognition for mentoring?
- How should our new teacher support program be evaluated and improved so it will be more effective?
- What are the proven, yet practical, best practices we should use so our program has the impact we seek?

Whether you are planning to develop a new induction program or are trying to refine an existing mentoring program to increase its impact, you must eventually address these and many other challenging questions. Furthermore, you must be sure your answers to these questions are aligned with your program's goals and that you do not create more problems than you solve. If you are intrigued by questions such as those stated above, this book will be very helpful.

DEFINING MENTORING, INDUCTION, AND PEER COACHING

For the sake of clarity, the following are the key terms I use in this book. Whether you use these terms makes no difference, but be sure that everyone in your school district understands *your* vocabulary.

Common Vocabulary for Uncommon Roles

- *Beginning educator:* A brand new educator who has little or no previous paid experience as an educator.
- *New teacher:* An educator with at least two or more years of paid recent professional education experience, but who has recently been hired by the district.
- *Protégé:* A beginning or new educator who is working with a mentor.
- *Mentor:* The title and status given to a person who assumes the primary responsibility for providing mentoring. The mentor is a more experienced, and frequently more senior, person who works in a similar location and has a similar level of job responsibility as their protégé.
- *Mentoring:* Mentoring is the complex developmental process that mentors use to support and guide their protégé through the necessary transitions that are part of learning how to be effective educators and career-long learners.
- *Team mentoring:* This approach to mentoring divides the tasks of mentoring among several veteran educators who share the responsibilities based on their individual strengths. Each contributes in different ways to the development and support of the protégé.
- *Induction:* The activities and processes necessary to successfully induct a novice teacher into the profession and develop a skilled professional.
- *Coaching:* The support for learning provided by a friend who uses observation, data collection, and descriptive, nonjudgmental reporting on specific requested behaviors and technical skills. The goal is to help someone assess their own patterns of behavior by looking at themselves through someone else's eyes. This prompts reflection, goal setting, and action to increase desired results. Coaching should include the beginner's observation and coaching of the mentor.
- *Peer* coaching is done between equally experienced persons. Therefore, the label *peer* coaching makes better sense when it is applied outside of or after mentoring relationships to extend the support for ongoing inquiry into best practices. Peer coaching may also include experienced persons who were not in mentoring, but who want to improve their own practice.

The process of developing an excellent, self-sufficient, but interdependent teacher is complex and multifaceted. That is why the processes of mentoring and induction take several years, talented leadership and insight, considerable training, and ongoing support to achieve their goals.

Induction is the "umbrella" label for the process of welcoming beginning educators to their new profession and preparing them to effectively assume the full responsibilities of the career. Those responsibilities include far more than effectively working with students, although that remains the core task. For all students to achieve at high levels, all educators must collectively apply their varied strengths in an ongoing schoolwide effort to meet the needs of an increasingly diverse student body. Effectively preparing beginning educators for success in that role requires a rich and coordinated mix of seven components. The first five components are

1. Orientation to the school, district, community, job expectations, and the curriculum

2. Staff development designed specifically for beginning teachers' needs

3. Peer support activities, necessary both for new educators and for the mentor's continued growth

4. Observation by new educators of the work of excellent, experienced colleagues, followed by analysis of their observations to learn from them (ideally, a mentor facilitates this process)

5. The provision of individualized support to beginning teachers. Mentors also guide planning and application in teaching of what protégés learn in the other induction program areas

In addition, professional teaching standards necessitate that induction includes two other components:

6. Professional development goals and plans based on a comparison of the protégé's current performance to the professional standards

7. Professional development portfolios, which must document involvement in professional development and improvement of practice

THE INCREASING IMPORTANCE OF MENTORING AND INDUCTION

It has always seemed logical to assign an experienced expert as the mentor for a beginner. Teachers especially know effective teaching is challenging work, requiring several years to learn fully. However, today mentoring has become much more than "the right thing." School districts that never assigned mentors now feel they must, and those that only assigned mentors and did little else now want the mentoring experience to dramatically improve the results of that process.

> Induction and mentoring are a compelling and unavoidable strategy that schools are deciding must be utilized to improve instruction and student learning.

THE COMPELLING RATIONALE FOR MENTORING AND INDUCTION

What happened to create such pressure for high impact mentoring and induction? Eleven crucial issues have surfaced that must be addressed because together they are very compelling.

The definitions for excellent teaching and student success have changed

Rather than preparing students for roles in an agrarian or industrial economy, today's schools need to prepare students for a twenty-first century information-based society. What we need now are teachers who successfully engage their students in problem solving, critical thinking, and discovery. In addition, with the advent of the No Child Left Behind Act of 2002, every U.S. student must achieve at high levels compared with the standards. However, few current teachers have observed the modeling of such student-centered teaching and learning.

New teachers have unique training needs

Training new teachers to improve student achievement requires a system that targets the unique and evolving needs of teachers new to the profession. Yet thirty years of efforts have shown that, by themselves, workshops are insufficient to improve teaching practices. For better results, we need to provide follow-up support in the teacher's classroom for guided practice and correction, problem solving, adaptation, and implementation of the training in work.

We need over two million new teachers in the next decade

The "baby boomers" who became teachers in the 1960s are now reaching retirement age. Some of our most experienced and gifted teachers are leaving without passing on their experience and wisdom. When this experience is not available to new teachers, they must start from "scratch" to learn the same lessons all over again. Mentoring allows us to capture and share the experience and wisdom that new teachers need and to honor those who serve as mentors for sharing their wisdom.

> Some of our most experienced and gifted teachers are leaving without passing on their experience and wisdom.

We retain only about half of the new teachers we hire

Beginning teachers are typically given the most challenging assignments. If left with little feedback or help, as many as 30 percent of novices leave in the first three years and 50 percent are gone after seven years. How can we meet the increasing demand for more and better teachers when we retain only half of the teachers who enter the profession?

Quality mentoring and induction retain as much as 96 percent of new teachers

Most new teachers who leave the profession do so because of a lack of support and because they feel unsuccessful as teachers. They chose the career because they wanted to make a difference in the lives of students, and they leave if they feel they cannot succeed in that. Mentoring ensures new teachers have the support and guidance they deserve to quickly learn how to positively impact the success of students. That translates into teachers who stay in teaching.

The cost of *not* retaining teachers is *more* than the cost of effective induction

The costs of teacher attrition are huge and include finding and recruiting the teachers we need, then orienting, training, supervising, and evaluating them. Other costs are lost administrator time and loss of momentum in school improvement when we have to start over. Recent research has shown that individual states are losing hundreds of millions of dollars a year to teacher attrition. Mentoring and induction are very cost-effective because they plug the leak and save money lost every year.

Many schools want to become communities where everyone succeeds as a learner

High impact mentoring and induction are powerful school improvement tools! Quality mentoring challenges traditional, outmoded norms and the superficial relationships of isolated professional practice. Mentored new teachers are not just oriented to the school, but can grow to become the kind of team-oriented teachers our students need. These novice teachers develop under collaborative norms in which adult learning is as frequent and expected as student learning. Mentoring provides the kind of professional relationships and the reflective and shared practice that characterize effective schools.

Not providing mentoring has a negative impact on the quality of teaching

Whether learning to teach within or without an induction program, the habits formed during the earliest years of a teacher's career lead to a disposition toward professional practice that endures throughout the teacher's career. A "trial and error" approach is ineffective and results in the adoption of coping mechanisms and teaching styles that are controlling and teacher-survival focused, rather than the student-centered, constructivist practices needed today.

Quality mentoring has a positive impact on new teacher performance

Research studies provide evidence of the positive impact of induction on the improvement of new teacher performance. Review of publication dates for these studies demonstrates we have known for a considerable time the negative impact of a trial and error approach to learning to teach, and the positive impact induction has on teacher quality.

> Research studies provide evidence of the positive impact of induction on the improvement of new teacher performance.

Quality mentoring improves the mentor's performance too

Mentors routinely report that they learn more than their protégés. This occurs for many reasons, including the need for mentors to consciously reflect on and examine their own practice as a part of the process of teaching their protégés what an expert teacher actually does. Mentors want to be effective models of excellence for their protégés, so they challenge themselves to always be at their best. Also, forming the questions that a mentor must ask the protégé causes the mentor to explore and evaluate his or her own thinking processes and decisions.

Schools are addressing the obstacle of time for effective mentoring and coaching

In traditional schools, time for adult learning competes with time for student learning. Student learning prevails, and little time is left for teacher improvement because it is not built into the school day. Since increased adult learning is the prerequisite for higher levels of student success, schools are rethinking their traditional use of professional time. Strategies such as block schedules, team planning time, and more time for mentoring and coaching are being implemented.

No wonder effective mentoring and induction have become so important! And no wonder this book is so important. It tells you exactly how to use mentoring and induction to cause increased teacher and student performance.

1

Getting Off to the Right Start

When I use the label "high impact" induction and mentoring, I refer to a program that works one relationship at a time to transform schools into true learning communities in which both educators and students perform at high levels. In these places, those who recently join the community are not just oriented and helped; they begin a career-long collaborative journey to become the kinds of teachers their students need in order to succeed.

In this chapter, I share a number of foundational concepts, models, and processes that you should consider before designing your program. With this foundation, the program you build will increase the performance of educators and students. However, any review of the induction and mentoring literature shows that the exciting results just described are not typical. This indicates that such programs are difficult to develop and sustain. This is true because most programs lack a solid foundation.

> Any review of the induction and mentoring literature shows the exciting results just described are not typical. This indicates that such programs are difficult to develop and sustain. This is true because most programs lack a solid foundation.

DIFFERENCES MAKE ALL THE DIFFERENCE

If I were to reduce all the best practices and learning I have gathered in this field to just one statement, it would be, "You must *be* different, if you want to *make* a difference." To make a big difference in *student success*, you must honor differences in *teaching* and create a different process for *learning* to teach. These three aspects are interconnected and must be addressed together. Of course, such comprehensive changes can lead to friction, discomfort, and disagreement. Nowhere is this discomfort more evident than when a cultural and performance improvement effort exists alongside the traditional egalitarian culture of schools. Traditionally, everyone acts as if all teachers are the same except for differences in teaching style. Yet how can we learn from the wonderful differences we each offer and also avoid the "sibling rivalry" and resulting ostracism that can occur when teachers are singled out as unique (Magee, 1999). This is a crucial question, since that is exactly what happens when a person is named as a "mentor." In order for teachers to offer themselves as resources for professional responsibilities like mentoring and to move beyond "just" teaching (Gusky & Peterson, 1996), there must be an acceptance of the often enormous differences among teachers. Otherwise, there is no basis for learning from and helping each other improve.

> Nowhere is this discomfort more evident than when a cultural and performance improvement effort exists alongside the traditional egalitarian culture of schools.

Nowhere are these differences more *useful* than in mentoring. They are the very things we look for when selecting and matching mentors to novice teachers, and they are the foundation for the expectation that considerable transfer of experience and professional learning will occur.

The differences between partners will challenge assumptions, lead to discoveries, and prompt professional growth for both of them. Without the differences, the new teacher's assumptions about the ability of all students to learn, the role of the teacher, and even the career of teaching remain those that were formed earlier as a student while observing traditional teaching. That is why effective mentoring can never really be a peer relationship.

Still, traditional school cultures reinforce "peer" relationships, and this can make mentors uncomfortable when they feel singled out for different status and use of time (Moller, paraphrased in Richardson, 1997). This dilemma (Bird, 1986) must be explicitly addressed in program design, and mentors need to be prepared during their mentor training to deal positively with it. People who are not involved in mentoring may be uncomfortable with teacher leadership, and these colleagues may make comments reflecting that discomfort. Responding positively to the discomfort can ultimately save a program from ineffectiveness because the mentor's role becomes too scary to undertake.

CRITICAL DISTINCTIONS

Clear vocabulary is a good starting point for learning to work with distinctions. For example, when coaching occurs *within mentoring* it is not *peer* coaching, although many programs use that term. The label "peer" seems imprecise when the job description ("teacher") may be the same, but there are several significant differences between the new and experienced teacher in a mentoring pair. The term *peer coaching* should be reserved to describe what occurs between two or more veterans who may have differing strengths, but whose years of experience are more similar. Those who choose labels such as "peer mentoring" or call mentor coaching "peer coaching" are usually trying to distinguish it from the supervision by an administrator who is the novice's evaluator. Find other terms to make these vital distinctions, such as differentiating between the process and purposes of coaching compared with evaluation. Figure 1.1 offers guidance on this. More strategies for dealing with differences and related challenges are offered later.

> When coaching occurs within mentoring, it is not peer coaching.

Figure 1.1   Clarifying the Critical Differences in Roles

Features	Mentor Coaching	Peer Coaching	Supervisory Evaluation
The focus of the observation	Set by the interests and needs of the teacher to be observed, often after some other activity that prompts discovery of a need to improve.	A mutual inquiry by two or more experienced educators into increased use of the best instructional practices in both parties' teaching.	Comparison of the teacher's skills with a model of excellent teaching or a set of teaching standards to determine minimal competency.
The direction of the focus	Start with ⟶ Protégé Mentor ⟵	Best Practices ↗ ↘ Protégé Mentor	Teacher ⟵ Evaluator
The goals of the activity	• To develop a more trusting and collegial professional relationship. • To develop reflective, analytical, and self-assessment skills in protégés and mentors. • To develop more effective teaching strategies. • To improve student learning and achievement.	• To develop a more trusting and collegial professional relationship. • To develop reflective, analytical, and self-assessment skills of both. • To develop more effective teaching strategies for both. • To improve student learning and achievement in both classrooms.	• To judge teacher competence for decisions about certification and continued employment. • To create focus and to apply pressure to increase teacher performance and accountability. • To improve student learning and achievement.
Observation initiated by	Mentor, first by invitation to the protégé to observe the mentor at work. Then, after comfort is established, mentor observation in the protégé's classroom.	Either teacher in the peer coaching pair.	The supervising administrator in response to legal and contractual requirements.
The paper trail and use of the observational data	Copies kept by both. Each looks for own data patterns. Mentor asks protégé reflective questions to teach how to self-assess, reflect, set PD goals, and plan.	Given to the teacher who was observed to analyze. Coach asks reflective questions to prompt teacher's analysis.	Evaluator analyzes the data and prescribes needed improvement. Papers go into personnel file as documentation of evaluation (teacher gets a copy.)

EFFECTIVE AT WHAT?
TREAT INDIVIDUALS INDIVIDUALLY

We Must Not Treat All Persons the Same

Although this sounds unfair, in fact it is *more* fair to treat people individually. For example, in new employee orientation, *everyone* needs to learn certain critical information about their new employer and organization. However, people who have never worked full-time in a role do not have the same experience and judgment as other "new" employees. Those who have raised families and/or are changing from another career or a different district have very diverse levels of experience and skills. All "new" employees must be treated as individuals.

Treating individuals individually is exactly what mentoring is all about. It is the best form of support for professional growth because it is customized to address the strengths and needs of *each* learner. However, there are a couple of variations from the one-to-one approach that are just as effective because they also "treat individuals individually."

A mentor can work with several protégés at a time and still be addressing each person's individual needs

> Mentors can economize on their use of time because the small group activity is individualized to the protégés' needs, even if not done with just one individual.

This works *if* the protégés need to learn the same thing at the same time. Such protégé small group learning activity still addresses each person's individual needs and readiness. In other words, mentors can economize on their use of time because the small group activity is *individualized* to the protégés' needs, even if not done with *just one individual.*

Meeting individual needs must continue in induction program trainings

A trainer may present information to a class of twenty-three people and still meet their individual learning needs. *When participants are at different levels* of prior knowledge or skill, the trainer needs to design instructional activities to allow people to join the learning sequence at different times.

Some participants may already have the needed information and just need help preparing a plan to organize that knowledge for implementation, while others may not yet have all the basic knowledge the class has, and need an extra step in the process to get them to the point where they are ready to join the class.

How can a program be designed to "treat individuals individually"? Is there a tool to help us easily collect the information we need and plan for each individual's learning?

> As we learn how to individualize for adults, we eventually discover what works for our students.

How can we possibly lead groups when everyone is at a different place and needing different instruction? In today's classrooms, we feel we have limited flexibility to restructure what we do to increase student learning. However, in *adult* professional development there is greater flexibility. Through effective induction and mentoring, we learn to differentiate our instruction for individual adult learners. As we learn how to individualize for adults, we eventually discover what works for our students.

WHAT RECENT RESEARCH SAYS HAPPENS IN MENTORING

Fundamental to the success of assigning experienced teachers to help inexperienced staff is the fact that mentors have already traveled far down the path of teacher development. The mentor has already learned a great deal of what a beginning teacher needs to learn.

Basically, mentors are asked to show new teachers the "right way to go," the "dead ends" to avoid, and the "express route" to an expert level of practice. The idea of a "path of teacher development" makes sense. In induction and mentoring, we focus on facilitating others' progression along that path of development. Bartell (1995) maintains that findings from the Californian induction studies showed teachers who were supported and effectively mentored became more effective sooner in their careers, and made a faster transition from just surviving to being successful. Ten years later, Bartell (2005) defined the path concept further, stating that the most effective induction programs were more concerned with moving teachers towards expert practice and high-quality teaching than simply with the "survival level" of teacher development. To help new teachers quickly attain high levels of practice, we need to know more about that "continuum of teacher development."

> "If you want your program to cause the professional development of teachers, what model of teacher development are you using to guide your work?"

USING A MODEL OF TEACHER DEVELOPMENT TO GUIDE PROGRAM AND PRACTICE

In my work as a mentoring and induction consultant, I often ask clients, "If you want your program to cause the professional development of teachers, what model of teacher development are you using to guide your work?" Rather than experimenting in the hope of discovering what causes professional growth, effective teacher development programs must be built from the start on solid research, tested theory, and expert practitioner wisdom. While some may consider such structured guidance unnecessary, my experience shows that many programs flounder because the leaders have relied on intuition rather than a research-based model of teacher development. These less effective programs typically include the following:

- New teachers attend several days of district orientation and training.
- New teachers attend required training on topics that research says new teachers need.
- Mentors are recruited, selected, provided with basic training, and matched to protégés.
- Surveys assess the success of mentoring and induction efforts.
- Novice teacher retention increases moderately.

When evaluating these programs, I usually find that novice teacher performance has improved only marginally and program leaders want to increase program impact and gain better results.

As a result of my work in mentor program evaluations, I know our instincts are an insufficient guide and can sometimes steer us *wrong!* There are clearly many more things we need to develop a high impact program.

> I know our instincts are an insufficient guide and can sometimes steer us wrong!

What is needed is to base program design and implementation, the conduct of program leaders, the mentor training, support, and program evaluation on a proven model of teacher development. In my work with induction programs and mentor and protégé development, I have found no better model than the Concerns-Based Adoption Model (CBAM).

In addition, I have been on an eighteen-year "best practice search" to discover what must be done to ensure that mentoring leads to improved performance and results. The

> The best practices I identified work effectively because, together, they facilitate teacher growth across the CBAM.

integration of that eighteen-year journey is the "High Impact" model I have developed and will share in this book. Over time, I have come to realize that the best practices I have identified work effectively because, together, they facilitate teacher growth across the CBAM. The CBAM is not just the model we need to use to grow mentors and protégés; it is the model on which we need to build every component of our program!

THE CONCERNS-BASED ADOPTION MODEL (CBAM)

The Concerns-Based Adoption Model (CBAM) is a very comprehensive teacher development model. We will use only the "Stages of Concern" from CBAM. It is the single most powerful and useful staff development model I know.

The Research & Development Center for Teaching at the University of Texas (Hord, Rutherford, Hulling-Austin, & Hall, 1987) analyzed the ineffective educational initiatives of the 1970s and found the change process always failed in the implementation stage. Further analysis revealed the following information:

- Learners go through a *predictable sequence of stages* as they hear about, learn, implement, build skill with, and master an innovation.
- Staff development programs to facilitate improvement must be based on *long-term* plans that provide *what learners need at each level* of their development and implementation.
- Staff development programs to facilitate improvement must support *individual adaptation* of innovations to each learner's setting and *integration* of the new knowledge and skills with the learner's existing strengths. They must "treat individuals individually!" Other researchers (e.g., Berlinger, 1988; Burden, 1990) have found developmental stage patterns similar to the CBAM.

The research was then used to develop a model that could lead to full adoption and implementation of educational innovations. The result was the Concerns-Based *Adoption* Model, which defines the steps needed for individuals to understand, adapt, and implement innovations to the point of mastery. This model has been validated by over twenty-five years of research in a wide variety of applications.

A person's "Stage of Concern" is identified by listening for clues in their comments and then comparing those statements to the CBAM Stages of Concern. By doing this, program leaders can know where individual learners are in the learning and implementation process, and can design interventions to address learner needs at that stage. Leaders also then know how to challenge and assist learners moving to the *next* level of development. Finally, collecting data about each learner's growth allows programs to document the levels of growth, diagnose development "bottlenecks," and design program improvements that deliver improved results.

THE CONCEPT FOR EACH CBAM STAGE OF CONCERN

Review Figure 1.2 for basic information about the CBAM stages of concern. Then read the following to learn more about how to distinguish the different levels and how to use the CBAM to effectively design and improve your program.

Figure 1.2　The CBAM Stages of Concern

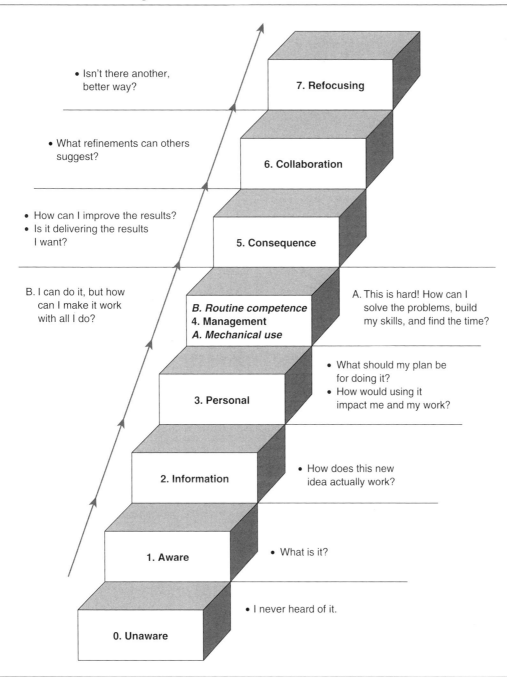

- Isn't there another, better way?

7. Refocusing

- What refinements can others suggest?

6. Collaboration

- How can I improve the results?
- Is it delivering the results I want?

5. Consequence

B. I can do it, but how can I make it work with all I do?

B. Routine competence
4. Management
A. Mechanical use

A. This is hard! How can I solve the problems, build my skills, and find the time?

- What should my plan be for doing it?
- How would using it impact me and my work?

3. Personal

- How does this new idea actually work?

2. Information

- What is it?

1. Aware

- I never heard of it.

0. Unaware

0. Unaware—The learner is largely *unaware* of a topic or concept and how to successfully complete related tasks. The learner is not even sure of all the questions that might need to be asked. This corresponds with Gordon's (2000) Unconsciously Unskilled level (Gordon, 2000, Figure 5.12), in which learners do not know what they do not know. For example, before reading the last couple of pages, were you previously aware of the CBAM? If so, you are at a higher Stage of Concern. If not, you too were at the Unaware level, but your reading will move you to the Information level.

1. Aware—The learner is just *acquainted with* the topic but does not know what is needed to successfully complete related tasks. In Gordon's (2000) model, this is the Consciously Unskilled level, where the learner knows what they do not know.

2. Information—The learner wants to *know* background information and understand the topic, but doesn't yet know all that's needed to plan and complete related tasks.

3. Personal—The learner has *sufficient information* and *conceptual* understanding of a task and how to do it, but has little or *no experience in doing* it. Learners at this stage focus on implications of the information and task for their own work. They want to know what is expected of them, and then they want to *plan* what they should do to implement what they know.

4. Management—The learner understands a task and his or her responsibilities for it, *has a plan* for using this knowledge, and *implementation has started.* The learner is focused on *building the skills* needed to *adequately* do the task.

A. At first, the focus is on just finishing the task. The process feels *mechanical* and takes the learner's full attention to complete correctly. In Gordon's (2000) model, this is "Consciously Skilled."

B. As the learner's skills at managing the task increase, it becomes more *routine* and the learner is more comfortable, confident, and competent doing it. This established routine means the activity no longer requires the learner's full attention to execute it properly. In Gordon's (2000) model, this is the Unconsciously Skilled level.

5. Consequence—The learner has sufficient skill to *competently* complete the task and now wants to increase the effectiveness of that work to *achieve better results.* At this stage, learners still try to do as much as they can *on their own,* and typically do not yet seek others' help.

6. Collaboration—The *results of the task are acceptable,* but not as high as needed. The learner *has done as much as possible* to *individually* improve results, and so seeks the advice of others to increase results. Sadly, the traditional structure of time use in schools rarely allows individuals to work and learn at this level, so typically it is not attained. In a recent article, DuFour (2003) wrote of the lack of collaboration in schools, saying that it "puts student achievement on a starvation diet." CBAM shows that collaboration is needed to attain the most effective level of practice.

7. Refocusing—The learner has mastered a task and easily produces a high level of results. Since even better results are not currently possible, this learner seeks and is ready for *a new task,* strategy, or responsibility which might offer even better results.

Note that Gordon's (2000) model helps us understand cognitive levels during development, but it is not as discriminating as the CBAM regarding subtle changes at high levels of practice. However, we will consider Gordon's model again in Chapter 6 when discussing new teacher thinking.

A Practice Exercise

Not only is it crucial that you understand the CBAM, it is a vital step in preparing yourself to understand and be able to use much of the rest of this book. I suggest that you practice it by completing the following activity:

Figure 1.3   CBAM Stages of Concern Practice Activity

Once you have read and understood the text description of each of the CBAM Stages of Concern, use this practice chart to try to write the six stages from memory, without referring to the text. The first step is already completed for you.

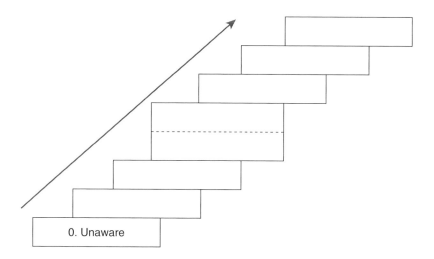

0. Unaware

When your memory list of the Stages of Concern is finished, follow the directions in the text for the next step.

1. Using a *copy* of Figure 1.3 and your *memory* of CBAM, write in order the seven steps of the CBAM Stages of Concern, starting at the bottom with "Unaware" (already done for you) and working up.

2. When you have completed the list to the best of your memory, compare it with Figure 1.2.

3. Mark your version of the steps with the numbers of the actual step in the model.

4. Notice whether you got any stage out of order or forgot any, which tells you the information you need to reread for better understanding. Then take the memory test again. In CBAM language, what you just did was check to see whether you have all the *information* you need to move to *implementation*.

We'll reference the CBAM throughout this book. Watch for the CBAM Steps icon in the margin.

ASSESSING AND USING DATA ON NEW TEACHER NEEDS

Each new educator has distinct needs at each stage of his or her development. To start planning your work, you need the following information for each new teacher regarding each potential learning topic:

1. What is the expected performance for the new teacher? (a standard)

2. What knowledge and skills does he or she already have? (current level)

3. What does he or she need to learn? (gap between current and standard)

4. What problems are obstacles to his or her further growth?

Question one is answered by our professional and governmental agencies. Question two is the focus of your needs assessment. Question three is answered when you compare the standard and the answers to question two. Question four is also answered by the need assessment. Remove these obstacles to create growth.

When you have obtained the answers to these questions, record this "baseline" data and your specific conclusions for later use.

Specifically, the way you can best answer these questions is through use of the CBAM Stages of Concern. First, base the design of your need assessment on CBAM, and second, display the response data on the Stages of Concern. The first action makes the second one easy. Step-by-step processes for doing this are outlined in Chapter 3.

In addition to your assessment of needs, other sources of crucial information are:

- The research on what beginning teachers need
- Your own experience as a beginning teacher
- Principals' and other experienced educators' views of what new teachers need
- What the new teachers themselves say they need

THE NEEDS ASSESSMENT PROCESS

The seven steps of the needs assessment process are described on the following pages.

1. Examine the Research on Needs of Novice Teachers

I recommend that you begin with the seminal work of Simon Veenman (1984), who studied *un*supported beginning teachers, and Sandra Odell (1986), who studied beginning teachers who *were* supported. While the findings of these studies are striking, a comparison of them is even more revealing! Both studies are "meta-analyses," meaning the researcher collected a large number of studies on the topic, compared all the findings and reached conclusions based on the patterns found. This powerful method tends to "average out" unusual or atypical findings that will not occur in most circumstances.

Veenman reviewed eighty-three research studies of organizations with *no support programs* or mentoring for novice employees. His findings are shown in Figure 1.4. Odell completed another meta-analysis. Her 1986 findings are shown in Figure 1.5. Remember, this analysis was of new teacher needs when they had received a year of support. There is obviously a big difference in the two studies that shows the power of induction to improve teachers!

In the "no support" study, new teachers continue to struggle with class management and their own survival even after one year. Concerns for *student* success are far down this list. In the "support provided" studies, new teachers have moved past concern for their own survival to the higher Stage of Concern for the effectiveness of their instruction and their students' success. According to Odell (1986), schools can help reduce their discipline problems by giving new teachers structured support in their first year of teaching; the result of this is that new teachers are able to focus on students' instructional needs—just as experienced teachers do.

Figure 1.4   The Perceived Needs of Beginning Teachers: Veenman's 1984 Meta-Analysis

Perceived Problem	Frequency = # out of 83
• Classroom discipline	77
• Motivating students	48
• Dealing with individual differences	43
• Assessing students' work	31
• Relationships with parents	27
• Organization of class work	27
• Insufficient materials and supplies	27
• Dealing with problems of individual student learning	26
• Heavy teaching load, insufficient preparation time	25
• Relations with colleagues	24
• Planning of lessons and school days	22
• Effective use of different teaching methods	20
• Awareness of school policies and roles	19
• Determining learning level of students	16
• Knowledge of subject matter	15
• Burden of clerical work	15
• Relations with principals/administrators	15
• Inadequate school equipment	14
• Dealing with slow learners	13
• Dealing with students of different cultures or backgrounds	12
• Effective use of textbooks and curriculum guides	11
• Lack of spare time	10
• Inadequate guidance and support	9
• Large class size	8

These findings are from a huge meta-analysis of eighty-three separate mentoring research studies that was done by Simon Veenman (1984). He studied settings where beginning teachers had no formal system of support, so *be careful* about the situations to which you apply this information.

Figure 1.5   The Perceived Needs of Beginning Teachers: Sandra Odell's Research, 1986

Perceived Problem	Rank Order of Needs
• Ideas for better instruction	1
• Personal and emotional support	2
• Advice on locating and accessing resources and materials for teaching	3
• Information on school and district policies and procedures	4
• Ideas for additional techniques on classroom management.	5

This research and the *differences* can help you gain early program support. What school doesn't want teachers focused on student success? However, there are three cautions concerning use of this research:

- Be cautious regarding your own assumptions about the timing for targeting these needs with induction program components. The CBAM tells us that the list of topics and the protégé's development level on each topic change over time.

- Research is conducted in context. Study dates and other details should be considered when planning to use data. In the mid-1980s, topics like standards and state testing were not as significant as they are in the current educational environment.
- As significant as this research is, it may be useful only in gaining *initial* support for an induction program. That support is unlikely to last more than two or three years. You will also need your own local needs assessment and results replicating those of these studies.

2. First Assess to Discover Priority Training Topics

Do *not* use the CBAM to determine what training topics are someone's priority. Its value lies in indicating a person's level of development for a specific topic.

- Use an assessment such as Figure 1.6, New Teacher Topical Needs Assessment, which is built from research such as Veenman's (1984), but which also includes current topics of concern such as teaching standards, student learning standards, the focus on state assessment scores, and so on.
- Limit the assessment to one side of a page if possible, and group the items by similar topics. Add a 1–5 scale, labels for what those numbers represent, and a return due date.
- Mail one to each protégé using the schedule described in step 6 below.
- After tallying responses, rank order the topics with greatest interest first.
- Remember, the rank order tells you what protégés *perceive* at that time to be their biggest need and importance. Use that data with a bit of flexibility. For example, you may know that because of an upcoming state test, a topic that was rated as a low priority actually needs to be a higher priority at a certain time. Of course, you should go ahead and schedule training on that topic. Just realize as you plan a training that protégés may be on the lowest stage, "Unaware."

3. Once You Know Topic Priorities, Assess for CBAM Stages for Each Topic

Trainers should design a one-page needs assessment so one or two items reflect each Stage of Concern for the topic. About two weeks before the training, send that assessment to enrollees to determine their level of knowledge, skill, and experience with the training topic. Don't do this too far in advance since protégés are growing and you want current needs to be the basis for your plans. Details about how to do this are provided in Chapter 3 under "Protégé Training."

4. Design a Local Needs Assessment to Allow Comparisons

Don't assess only what beginners *perceive* they need at *one* moment. The assessment should tell you other things you need to know, such as whether or not educator perceptions change over time. Other questions you need to answer require comparisons of data from different sources. You need to compare factors such as

- What *new but experienced* staff know and can do versus *novice* staff
- What trainees know and can do before versus after a training or development process

Figure 1.6   New Teacher Topical Needs Assessment

The Induction Program is designed to support your professional growth. To help us do so, please tell us the level of concern you *currently* feel for the following topics. Thanks.

Name _____   School _____   # years teaching _____

	None	Some	Very Concerned

Expectations

1. District curriculum	1 - 2 - 3 - 4 - 5
2. Grade/subject standards for student learning	1 - 2 - 3 - 4 - 5
3. School/district policies and expectations	1 - 2 - 3 - 4 - 5
4. Using technology as a tool for learning	1 - 2 - 3 - 4 - 5
5. Evaluation of teacher performance	1 - 2 - 3 - 4 - 5

Teaching

6. Determining student academic ability	1 - 2 - 3 - 4 - 5
7. Effective use of teaching strategies	1 - 2 - 3 - 4 - 5
8. Differentiating for individual students	1 - 2 - 3 - 4 - 5
9. Unit and lesson plan design	1 - 2 - 3 - 4 - 5
10. Effective use of textbooks and curriculum	1 - 2 - 3 - 4 - 5

Classroom Management

11. Student discipline	1 - 2 - 3 - 4 - 5
12. Preparation time	1 - 2 - 3 - 4 - 5
13. Assessing/grading student work	1 - 2 - 3 - 4 - 5
14. Organization of the classroom	1 - 2 - 3 - 4 - 5
15. Management of paperwork and reports	1 - 2 - 3 - 4 - 5
16. Accessing materials, supplies, equipment	1 - 2 - 3 - 4 - 5
17. The budget for instructional materials	1 - 2 - 3 - 4 - 5

Relationships

18. Parents and community members	1 - 2 - 3 - 4 - 5
19. Principals, administrators, Board of Education	1 - 2 - 3 - 4 - 5
20. Colleagues	1 - 2 - 3 - 4 - 5
21. Motivating and rapport with students	1 - 2 - 3 - 4 - 5
22. Cultural diversity of students	1 - 2 - 3 - 4 - 5

Other Concerns?

23. _____	1 - 2 - 3 - 4 - 5

- What novice teachers think they need *versus* what the research suggests they need
- What protégés perceive they need *versus* what mentors and supervisors perceive

The most effective way to plan such an assessment is to think about the kinds of questions your program needs to be able to answer in the future. *Then work backwards* to plan when, how, and from whom to collect the data that will give your program the answers needed for decision making. For example, *pilot* programs are an excellent strategy for implementing a program plan and collecting comparison data to assess the program's effectiveness. Pilots are valuable because they create two groups: those with and those without improvements you wish to test. This approach also gives you a base of experience and builds leadership capacity.

Collecting data like these is so critical that it is better not to make any major changes in use of time, money, or other resources *until* you have the relevant *comparison* data. This is the only way to be sure that such changes are likely to result in the desired improvements. Without such data, you may get lucky and cause improvements, but *you may not be able to sustain those improvements* because you do not know enough about *why* the improvements happened.

5. Design Assessments to Distinguish Needs of People With Differing Experience Levels

Do not treat all persons the same. Your needs assessment process should capture the extent of prior knowledge and skills for the topic and allow you to plan appropriate support for professional growth by each learner. Check existing knowledge and skills for

- Beginning employees
- New employees with prior experience in the same job
- New employees moving from a different career
- Junior or less experienced teachers who are identified for leadership development
- Other staff who receive mentoring, coaching, or other support for professional growth

To design for diverse experience levels, reframe the questions to include people of many levels of experience. Change your language to be more general and inclusive. Don't say "teachers," say "educators." Instead of "first-year teachers, new teachers, or novice teachers," say "protégés." Saying "principals" leaves out assistant principals, deans, and others, so say "administrators." Then one assessment works for all.

Embed hidden or subtle markings so you know the experience level of respondents. To use one assessment but know the experience of respondents, underline the title for those going to staff with a year or less of experience, capitalize all letters in the title for more than five years, and use normal caps and no underline for those with one to five years' experience. Then you can separate and compare the data from different groups of people to determine how best to support their different professional development needs.

6. Use Needs Assessment for the Same People
Across Time to Reveal How Perceptions of Needs Change
as Employees Gain Professional Experience and Maturity

This crucial step will help you design trainings and other supports during the later years of your program. During the first year, I recommend assessing protégé perceptions of need four times:

- Immediately on hiring, to find baseline perceptions prior to any training, orientation, or mentoring. Comparisons made later will show the effects of mentoring.
- Within the first three to four weeks of being on the job. This shows changes in perception of needs due to the realities of being in the job for a few weeks. Reality is a great teacher, so expect needs to have changed—for some, dramatically.
- About three months after beginning the job. See what protégés perceive their needs to be after working for a while, learning the "ropes," and getting past the initial challenges of learning the job and orientation.
- About nine to ten months after starting. By this point, protégés have learned a great deal. Their perception of needs could be changing again. Now, find out whether protégés are aware of the need for continuing professional growth or whether they feel they are mostly done with learning. Either way, these data tell you what to do next with protégés, perhaps during summer.

7. Assess the Needs of Your Organization

Needs assessments typically focus on protégés, and perhaps even mentor needs. That is a critical place to start, but your mentoring program must be perceived as "worth it" by decision makers in the organization if it is to remain sustainable. That means that your needs assessment must also address valued organizational needs, such as

- Increased retention of new employees and the associated cost savings
- Bringing new employees up to the level of veteran employees regarding knowledge of and commitment to organizational mission, initiatives, and expectations
- Accelerated "learning curves" for new employees
- Improved job performance of both protégés and their mentors
- Increased "bottom line" results, like student achievement, that the district needs

Assessing these "needs" will likely require collecting data that already exist (at, for example, the central office), as well as developing ways to assess new indicators. This may initially take extensive time, but over time the task will become simpler and faster. These data are crucial because district needs are typically much more important to decision makers than the development of persons. Program leaders would be wise to keep this reality in mind.

THREE CONCEPTS ESSENTIAL
FOR PROGRAM SUCCESS

The most essential concepts for program success are first, that your program must have all the needed program components; second, that each component must be working at a best practice level; and third, that the way you conduct each component's activities should develop synergy among the parts.

Your Program Must Have All the Right Program Components

For maximum participant development, needs of people at each Stage of Concern must be anticipated and addressed through program components. If one of the stages of concern is not supported, people will be left to "figure it out on their own." In a high impact program, we want to ensure that growth is accelerated and continuous across all Stages of Concern.

Each Component Must Be Working at a Best Practice Level

In a high impact program, we don't only recruit, select, and match mentors to new teachers. The goal is not to have mentors in place. The goal is mentoring that transforms teaching practices and student results. Therefore, we design the recruiting, selection, and matching processes using those practices proven to lead to highly effective mentor and protégé pairs.

In addition, we train and support mentors so that when mentors and protégés meet, mentors use strategies we know will cause improvements in performance and student results. This book describes how to effectively design and conduct each program component to get the maximum impact from every activity, and also explains how to evaluate and diagnose any "road blocks" when things don't work as expected.

The Way You Conduct Each Component's Activities Should Develop Synergy

Synergy is an almost magical result in which there is a multiplying effect within the program. Synergy happens when each program piece plays its part in the developmental sequence *and* does what it can to set up other program pieces to succeed. Here are a few examples of potential synergistic results:

- Mentors' own learning will increase and their teaching will improve.
- Principals will report that protégés are attaining the levels of practice in one year that used to take most teachers three years to reach.
- Guides who first refuse to be mentors will volunteer to become mentors later.
- The quality of your new staff will improve, exceeding what mentoring alone could have caused. This is due to the drawing power of your induction program during teacher recruitment and the resulting better pool from which you can hire.
- Principals will report that their interaction with teachers during supervisory evaluation conferences has improved.
- Positive teacher leadership in your schools will become more common.
- Teachers will discover that "Great mentoring is also great teaching," and will use mentoring strategies with their students, leading to better results.

What does it look like to create a complementary, multiplying, synergistic effect? As an example, ask yourself, "How can what we do during mentor recruitment help us during mentor selection and matching? Mentor training? Provide mentor support? How can what we do during mentor recruitment assure a productive relationship with the program coordinator?" Another example is, "How can mentor roles and tasks be used to create a job description and application, in selection and matching, in training and support and to guide the program coordinator?" Figure 1.7 is an example of building synergy for the mentor roles and tasks component.

THE BIG PICTURE: THE HIGH IMPACT PROGRAM COMPONENTS

Finally, we can look at the "big picture" of all the components in a high impact induction and mentoring program.

All the items shown in Figure 1.8 are under the "umbrella" of the New Teacher Induction Program. In other words, the Mentoring Program is one strategy in the induction process.

Review Figure 1.8, starting with the box titled "Novice Teacher Development." In that box are the seven program components required to ensure that the protégé's growth accelerates across the full CBAM Stages of Concern and the protégé quickly becomes a high quality, student-centered educator.

1. Initial protégé orientation is usually done the week before school starts at the end of summer. It is called "initial" because the mentoring process (step 7) includes ongoing orientation of the protégé to any first-time experience later during the year. Orientation is done to increase the protégé's opportunity for success the first time they go through each new experience.

2. Protégé training is the district training specifically designed based on national research and your local data on individual novice teacher needs for learning.

3. Protégé observations of expert teachers gives novices the opportunity to see excellent practice. Usually observations are selected by the protégé in consultation with the mentor and designed to focus learning on one or more of the protégé's professional growth goals.

4. Protégé peer support activities are carefully structured and facilitated opportunities for novice teachers to learn from and support each other. This component is critical because peer influence is often as powerful as mentoring but needs to be focused on learning best practices. These are either separate group meetings or activities that are integrated into trainings to reduce the demand on novice teachers' time.

5. Protégé professional development goals and plans are essential to teaching novices the skills of and dispositions toward reflective practice and continual improvement. Most often, setting these goals and making these plans is a process facilitated by the mentor. This is based on mentor feedback and guidance through self-assessment of the protégé's own practice and comparison to the professional standards.

6. Protégé professional growth portfolios are a requirement because reflecting on actual work products and other artifacts is more powerful than reflecting on one's memories. This component takes extra time for a busy novice and can become counterproductive if not handled appropriately.

Figure 1.7 An Example of Creating Synergy by Using One Program Component to Increase the Impact of Other Components

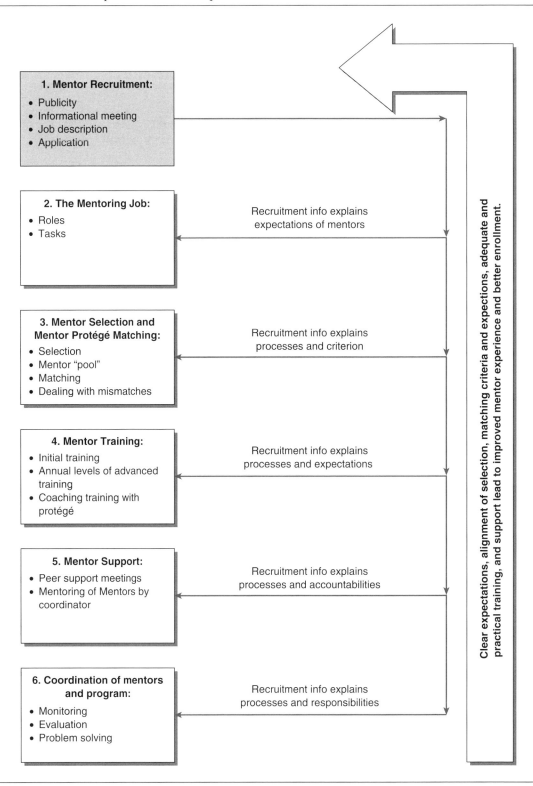

Figure 1.8   Components Needed for High Impact Induction and Mentoring Programs

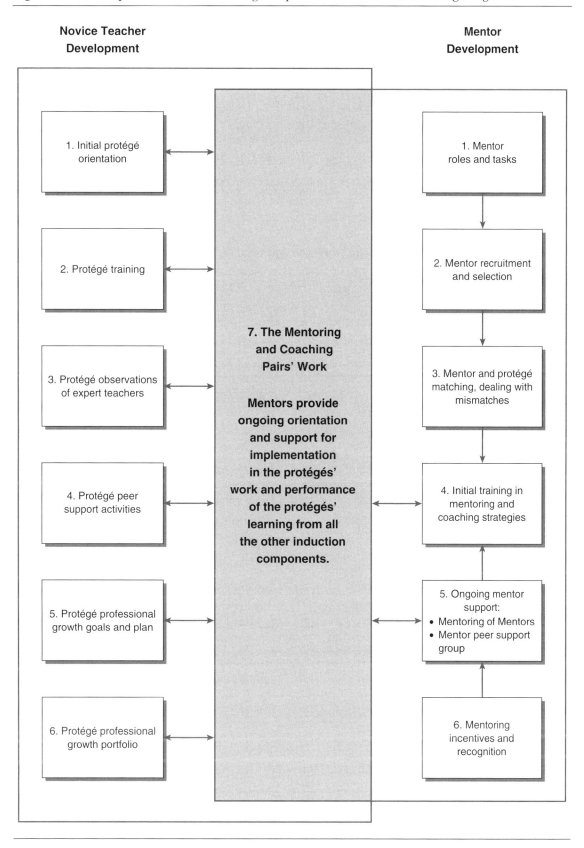

7. Mentoring and coaching pairs' work. At this intersection of the induction and mentoring programs, the mentor guides the protégé to integrate all the learning gained for implementation in the classroom.

Chapter 3 provides much more detail on each of these components, including best practices for each one.

Now we switch our attention to the right half of Figure 1.8 and the column titled "Mentor Development." This side is what we would call the mentor program. It includes the overlapping area representing the work of mentoring and coaching. The components are

1. Mentor roles and tasks. Roles describe what effective mentors need to *be* like and tasks describe what effective mentors must *do*. These are considered first because effective recruiting, mentor selection, training, and other components all build on mentor roles and tasks.

2. Mentor recruitment and selection. Recruitment is what is done to ensure there are a sufficient number of persons who want to become mentors. Recruitment works with mentoring incentives to attract and prequalify persons. Recruitment includes information on websites, flyers, announcements, and other outreach tools, including a mentoring information meeting that informs and attracts potential mentors and discourages those who should not become mentors.

3. Mentor and protégé matching and dealing with mismatches. Matching is identifying the mentor with the most appropriate match of characteristics and strengths to address a specific protégé's needs. Mismatch problems are often resolved by the program leader; however, when a mismatch cannot be resolved, a specific process must be already in place as a guide.

4. Initial training in mentoring and coaching strategies. The initial training is the first training the mentor attends. *Ongoing* mentor training is best integrated into mentor peer support meetings. Often the first mentor and protégé (both) coaching training occurs near the end of the first semester, the point at which most program leaders feel protégés have their "feet on the ground."

5. Two kinds of ongoing support for mentors. Peer support is when mentors meet to learn from and support each other. Mentoring of Mentors is the work of a program leader, and ensures that mentors have the support and accountability they need.

6. Mentor incentives and recognition. Although some districts do not offer stipends, others find it necessary to offer an incentive. Almost every program includes some form of mentor recognition. Specific best practices can help programs retain a sufficient number of mentors.

7. The practice of mentoring and coaching. This is where the components and efforts come to fruition. If your program has cultivated the whole process, you will be able to reap the harvest you expect.

ARE ALL OF THESE PROGRAM PIECES REALLY NEEDED?

Think about the CBAM steps we need to make sure learners are successful at each stage in their development. If our programs and practices provide the right mix of challenge, guidance, and support at each step along the way, protégés' and mentors' growth is accelerated and reaches new, higher levels. How exactly does the CBAM align with all these program components? Look at Figure 1.9 for help in answering this question.

Each component has both a typical (dark line box) and exemplary (broken line box) range it addresses on the CBAM. You can easily see that each component provides support at different CBAM stages. As a complete set of components, the mix ensures that a person has several opportunities to learn and improve at each step of development. Then the separate experiences of the development process are integrated by the mentor and the reflection components of professional growth goals, plans, and a professional growth portfolio. Together, these cross all CBAM stages and ensure that it makes sense as a whole to the learner.

Each of us has different learning preferences. The mix of High Impact Program elements ensures that, regardless of a person's preferences for learning, learning will be supported adequately. Whether you prefer face-to-face collaborative settings, online options, individual professional reflection, or working with materials, the High Impact Mentoring and Induction Model works to meet your needs.

Are all these program pieces really needed? If the induction program is to help protégés at every step of their development process and the mentoring program is to help mentors at every step in their development process, the answer is definitely "yes."

Figure 1.9 How Typical and Exemplary Induction Program Components Support Protégé Growth on the CBAM Stages of Concern

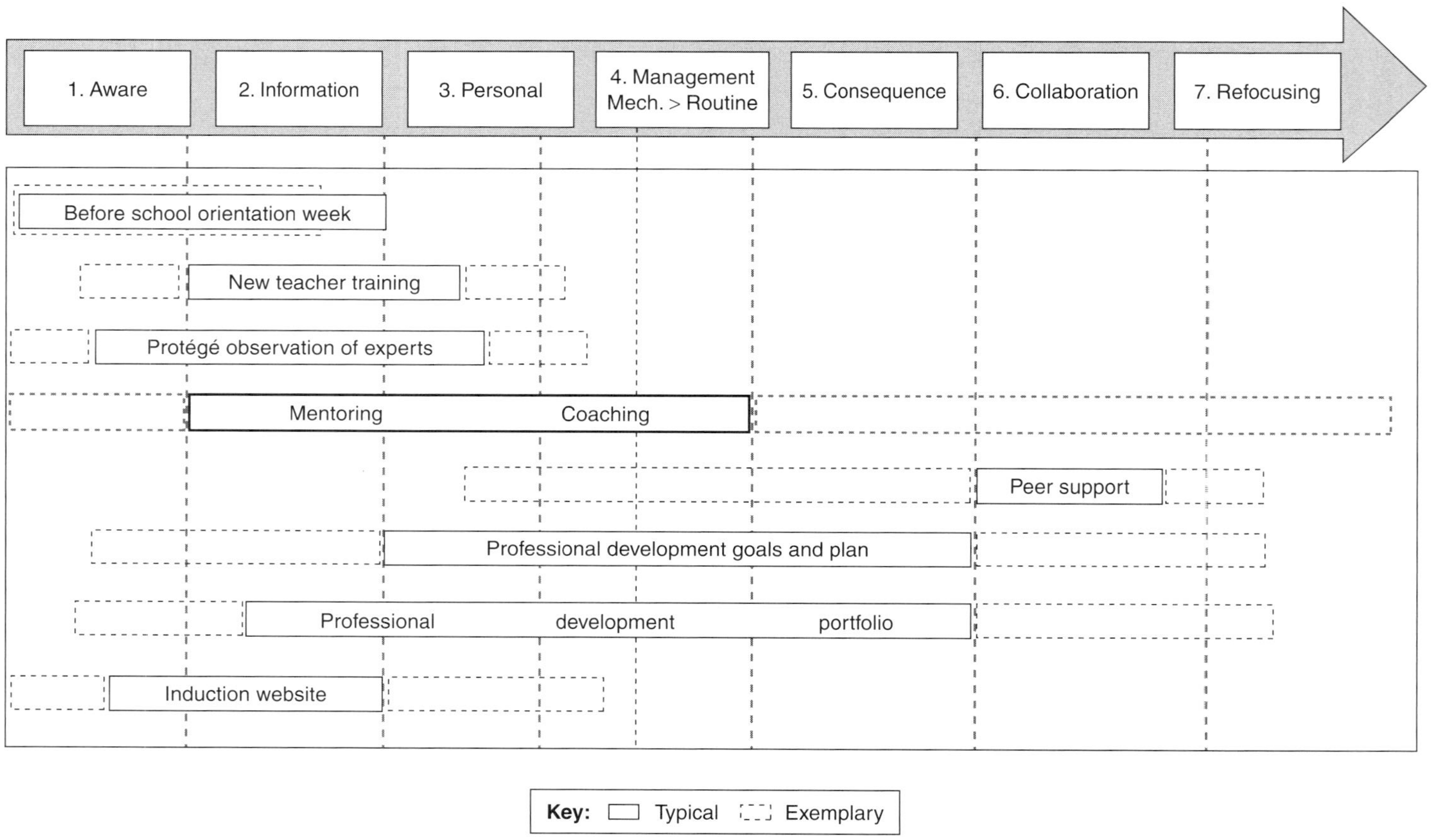

2

The Program
Design Process

This chapter describes a proven, effective process for designing a High Impact Program. Using this process will ensure that you develop a successful program right from the start.

DESIGN FROM THE DESTINATION

In an effective program, the decision about program purpose determines program goals and drives every other decision. This means *purpose* should be decided early and referred to often as you make later program decisions. As part of your school district, your program's sole purpose is the same as for all other programs: improvement of student achievement.

The surest way to create a program that accomplishes that purpose is to start from that desired result and *define in reverse* all steps needed to arrive at the starting point of program-level decisions. For your mentoring and induction program's part in supporting student learning and achievement, these steps or "links in the chain" include:

- Student learning strategies and achievement
- New teachers' teaching strategies
- Mentors' mentoring strategies
- Protégé and mentor training strategies
- Induction program leadership and Mentoring of Mentors strategies
- Program strategies

Figure 2.1   Chain of Causes and Effects

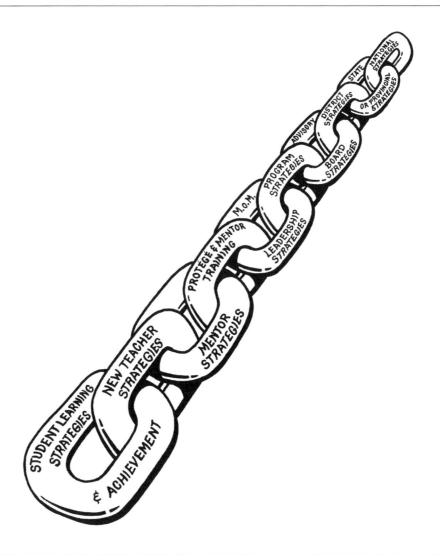

Previously, we discussed the three essentials for program success, including all the right components, each component functioning at the best practice level, and all components needing to set up the others for success (synergy). We can relate these program essentials to our design sequence, what we will call the Chain of Causes and Effects:

- Each link is necessary or the Chain of Causes and Effects is broken.
- Each link must be strong, which means each must use best practices.
- Each link in our chain must build on what is provided by the previous link and must anticipate and provide for the needs of the next link in the chain.

The idea of the program as a Chain of Causes and Effects links means that right actions at the program level will cause cascading effects at the other levels of practice. Careful design of the Chain of Causes and Effects ensures that each link in the chain is excellent and supports success in the *next* link, all the way down the chain to the student impact at the end.

Getting the right sequence, strong links and synergy in the chain is complex. This explains why educational initiatives are hard to implement well, hard to improve when a link fails, and hard to diagnose when student improvements don't result. If the whole chain is not there and working correctly, the ultimate desired effect cannot happen. Our challenge is to use this Chain of Causes and Effects to build and implement a program system. It's a "system" since, after program design, the chain will also guide program implementation and evaluation.

Figure 2.2   Think of *Design*, Implementation, and Evaluation Together

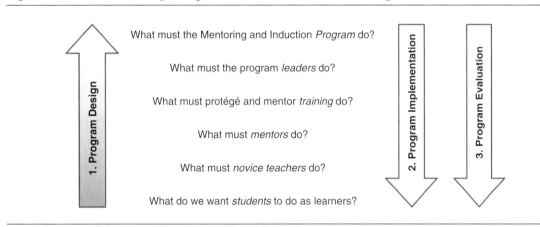

Figure 2.2 presents a simplified version of the Chain of Causes and Effects. This version helps us to move our focus from the drawing of the chain to the ideas it represents. The left side shows that we will *design* starting at the student end of the chain and work *up* the chain. However, we must *implement and evaluate* the program from the program level and work *down* the chain. Basically, we need to implement the program strategies "link" first. That will tell us how to recruit, select, match, train, and support. Then we'll put those decisions in place with the Mentor of Mentors/coordinator who also trains and supports the mentors. Next comes design of trainings and the mentors. First, let's finish discussing the design process.

START WITH THE STUDENTS

The final link in our Chain of Causes and Effects, student learning and achievement, is the first to be defined. If what we design is not aligned with the desired kinds of student learning and achievement, the program will not help achieve that result.

Most induction and mentoring programs state that improved student learning is their ultimate purpose. However, few are *designed* to attain that purpose or actually do it. Mentoring and induction can improve learning for students, and in some places it does. However, mentoring and induction cannot accomplish that purpose if there is no agreement on what the desired student learning actually looks like. Rather than defining *achievement* as test scores, we need to focus on *what successful learners do while they are learning well*.

Schools that succeed at increasing student learning and achievement do so because all staff have agreed on what the desired learning behaviors should look like in classrooms

> Schools that succeed at increasing student learning and achievement do so because all staff have agreed on what the desired learning behaviors should look like in classrooms and have then aligned all actions to attain that vision.

and have then aligned all actions to attain that vision. While your program may not be able to determine this for your district, it is important that your program planning group analyze the district mission, vision, board goals, or strategic plan for what they state student learning should *look* like. If those sources do not provide this, check the staff development program to determine where the district is investing time and resources. Is it on use of active, engaged learning? Differentiated learning? Use the district's focus to write your brief vision of what student learning should look like. Then the mentoring and induction programs will align with improvement efforts the district already values.

For example, let's assume your district says it wants students to be active and engaged learners whose learning needs are met by individualized instructional strategies. Use those desired results as the basis for planning the next link moving up the chain.

DEFINING THE KIND OF TEACHING NEEDED TO INCREASE STUDENT SUCCESS

As shown in Figure 2.1, the next step is to improve the quality of novice teachers' instruction. To do this, you must reach a consensus about the kind of teaching that promotes the desired kinds of student learning. So if you want students to be active and engaged learners whose needs are met by individualized instructional strategies, then teaching must utilize those methods. However, when new teachers were students they may not have observed many of their own teachers using individualized instruction strategies, nor

> Beginning teachers must observe excellent instruction that demonstrates the desired methods, and then novices must have intensive coaching and support if they are to implement these methods in their work with students.

would they necessarily know what engaged, active learning is like. In this case, they may have difficulty using the desired approaches in their own teaching.

To master these desired methods, new teachers must personally experience learning opportunities that are active, engaging, and individualized. Also, they must explicitly understand the expectation to learn and use that kind of instructional approach with their students. Finally, beginning teachers must observe excellent instruction that demonstrates the desired methods, and then novices must have intensive coaching and support if they are to implement these methods in their work with students. It makes no sense, for example, to lecture beginning teachers about individualized instruction and then provide no individual mentoring. The means to an end must be compatible with the end, or that end will not be reached.

DEFINING THE KIND OF MENTORING NEEDED FOR TEACHER AND STUDENT SUCCESS

As we travel back up the Chain of Causes and Effects, we reach the link of mentoring. From our previous work, we can see that to cause the kind of teaching we envision, engaged, active, and individualized instructional strategies must be utilized when mentors work with protégés. We don't just want mentors with the answers. We also want mentors who actively engage new teachers in developing their own plans and assessments, and who involve protégés in learning and using reflective decision-making skills.

If we ask mentors whether they know how to model and teach their protégés these desired techniques, there is a very good chance that they will say "No." This is likely, since mentors may not have had opportunities to learn these strategies or to see them demonstrated. With changes in the definition of excellent teaching, even our best teachers are trying to catch up and become the teachers they know they need to be. To ensure that mentors will be successful at teaching novices the desired instructional methods, the mentors will need training and support in order to learn how to use them.

DEFINING A TRAINING TO INCREASE MENTOR, TEACHER, AND STUDENT SUCCESS

The next link in the Chain of Causes and Effects is the effective training of protégés and mentors. Chapter 3 discusses how to design and conduct effective *protégé* training. Mentor training will be covered in Chapter 6. All we need to say here is that *mentor trainers* must use the same active, engaging, and individualized strategies in mentor training that the mentors must learn to teach to their protégés, and *mentors* must learn about the Chain of Causes and Effects and what their role is in continuing the flow of positive effects to new teachers.

LEADERSHIP AND PROGRAM STRUCTURES TO INCREASE MENTOR, TEACHER, AND STUDENT SUCCESS

The next link, moving up the chain, is developing the leadership needed to support the mentors' implementation of the desired strategies. The modeling of mentor trainers during training, and the work of the Mentor of Mentors after their training, is exactly what mentors need. Finally, we need program processes and structures that are active and engaging of individual mentors in their own learning and that support the kind of leadership, mentor training, mentoring, and teaching we need to produce the desired result in students.

> We need program processes and structures that are active and engaging of individual mentors in their own learning and that support the kind of leadership, mentor training, mentoring, and teaching we need to produce the desired result in students.

The induction and mentoring program-level activities like recruiting, selecting, matching, and motivating mentors must each be conducted using the same models of individualized, active learning that are desired at the end of the chain. Members of your collaborative planning group and the mentor program coordinator must experience their work as an active and personal learning process, not just as a committee function with a management and coordination role. They must conduct their work as an experiment in which decisions are tested out in practice, data are collected, analyses and interpretations are made of the data patterns, and conclusions are reached regarding the efficacy of the experiment. Specifically, the focus must be to assess the effectiveness of the use of the Chain of Causes and Effects to transmit the model of active, engaged, and individualized learning down each link in the chain to the students.

When a clear vision of the intended learning approach and the kind of excellent teaching needed to produce it has been defined, and when that model of excellent instruction and support is implemented in everyday activities at every level of the program, then the induction and mentoring program *will* fulfill its purpose.

THE SEQUENCE FOR CREATING A SUCCESSFUL PROGRAM

The next challenge is to use these concepts to design the induction program. The program development process can be complex, since numerous components may be developed simultaneously and many of the necessary decisions are interconnected.

Figure 2.3 shows how the different parts in the design process fit together. The figure looks complex because the process is comprehensive, but this book provides the detailed information you need to implement it. In fact, earlier sections of this book have already addressed some of the early steps. The steps are as follows:

1. Establish a planning group.

2. Identify a program coordinator.

3. Define a brief Teaching and Learning Vision statement, and then Purpose statement.

4. Read this entire book.

5. Divide the planning group into task forces, assigning each to conduct research on needs of district novice teachers and search the literature on the needs of novice teachers.

6. Reach conclusions about needs and best practices to address needs.

7. Set program goals that target the priority needs.

8. Define expectations, roles, and tasks for participants.

9. Assess what each participant group already knows and can do related to expectations.

10. Design selection and matching processes and criteria.

11. Plan recruitment of and incentives/recognition for participants.

12. Design mentor training.

13. Design mentor support activities.

14. Discuss, define, and plan other necessary induction program activities and their coordination.

15. Plan the program evaluation.

16. Discuss a plan for program implementation and set an implementation time line.

17. Define resources and budget needed to support the program.

18. Prepare a program proposal and budget.

19. Communicate with and seek program support from stakeholders.

20. Communicate with and seek support from key decision makers and grantors.

21. Implement plans according to the implementation time line and budget, then monitor.

22. Collect evaluation data.

23. Analyze collected data and reach conclusions about what those data mean.

24. Report to decision makers.

This entire planning sequence *is* complex, but every step is addressed in this book. Just follow the process one step at a time.

THE FIRST STEP: ESTABLISH A PROGRAM LEADERSHIP GROUP

You will definitely need help. Without it, the time you can give will be limited and so the growth and success of your program will be limited too. That's not desirable. There are people whose work on the group will better position them to understand and value the program. Involve them to create program advocates. What stakeholder groups do you want to have an in-depth understanding of the work of effective induction and mentoring? Who has a viewpoint you need?

> Your leadership group should be representative of diverse backgrounds and values. This isn't just politically correct. There are decisions that will fail, or at the very least meet resistance, if they don't honor the diversity of your community and students and capitalize on the strengths that diversity provides.

Your leadership group should be representative of diverse backgrounds and values. This isn't just politically correct. There are decisions that will fail, or at the very least meet resistance, if they don't honor the diversity of your community and students and *capitalize on the strengths* that diversity provides.

Decide whether your planning group will be advisory or a board that makes the decisions. If you have a funding source already identified, check with the source, as many grants define how these boards must be structured. Decide whether the leadership group should include other program partners, such as a university preservice teacher preparation program. If you include other partners, develop and sign a formal, written governing agreement for the partnership.

THE NEXT STEP: IDENTIFY A PROGRAM COORDINATOR

On the surface, coordinating an induction and mentoring program is not that different a process from coordinating any other developmental program. Most effective administrators

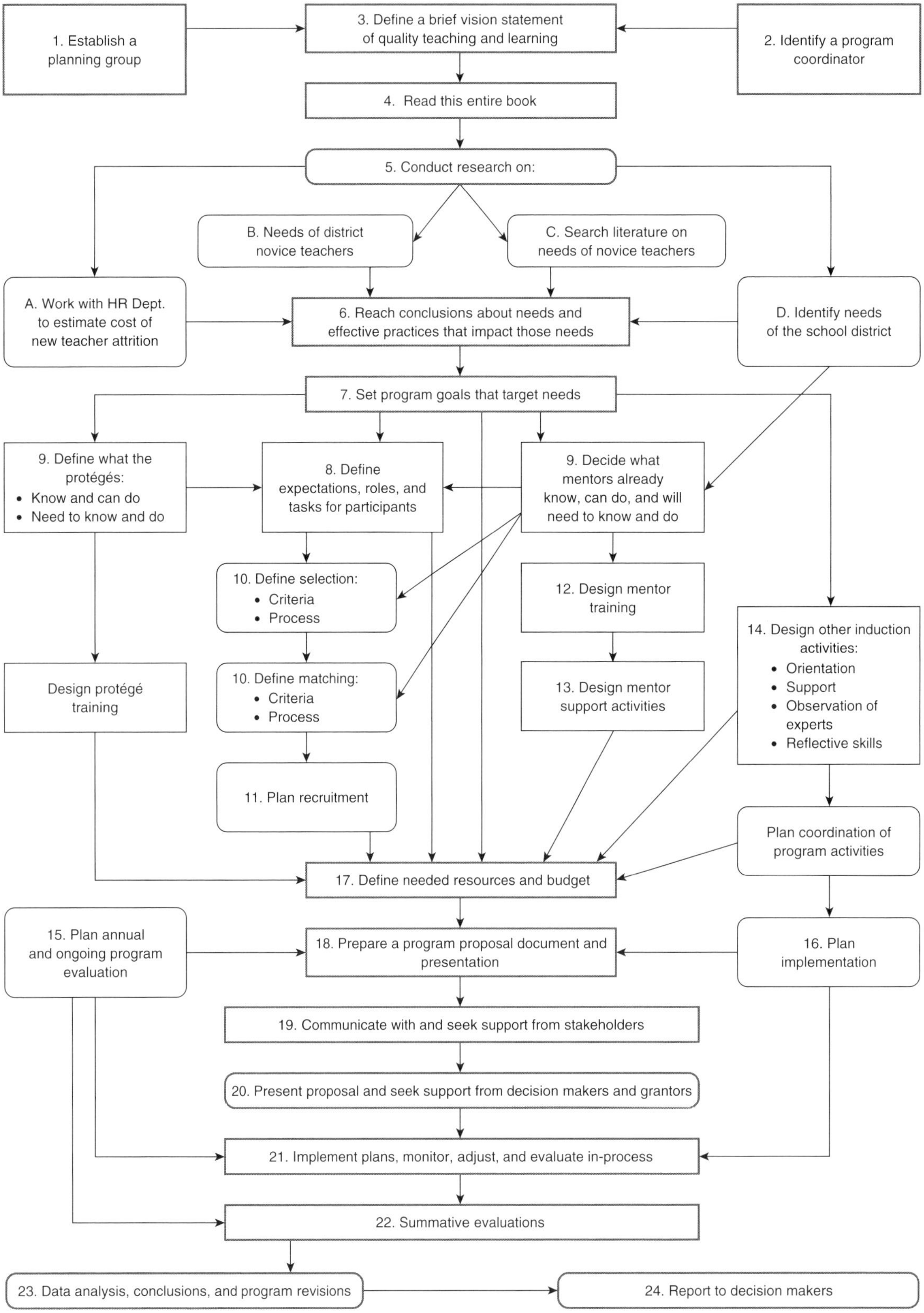

Figure 2.3   Best Practice Sequence for Induction Program Design

or teacher leaders can do it. However, a more crucial leader-ship issue exists if the program will seek to change teaching practices or establish the more collaborative norms of a learn-ing community. Then leadership must be particularly vision-ary, and by its own actions provide an effective model of the desired behaviors so that people can see the goals come alive.

> Leadership must be particularly visionary, and by its own actions provide an effective model of the desired behaviors so that people can see the goals come alive.

Optimally, an induction and mentoring program coordi-nator should be a *teacher* who has shown natural leadership strengths. The reasons for this are many:

- Teacher leaders have an immediate rapport with other teachers.
- Teacher leaders will keep the focus on improvement of instruction and student success.
- Teacher leaders can be released part or full time to quickly build their knowledge of effective induction and mentoring and their capacity to build a strong program.
- Teacher leaders will be very motivated, and many will eventually develop into administrators who will know how to grow the capacity of their faculty.

However, teacher leaders will need support for learning management of programs, budgets, grants, and people. Will your best teacher candidates willingly leave the students? Teachers are motivated to help colleagues too. The following e-mail reflects the rewards teachers find in leading an induction and mentoring program.

Hi Barry,

I must tell you that I never thought anything could fill my cup the way teaching children did, but I am finding the challenge to nurture and grow a strong mentoring program for my district to be amazingly rewarding. Also, I discovered I am still a teacher.

I was at a sandwich shop yesterday and saw one of our mentors. After we chatted and I left the table his girlfriend said, "Who was that?" and he replied, "That's Mary, she's my teacher." My heart soared!!

Mary C. Hasl, Mentor Coordinator
Poudre School District, Fort Collins, Colorado

ROLES OF THE PROGRAM COORDINATOR

The induction and mentoring program coordinator's job is highly complex and time con-suming. A program must have such a leader if it is to become a "high impact" program. Ellen Moir, Executive Director of the New Teacher Center at the University of California, Santa Cruz, advises, "Programs should be staffed with innovative, full-time program administra-tors with training, time, and resources to establish and run excellent programs" (Moir, 2005).

My own research clearly shows that an effective program coordinator is the second most important factor in developing and sustaining a high impact program. It is second only to an effective mentor training. What does this program leader do that makes the role so crucial?

Program Coordinator Responsibilities

- Set the agendas for, and facilitate the meetings of, the program leadership group.
- Train and monitor volunteer and program staff to ensure the use of best practices like the CBAM in their work.
- Lead program activities like mentor training, quarterly mentor peer support meetings, and special events such as a mentor recognition night.
- Maintain personnel records for participants, such as documenting induction involvement to gain a standard certificate for protégés and mentor information as part of the Mentoring of Mentors and for use in future mentor-protégé matching.
- Undertake the Mentoring of Mentors, model best mentoring practices, and coach mentors to adopt those practices.
- Track and schedule program activities such as with time logs.
- Document and monitor effectiveness of mentor and protégé matches.
- Serve as program historian to save evidence of what was changed and when—data which are crucial for discovering how program changes improve outcomes.
- Capture program wisdom and best practice, and create policies which codify these.
- Monitor policy implementation to ensure the "spirit" of the policies and their goals are flexibly attained and they don't become obstacles to best practice.
- Plan, manage, and document program evaluations.
- Plan the program budget, manage program finances and associated reporting.
- Seek a diverse stream of funding beyond what the district can provide.
- Serve as program and mentoring advocate in the community.
- Regularly communicate with district decision makers and participants.

DECIDING THE SEQUENCE FOR IMPLEMENTING PROGRAM COMPONENTS

Improvements in teacher and student performance are often missing because programs are not *designed by starting with the end* in mind. Programs also have decreased impact when program components are not implemented *in the best sequence.* To see what I mean, look at a variation of an earlier diagram of the Chain of Causes and Effects (see Figure 2.4).

We first used this diagram to discuss the best sequence for program *design,* which the arrow on the left side indicates. Now look at the right side of the diagram for the emphasized arrow that's labeled "Implementation." Notice that this arrow is pointing down. That means that the best way to implement program components and to ensure that the Chain of Causes and Effects is maintained is to implement as follows:

1. Establish the *program leadership group* and design the *full* best practice program for both induction and mentoring. Make sure that all the decisions about program level strategies reflect the use of the Vision for Excellent Teaching and Learning for the program. For example, if the desired *student* behaviors are "constructivist," then mentor selection criteria should include people who are continually improving their skills as teachers and willing to do so as new mentors.

Figure 2.4   Think of Design, *Implementation*, and Evaluation Together

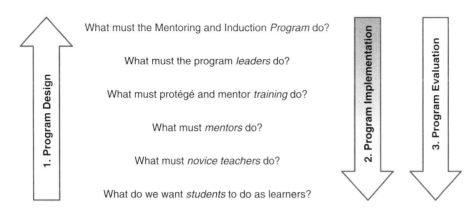

2. Now, implement the work of the *program coordinator,* especially as it relates to leading the mentor training. That training will maintain the Chain of Causes and Effects *if* it teaches mentors the vision and models that same kind of teaching and learning.

3. Implement the coordinator's role as *Mentor of Mentors.* That role must also reflect the program's Vision for Excellent Teaching and Learning. Mentor of Mentors activity must demonstrate the desired model of instruction. If mentors experience the kind of mentoring they are to implement, their understanding of what to do with their protégés will be clearer than any training alone could teach. Finally, the Mentor of Mentors helps mentors plan how to demonstrate and teach that same vision to their protégés. Then the Chain of Causes and Effects has another link added to it, and implementation of that vision has moved a step closer to that protégé's classroom.

4. The next step in the chain is the *mentors,* who must use the visionary teaching model with their protégés. The protégé first experiences the model, then mentors teach their protégés about the model, and finally mentors help protégés plan how to implement the model with their students. The chain is intact and the effects have continued along the chain, one link at a time, as each link passes the vision on to the next link.

When you are implementing from the top of the chain down, implement each step one at a time, but only when the next component is ready to do its job well. If one link in the chain is not ready to effectively use the visionary model, then it is not yet time to implement that step.

APPROACHES TO IMPLEMENTING THE PROGRAM

If you follow the guidelines mentioned previously, you will be using the "phased in" approach (see Figure 2.5A and B) rather than trying to implement the whole program all at once before it can work.

However, you must start by *designing a full program* that reflects as many best practices as possible. This means that as you implement each step it works well and, when all components are finally implemented, all the program functions *in that plan* will work together as a whole Chain of Causes and Effects.

Figure 2.5A   Example of Gradually Implementing an Induction Program, Part A

Key: BT = beginning teacher, NT = new but experienced teacher

Component	Year 1	Year 2	Year 3
• New educator orientation	One day w/district and community reps and bus tour	Add two AMs of district curriculum, PM w/mentor	Add one day, AM district initiatives, PM w/mentor
• Program leadership	Create group and plan program		Add mentor coordinator
• BT professional development		1st year BT attend 12 clock hours	Add: 2nd year BT nine hours, 1st year BT nine hours
• Peer support for BT and mentors			Three meetings per year, facilitated and structured
• Mentor program		Add guide help for all new staff	Add mentors for only beginning teachers
• Mentor and guide training		Add for guides	Hire external mentoring and coaching trainer
• Guide program		For BT and NT	Just for NT
• Protégé observations of experts		2 days each for 1st and 2nd year protégés	Observe with mentor, then confer after
• Professional development portfolio			1st year BT save "stuff" and reflect on it at year end
• Professional development goals and action plan		Informal between BT and guide	Informal between BT and mentor, formal goals for following summer
• Program evaluation	Assess needs of BT, NT and organization	Add assessment of all programs	Add assessment of mentor program and Yr. 2 program

In Year 1, a basic orientation is held, and other work is data collection, researching, and planning the whole new program. In Year 2, the program design is used to increase orientation, add BT training, observations, guides, guide training, informal reflection and assessment of new programs. In Year 3, mentors and mentor training are added, there is more orientation, a program coordinator, portfolios are added, and assessment of the new mentor program takes place.

The logic here is to implement only what you have the leadership capacity to do very well, and only when participants are ready for that step in the process. For example, don't start training mentors until all the previous links in the Chain of Causes and Effects are functioning according to your Vision for Excellent Teaching and Learning and you have a mentor training plan and trainer(s) who will follow that vision too.

If you start by developing the whole program plan, even though you are initially only going to implement some parts of the program, when the remaining parts are added, they will all function effectively together. In addition, if the members of the leadership group change over time, the new members will still be able to follow the original "roadmap" and vision, and will be able to maintain the Chain of Causes and Effects you have designed.

Figure 2.5B   Example of Gradually Implementing an Induction Program, Part B

Year 4	Year 5	Year 6	Year 7
			→
Add Mentor of Mentors role			→
			→
			→
			→
Do own two-day mentor training. Hire coach trainer	Add own mentor and protégé coaching training	Add peer coach training option for experienced staff	→
			→
Choose from new demonstration teacher directory			→
2nd year protégés add "stuff" related to teaching standards. Organize to show growth	Add structure to guide assessment of actual versus standards. Add written reflections.		→
Formal, standards-based portfolio, BT and mentor roles defined			→
Assess portfolio and goals as help for professional development	Add assessment of BT skills versus standards	Assess increase of BT skills versus standards	Add assessment of impact on student learning and achievement

Year 4, coordinator adds Mentoring of Mentors, district does own mentor training and hires expert to lead first coaching mtg. New demonstration teacher directory is created, Year 2 stuff is added to formal portfolios, standards are more the focus, and portfolios are assessed. Year 5, mentors and protégés get in-house coaching training, a form for comparison with standards, and district assesses BT skills. Year 6 add training for all experienced staff to peer coach. Year 7 add assessment for student impact.

WHAT IF YOU ALREADY HAVE A PROGRAM STARTED?

Of course, the advice just given is for starting a *new* program largely from "scratch." If you have an existing program with a few components already in place, start by comparing those components to the Chain of Causes and Effects. Identify any links in that chain that may be missing, and determine whether the existing links *use the best practices* described in this book.

While you are making improvements to the existing components, develop an implementation plan for missing components with logical steps that will take you from where you are to the next link in the chain that you are, or soon will be, capable of supporting and leading. Make sure that the next links you add will effectively continue the Chain of Causes and Effects by using and teaching the Vision for Excellent Teaching and Learning.

To determine whether it is the right time to implement a new program element, conduct an assessment of the needs of teachers and the needs of the district. These results can dictate which components of the program are needed and when they should be implemented. For example, it may make sense to start a beginning teacher staff development series but then to gain experience in those trainings before adding beginning teacher support activities to them. To decide what to implement, rely on the CBAM Stages of Concern.

USE THE CBAM TO GUIDE IMPLEMENTATION DECISIONS

When analyzing the program components that are in place and deciding what the next step might be, let the way people learn guide you. Use the CBAM Stages of Concern to chart the levels of practice and implementation for participants in your current program.

> Consider implementing as your next component those activities that will move people a step higher on the CBAM Stages of Concern.

Use data collected at events as well as careful observation to determine when people are comfortable with new skills and when they feel the need for continued improvement. This reveals the readiness of people to take the next step. Then consider implementing as your next component those activities that will move people a step higher on the CBAM Stages of Concern.

DEFINING PROGRAM PURPOSES, GOALS, AND OBJECTIVES

People frequently use the terms *purpose, goals, objectives*, and *activities* interchangeably. The definitions here will help you understand how the terms are used in this book. Also, these meanings correspond with those used in most grant applications, so using these meanings when writing your program plan will facilitate the grant application process.

The *purpose* of your program should be the same as every program in the district and should focus on teacher effectiveness and student learning. Write out your program's variation, starting with, "The purpose of the Induction and Mentoring Program is to . . .," but say little else. Clarify that your program is designed (and should be supported) because it supports the district mission.

Program *goals* are permanent and define the *unique* things mentoring and induction will contribute to accomplish the district purpose. State these so *no other program* can attain your goals. This helps create the understanding that your program is essential to attaining the district's purpose. Generally, induction and mentoring program *goals* fit within four broad categories:

1. Orientation to a new setting, curriculum, and responsibilities

2. Induction into the responsibility and career of teaching

3. Instructional improvement

4. Transforming the school culture to that of a learning community

These are comprehensive, but they are not specific enough for designing a program or program evaluation. Each of the four categories implies more specific goals that are better guides for design and evaluation. A review of many programs reveals a more specific and helpful list:

- To accelerate new employees' learning of a new job and skills
- To reduce the stress of transition to a new career
- To improve novice performance through modeling and coaching by a top performer
- To attract more skilled and diverse faculty in a competitive recruiting environment
- To retain new employees and to protect the district's investment in new teacher recruitment and development
- To increase retention and recognition of excellent veteran staff by creating a setting and roles in which their contributions and wisdom are highly valued
- To develop increased numbers of positive teacher leaders
- To respond to state, district, or contractual mandates for new teacher support or instructional improvement
- To benefit from a partnership with a university and/or regional service center that has resources to support new teachers
- To socialize new staff into the school family and its positive values and traditions
- To transform the school culture by establishing more collaborative norms within which beginning teachers are inducted into the profession and have the chance to experience a learning community

Figure 2.6 Definitions and Examples: Purpose, Goals, and Objectives

Purpose	Goals	Objectives
Purpose • *Definition:* Everyone and every program works toward the *same* purpose, the overall reason your school district exists. • *Example:* "Every student will meet the state standards in all subjects, will graduate from high school, and will succeed at the next level of their education."	*Definition:* The broad ways each program and each person in a program contributes to achieving the overall purpose of the district.	*Definition:* The annual steps taken to move closer to the desired goal.
	Mentoring Example: • Help all new teachers to develop all the routines needed to be high quality teachers and to focus on meeting each student's needs for academic success. • Help new teachers to internalize dispositions and the skills of reflective practice and continual improvement.	**Mentoring Example:** • By 12/06, revise the new teacher orientation program to focus only on what is needed for success during the first month of school and to give novices more time with their mentors in classrooms during Orientation Week to better prepare for quality instruction.

This list is too long for a program to use as it is, so narrow it to those goals most relevant to your setting and needs. You can use a goal for each need or allow each goal to address a number of new teacher and organization needs.

Finally, program goals must be general and flexible enough to allow you to address the varied length and kinds of prior experience of program participants. What is appropriate for a beginning teacher may be unnecessary for a new teacher hired from another district or someone entering the profession through an alternative route. Allow age and the professional and life experiences of new employees to suggest the specificity or generality of your goals language.

The following sample statement may be more detailed than you need, but notice that there is no doubt how the program will accomplish what it intends. The bullet statements could be eliminated if desired.

Sample Induction Program Purpose and Goals

Purpose

The City School District Induction and Mentoring Program's purpose is to provide an effective professional development and support system that attracts and retains a caring and high quality professional staff that values collaborative work and effective teaching and is dedicated to the success of all our students.

The Goals of the Induction Program Are to Provide

1. *Orientation to the new job and the local setting, including*
   - Knowing the key people and expectations of the district, school, and community
   - Learning to access school, district, community and other resources
   - Reducing the stress of job transition
   - Becoming familiar with the setting and the instructional program
   - Learning staff and administrative roles and the school and district procedures

2. *Induction into the teaching profession, including*
   - Developing skill in the roles of the professional educator
   - Management of learning environment
   - Time management
   - Instructional leadership
   - Meeting individual student needs
   - Learning and implementing effective teaching practices so as to gain the state's standard license
   - Contributing to the school community and its groups

3. *Induction into our vision for our profession, including*
   - Committing to continuous, individual professional improvement
   - Defining learning according to recent brain research
   - Defining teacher roles as:
     - team-oriented, where diversity is used as a strength
     - learning from and supporting the learning of others in a learning community

---

> – focus on student learning success, not just teaching
> – facilitating application of learning, not just sharing of knowledge
> – shared leadership and decision making
> • Aligning instruction to the school improvement goals and state student standards
> • Contributing to improvement of the profession

Two other terms needing definition are *objectives and activities.*

Objectives are annually framed, measurable statements that describe what must be done to gain progress on a goal and what that progress will look like. Objectives are written to guide and evaluate specific improvements. An objective to support the goal of orienting new teachers might be, "To have at least 90 percent of orientation participants for 2006 report that orientation provided a sufficient level of support to successfully start the first month of the school year." There might be several activities to support that objective.

Activities are very specific statements of observable behaviors that are needed to achieve an objective. Using our objective example, two possible activities might be:

- "To provide each new teacher at orientation with a *New Teacher Manual* containing current schedules, contact information, curriculum information, teacher responsibilities, a district map, and other essential orientation information"
- "To provide a panel of second-year teachers during orientation to answer questions of teachers who are new to the district"

Objectives and their associated activities are too specific to be in a program plan. They could be found in an annual program evaluation report under a heading like, "Objectives and Activities for Program Improvement," or they could be in a program coordinator's "Objectives for My Role in the XX-XX School Year." For examples of good objectives, check out the "Transition to Teaching Goals and Objectives" found in a program's second-year evaluation report at http://t2t.fms.k12.nm.us/data/t2tdata_year2.pdf. Note that this report went to a grantor for annual funding support and that the statement does *not include activities,* so as not to limit what can be done.

The best way to achieve several goals is to design several specific activities for each goal. Program activities can also address multiple goals.

DEVELOPING COMPONENTS
THAT ADDRESS PROGRAM GOALS

What follows is a helpful structure for checking each program component's effectiveness and contribution to the program goals. Use the chart in Figure 2.7 to determine whether your program activities support the Chain of Causes and Effects you designed. I suggest that you *use* this chart *after* you have designed all the program components. It is included here since it relates to goals and activities. Activity examples are mentor support and guidance, mentor coaching, new teacher orientation, and new teacher training.

Once goals and activities are listed, compare each activity against each goal to see whether each goal is sufficiently supported. For example, assume one program goal is to provide high-priority information to new employees. That goal would be listed with other goals at the top of one of the columns under the heading "Induction/Mentoring

Figure 2.7 Ensuring That Induction and Mentoring Activities Are Led by Your Program Goals

Induction/Mentoring Program Goals

Induction Activities

Program Goals." New teacher orientation, which provides key district information, expectations, and policies, would be listed in the left-hand column under "Induction Activities." To consider exactly how an activity supports a goal, look at the intersection of the goals column and the activity row.

Each activity should be checked to ensure it is specifically designed to help the program attain as many goals as possible. If a program's goals include promoting individualized instruction, then the program should limit the use of group meetings for orientation, training, and support to just those deemed necessary to address common needs for all protégés. All activities of the program should be designed to reflect the priority placed on individualized support for learning.

Using Figure 2.7, you can decide to eliminate or revise any activities that are not supportive of your program's goals. This comparison also reveals where there are no, or too few, activities to accomplish a particular goal. Existing programs also can use this same structure to revisit their goals and activities.

Lastly, a completed version of this figure can guide those who lead each of the separate program activities. After a time, program planning decisions become more distant in memory, and program activities can become less focused and be shaped by individuals who may have forgotten the program's original intentions for their specific part in attaining program goals. Always ask that individuals responsible for activities refer to this figure as a reminder of the purpose of an activity. Building an ongoing awareness of goals is the *real foundation of a program's effectiveness* because it ensures continuity in practice of your Chain of Causes and Effects.

DO YOU NEED A SINGLE- OR MULTIPLE-YEAR PROGRAM?

Once program goals and purposes are written, other components that depend on those statements can be designed. For example, program goals help determine the number of years a new teacher should remain in a program. Other contextual factors also play a role.

Illinois provides an example of such factors. Like many states, Illinois gives beginning teachers an "Initial Teaching Certificate" for four years. At the end of four years, new teachers must demonstrate sufficient professional growth and competence to earn the state's "Standard Certificate." Otherwise, they cannot teach in Illinois. Completion of an approved induction program is one of the options approved for demonstrating adequate professional growth. Naturally, most new programs are multiyear programs providing three or four years of support to "Initial Certificate Holders." The training, observations, goals, portfolios, and mentoring have all been defined as multiyear growth strategies. On the other hand, some more complex and sophisticated activities are saved for the second year and thereafter, since first-year teachers need to spend almost all their available time planning instruction, developing materials, and preparing for the next day of teaching. Typically, as teachers return for their second year, activity becomes more focused on self-assessment against the professional teaching standards and on the accountabilities for demonstrating those things needed for the Standard Certificate. The program length of four years is a function of the program goal to support novices until they acquire their Standard Certificate. Since it is likely that your state, province, or country has similar requirements for teacher licensure, you should design your program to be supportive of new teachers over several years.

What follows is an *example* of how program activities may be transitioned from the start of a new educator's career through the next three years. Eventually, you should create a similar document showing what each year's support includes. This document will be crucial to new teachers and mentors, and will also be useful for administrators, induction trainers, and others. For example, it could be sent to the state or province as partial documentation of compliance.

Example: Narrative—a Three-Year Mentoring and Induction Program

Year 1

In Year 1 of the three-year induction process, the mentor and protégé begin by attending an initial training that prepares them for their work together. The essential work of a mentoring pair is orientation, learning the curriculum, and accelerating the protégé's transition from thinking like a student to thinking and behaving like an expert professional educator.

During this initial year, the mentor is constantly modeling and promoting discussion of a wide range of effective teaching practices. Practices emphasized are those that are dictated by research on the typical needs of beginning teachers and those identified as areas for growth by assessment of the needs of the specific beginning teacher. Growth areas are identified by the novice's comparison of his or her own actual practice with the teaching standards.

In January of Year 1, the mentor and protégé are trained in the skills of peer observation, nonjudgmental feedback and coaching for self-assessment, reflection, and analysis—all of which are focused on effective classroom instruction. Mentoring pairs complete at least one coaching cycle each quarter for the remainder of the year.

Evidence of the protégé's teaching and the mentoring pair's work together is collected throughout Year 1. This "save your stuff" approach is designed to initiate work on the portfolio and yet protect the first-year teacher's time for planning instruction. The culmination of Year 1 is mentor and principal feedback to the protégé, based on mentor-facilitated analysis by the protégé of materials saved in the portfolio and the protégé's self-assessment of his or her teaching relative to the state teaching standards. The final product is a personal profile of the protégé's teaching strengths, identification of two to three standards areas which are targeted for growth, and a professional development plan addressing those target areas.

Year 2

During Year 1, many of the protégé's basic survival needs are met and laid to rest. In Year 2, protégés continue to refine their teaching practices as they have greater ability and self-confidence to take a more critical look at their own teaching. To support this self-examination, the mentor-protégé pair conducts initial mutual observation and coaching, learning, and applying the process of action research. All of the coaching and action research is focused on:

- The implementation of their professional development goals and plan
- The collection of evidence of professional activity and growth and other related artifacts
- A continuous study of effective teaching practices and standards
- Reflection on and self-assessment of actual teaching versus the standards
- The increase of teaching skills in the targeted areas of the teaching standards

The protégé continues to collect evidence of professional growth, of the work with the mentor, and of teaching students. The mentor and protégé analyze this evidence, especially for its relevance to demonstrating growth in targeted areas of the state teaching standards identified in the professional development plan. This plan may be updated and extended as needed so it remains an effective guide.

The final products of Year 2 are the selected evidence of the protégé's growth relative to the teaching standards, the data collected from the observation of their teaching, and reflective writing by both mentor and protégé about the conclusions they have reached about their mutual work and growth.

At the end of Year 2, the mentor prompts protégé self-assessment, reflection, and conclusions about areas for growth relative to the teaching standards. The mentor provides feedback on the protégé's strengths and reinforces the protégé's accurate self-perceptions about areas for growth. When protégé and mentor perspectives are different, the mentor prompts protégé analysis of data collected and reaching conclusions about the need for growth relative to the teaching standards. Together, the mentor and protégé develop a professional development plan for their third and last year of work.

Year 3

Year 3 is a continuation of Year 2 in its focus on effective teaching practices, collection of observational and action research data, and implementation of the professional growth work plan. The major difference in Year 3 is a greater emphasis on documenting the results of the entire process. Specifically, the work with the professional growth portfolio is extended to include more evidence of the mentoring and teaching work of the third year. Also, evidence of the professional growth of the protégé relative to the state teaching standards is selected from the artifacts collected and prepared with explanatory comments. This work is an intense and time-consuming process, but its purpose is vital to the beginning teacher's credential attainment.

At the end of Year 3, the portfolio provides evidence of mastery of teaching standards, which supports the beginning teacher's application for a standard teaching license. After Year 3, the protégé is expected to have attained self-sufficiency and the skills of self-assessment and reflective practice that promote career-long learning. While there will always be collaboration, collegial support for and discussion of development, the granting of the standard teaching license is based on the demonstration that these skills and dispositions have been internalized by the beginning teacher, such that the protégé is worthy to be called a professional educator.

The above narrative will help some to understand what the changes might be like in a multiyear program. Some folks are more visual and may find it helpful to use Figure 2.8A and Figure 2.8B, which provide an example of a *four-year-long* induction experience. Notice how activities completed in one year ready the protégé for fuller implementation the next year. Other changes show how experience is being gained one year so the protégé can assume greater responsibility a year later.

Figure 2.8A   Part A *Example:* Transitions in a Four-Year Induction Experience

Component	Protégé's Year 1	Protégé's Year 2
Orientation	Initial week before the start of school, five mornings	• A few selected for panel at the initial orientation of others. • Two-hour "What's Up This Year?"
Mentoring	Starts on contract signing, four afternoons during first week. One to two hrs three days each of the next three weeks, one hr/week during rest of the first semester, two to three hrs/month in second semester	As needed. Minimum of one hour each of first four weeks, then two to three hrs/month rest of the year, focused on development of work-related skills identified in the protégé's PD goals
Coaching w/data analysis	Half a day each quarter with mentor who prompts self-assessment	Half a day each quarter with mentor who prompts self-assessment
Training	Eighteen clock hours total: six during initial orientation, six hours required—content set by district—during the year, and six hours of district-designed electives	Fifteen clock hours total required, w/content set by district, twelve hours of electives of district-designed content. One paid full day at an outside-of-district workshop
Protégé observation of experts	None first semester, half day a quarter second sem. Focus is a PD goal. Person to be observed decided in consult. w/mentor	Half a day each semester, PD goal focus, choice of whom to see is mentor facilitated
Protégé peer support	Half hour integrated into each protégé training event	Half hour integrated into each protégé training event.
Reflection: Professional development goals	Focused on protégé self-assessment facilitated by mentor, updated approximately once a month	Mentor facilitated, focused on protégé self-assessment vs state professional standards
Professional development plan	Focus is PD goals, facilitated by mentor, update as needed	Focus is on PD goals, facilitated by mentor, update as needed
Professional development portfolio	Not discussed as such, focus on the "save your stuff" strategy, mentor facilitates reflection on materials saved	District training on portfolio expectations, PD goals focus, first sem. "development model," second sem. add "assessment" model, all are mentor facilitated

Figure 2.8B   Part B *Example:* Transitions in a Four-Year Induction Experience

Component	Protégé's Year 3	Protégé's Year 4
Orientation	One hr. "What's Up This Year?"	One hr. "What's Up This Year?"
Mentoring	As needed. Minimum of one hr a month all year. Focus on work skills development as described by state standards and profess. dev. goals and plan half day each qtr with mentor who prompts self-assessment	As needed. Minimum of one hr a month all year. Focus on meeting Standard State Professional Certificate requirements. Work about half a day each qtr with mentor prompting self-assessment
Coaching w/data analysis	Half day each qtr w/mentor who prompts self-assessment	Half day each qtr w/mentor who prompts self-assessment
Training	Participate in regular district professional development	same > >
Protégé observation experts	Half day a year, with a focus on improving on a Professional Development goal	Half day a year, with a focus on improving on a Professional Development goal
Protégé peer support	One 1.5-hr event per year	One 1.5-hr event per year
Reflection: professional development goals	Mentor input, focused on protégé self-assessment vs state professional standards	Focused on protégé self-assessment vs state professional standards. Protégé shares with mentor
Professional development plan	Focus on PD goals, facilitated by mentor, updated as needed	Focus on PD goals, facilitated by mentor, updated as needed
Professional development portfolio	Mentor facilitated, uses both development and assessment models, goal is to demonstrate growth vs state standards	Protégé facilitates for mentor feedback, both models used, the focus is demonstrating growth vs state standards

A SUMMARY

Don't be discouraged by the level of in-depth information covered in Chapters 1 and 2. Following these guidelines will help ensure that you *succeed the first time* in building a program that improves teaching and student learning. Also, your mastery of these models and processes will continue to increase as you implement them. In the following chapters, I will often refer back to these models and practices. Focusing on them will lead to excellence in mentoring and induction.

Induction Structures for Effective New Teacher Development

When we use the term "induction," we are really defining those things that the *organization* should do to provide the needed support for new employees. You may ask, "why isn't mentoring enough by itself?" Mentoring can be a very powerful influence, but mentors cannot provide all the support that protégés need to succeed. No one has all the strengths and skills needed for every person whom they would try to help. Every classroom teacher knows how true *that* is!

That "mentoring can't do it all" has been the message emphasized by Harry Wong (2001) for the last several years. If we expect accelerated professional growth of protégés and the kind of performance needed to improve student achievement, an integrated partnership of mentoring and induction is essential.

> If we expect accelerated professional growth of protégés and the kind of performance needed to improve student achievement, an integrated partnership of mentoring and induction is essential.

COMPONENTS OF A HIGH IMPACT INDUCTION PROGRAM

Figure 3.1 shows the Induction Puzzle, a graphic representation of the components needed in a high impact induction program. Our task in this chapter is to design each of the pieces illustrated by this puzzle.

Figure 3.1   Components of a High Impact Induction Program

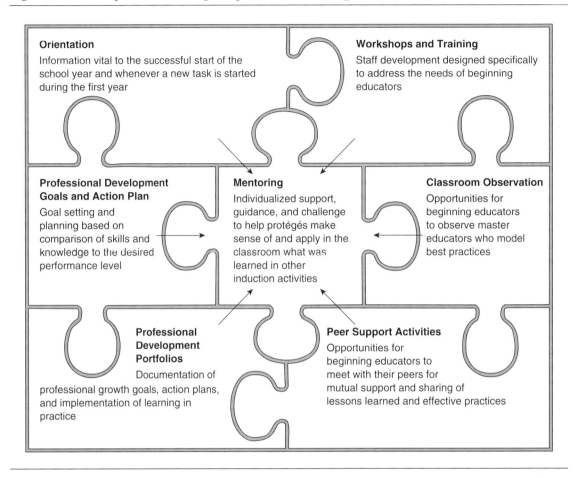

This chapter will explore each of these components in detail. However, we must start by first collecting information on our learners. As you probably know, the learners in our programs are always changing.

THE EVOLVING PICTURE OF YOUR PROTÉGÉS

It is often quite surprising to review the range and diversity of prior experience in the new employees found at a typical beginning-of-school orientation meeting. Some are twenty-two years old, recently graduated from college, and assuming their first paid position in a new career. A few of these have never held a paid position previously. Others may be in their thirties, parents of several children, and returning to a career they began fifteen years earlier. Some have actively been teaching for a number of years and are merely changing districts, schools, or grade levels. Still others worked for a number of years in a corporate position or the military, recently attained a teaching degree or certificate, and are changing careers to become teachers. A more recent phenomenon is the new employee who has worked in another career, has no formal teaching preparation, and is entering the profession via an alternative certificate program.

Induction programs must carefully seek ways to adjust the support provided to such a diverse range of "new" teachers so the assistance provided remains appropriate to the varying levels and types of experience new employees bring to their work. By addressing the individual professional development needs of each educators, the program explicitly models for teachers the importance of individualizing instruction for each student in their own classrooms. Tailoring an induction program in this way promotes the Vision for Excellent Teaching and Learning in each link of the Chain of Causes and Effects, resulting in effective classroom practice and increased student learning.

> A more recent phenomenon is the new employee who has worked in another career, has no formal teaching preparation, and is entering the profession via an alternative certificate program.

The need to adapt programs is heightened by the inclusion of teachers taking an alternative certification route to the profession. Research on this approach (Houston, Marshall, & McDavid 1993) reported on the challenges faced by alternatively certified teachers compared with traditionally prepared teachers. Recent research shows that alternative-route teachers usually begin their work with little or no formal teaching preparation (Bartell, 2005). Many alternatively certified teachers have strong subject area knowledge, but need assistance in learning how best to share what they know with students. To remedy this, some alternative certification programs require their new teachers to work with a mentor while obtaining a traditional teaching certificate in the evenings and summers.

Program leaders will need to ensure that their induction program components are structured for success. Orientation and new teacher seminars, for example, can begin with whole-group activities, but should be customized to grade or course level for introductions to curriculum and strategies that are specific to particular levels of instruction. The support should also be individualized. Mentoring is provided precisely to ensure that the critical knowledge gained in group settings is individualized to the needs of the learner, successfully mastered, and applied in every teacher's classroom.

One way to adapt the program to the unique needs of the protégés is to modify the roles and tasks of support providers. Chapter 5, on mentor program design, discusses the use of the guide or a buddy teacher to help new but experienced staff who don't need a mentor's more intensive help.

An example of a topical needs assessment to help you understand the specific learning needs of your new teachers was offered in Chapter 1. See Figure 1.6 to review that assessment.

USING THE CBAM TO DESIGN INDUCTION

Having previously discussed the CBAM as a valuable tool, we will now use it for planning. You may wish to refer to Figure 1.9 while reading this section. Our intention in using the CBAM structure is to both understand how each component of the induction program addresses the needs of protégés at specific places in their development process, and check that the program components we provide to protégés do not deliver more than is needed or deliver "help" that is inappropriate at one level of protégé development, but which would be needed or appropriate at a *different* level of development. We need to be sure that each component we design provides help at the levels shown as dotted lines in Figure 1.9 so those components work most effectively.

Figure 3.2 There Are Many Kinds of "Beginning" Educators

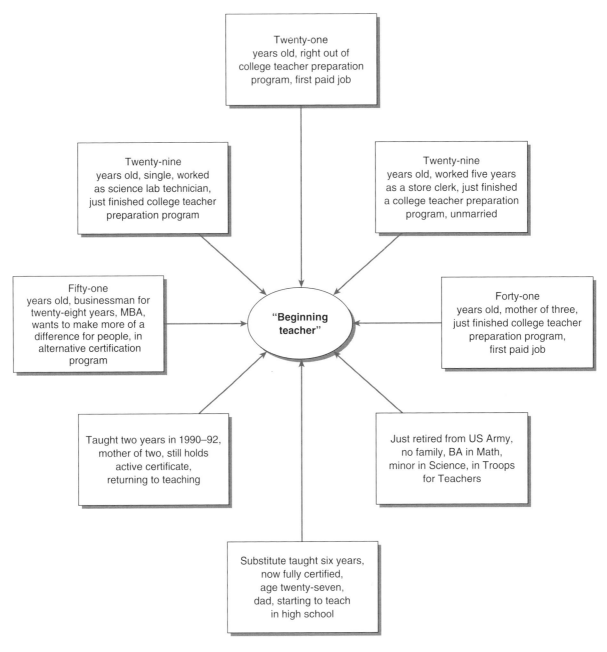

DESIGNING AN EFFECTIVE INITIAL ORIENTATION

Determining the essentials a new teacher needs to learn can be challenging.

The district wants to help its new teachers. It has lots of information, resources, suggestions, and guidance for them. District staff instincts are to provide all the in-depth information that all new teachers may need.

The mentor, too, has a great deal of information and resources, suggestions, and guidance for new teachers. Mentor instincts are to provide the in-depth information the new teacher needs throughout the following year, as well as to spend time getting to know their protégé and building a good relationship.

Other experienced teachers who are not in the induction program also have information, resources, suggestions, and guidance to offer. Since they know a mentor has been assigned to help the protégé, their instincts are to *minimize* the support and information that they offer to the protégé so as to avoid conflict with the mentor or giving the impression that they think the mentor is inadequate.

Given those good intentions, what is the *reality* of orientation processes? *New teachers* with previous experience may become bored with too much presentation of information. *Beginning teachers* with little or no previous experience may know a lot, but they are unaware of what they *don't* know, so they cannot ask for all of what they need. That leaves us to guess what is best to provide them.

Your initial orientation will be very welcome, especially if it is prioritized. However, you may become bored, especially if presentations repeat what you already know and waste precious time needed for classroom preparation. People can also easily become overwhelmed with too much information and too many choices, and much of the information may remain unused.

BEST PRACTICES THAT ADDRESS BEGINNING TEACHER NEEDS

Districts, principals, mentors, and others see certain needs that must be met, but novice teachers' perceived needs may not always match the needs seen by others. The conflict between perceptions of needs creates a challenge. Collecting data with a topical needs assessment from new teachers, principals, and mentors can help with this. You should compare these viewpoints and present the analyzed data to all. After being shown the diverse-needs data, the stakeholders will tend to give program leaders more flexibility to decide what is needed from their unique program perspective. Here are the suggested best practices that resolve this problem.

- *Define initial orientation to provide just what is needed to ensure beginning teacher success during the first month.* Then provide the district calendar showing trainings and other learning opportunities that have also been scheduled. Finally, ask novices what else, besides what is planned, they feel they need to learn right now. Then do your very best to provide for those needs as soon as possible. This is an important first opportunity in the program to model individualized instruction.

- *Differentiate* orientation for new, experienced staff versus beginning staff, as well as for teachers versus other nonclassroom specialists and administrators. Provide for the *whole group* only what *they all need* (Bartell, 2005). Then provide individual mentor support to meet the unique needs of each person.

Differentiate orientation for new, experienced staff versus beginning staff, as well as for teachers versus other nonclassroom specialists and administrators.

- *Prioritize* information to be covered so that it is just what is needed for the immediate future. Ask administrators, new teachers, and mentors to help develop sets of checklists that prioritize the different activities.
- Hold monthly beginning teacher staff development and orientation meetings after school. Include support group activities with the trainings.
- Provide checklists to mentors and explain that the checklists are to help them set priorities and to *avoid overloading* those they want to help.
- *Define* mentors' roles to include giving ongoing orientation for each "first time" experience all through the first year. Examples are the first parent phone call, first parent conference, first grade cards, first holidays, and so on.
- *Inform* all staff that it "takes an entire school to provide the support new teachers *deserve,*" and invite all forms of informal mentoring.
- If there are any issues *you* know are crucial to new teacher success, but you think that beginning teachers will not value them, use one of the "Words From the Wise" strategies (see below).

USING "WORDS FROM THE WISE" AT NOVICE TEACHER ORIENTATION

Peer pressure is a powerful force that induction programs can harness to encourage further best practice. To do this, induction program components must be redesigned to incorporate opportunities for selected second- and third-year "new" teachers to tell their peers what they have learned—particularly concerning such critical messages as listening to the program and mentors' advice (Sweeny, 2003). Because the tendency of the younger generation of new teachers is to defer to their peers for advice, we must find ways to use that tendency to ensure that what their peers tell them is valuable information.

> If the tendency of the younger generation of new teachers is to defer to their peers for advice, we must find ways to use that tendency to ensure that what their peers tell them is valuable information.

One certain method for capturing the attention of beginning teachers and communicating important content is to let them hear from the new teachers who have just finished their first year. This group has tremendous credibility with the group of new teachers. The mentors are also highly interesting to the new teachers.

A SECOND-YEAR TEACHER PANEL

During Orientation Weeks I designed, one of the most successful events was a second-year teacher panel provided for first-year beginning teachers. New employees really attend to the words of folks they consider to be "peers." Here are the steps.

Choosing Teachers for the Panel

If you are in your program's first year, use those first-year teachers who had good experiences with informal mentoring. Later in the life of the program, you can select three or four second-year teachers who also had a successful experience with a mentor.

Preparing Panel Members

Explain to second-year teachers the panel's goals:

- To help new teachers realize the extent of the challenge without scaring them.
- To help beginning teachers see that there is help available and to create an expectation/ permission to ask lots of questions and to seek help.
- To help new teachers understand that everyone has to go through this challenging transition and gain first-hand experience.

Provide the second-year teachers with a few questions ahead of time for them to think about what they can say, such as

- Was your first year what you expected?
- How was it similar to and different from what was expected?
- Was there a "low" time for you? What happened to help you get through it?
- How did others help you? What did they do?
- What advice can you offer about communicating with parents?
- What advice can you offer about asking questions and asking for help?
- What advice can you offer about the teacher evaluation process?
- What advice can you offer about dealing with the workload and time management issues?
- What else did you learn in your first year of teaching that you consider critical advice to share with beginning teachers this year?
- What helpful "hints" can you offer for new teacher class management success?

Have ready a supply of markers and a flip chart and paper pad on which you have written each question on the top of an individual page. To get the ideas on the papers, I prefer whole-group discussion so that *every teacher* benefits from all the ideas.

Have someone write the answers and ideas on the appropriate page. Type up the responses with a title like "Advice for First-Year Teachers From Your Second-Year Teacher Colleagues" and use it in a new teacher manual next year.

Holding the Panel Discussion During Orientation

Explain the goals of the panel to the *beginning* teachers. These are the same goals you discussed with the panel members.

It is usually sufficient to allow about an hour, but I always find it best to schedule the panel at the end of the group time together so it can go over time a bit if needed and interest is sustained. Give beginning teachers opportunities to ask questions of the panel.

TWO IDEAS FOR A MENTOR PANEL

Another wonderful activity for new teacher orientation is a mentor panel discussion. Experienced mentor teachers can be asked to prepare answers to some of the same questions as the second-year teachers. However, because of this panel's greater experience, the answers will probably be very different from those of second-year teachers.

When introducing the mentor panel to the new teachers, you might even ask the beginning teachers to expect some differences between the two panels and tell them they should be able to describe later how the two panels were similar and different. In that case, be sure to provide the time later in which they can discuss these differences. This will prompt a more attentive audience and can increase the new teachers' ability to reflect on and gain from the experience. It can also create, in the minds of beginning teachers, an understanding that *experienced teachers are willing and able to help in ways that are still not possible for second-year teachers.*

Reader Activity

Using Option 1: Sample Orientation Program Schedule provided in Figure 3.3, answer in the relevant columns:

1. If you were a beginning teacher at this event, how would you feel about the schedule? Mark a "N" for "No" in the first column next to any item you feel is *not good* for or needed by new teachers at this early point.

2. Mark an "X" in any of the other columns to indicate *whose* needs you feel the activity serves.

3. What are the conclusions you draw about the schedule, having done this analysis?

4. How could the value and impact of the schedule on novice teachers be improved?

DEVELOPMENTALLY APPROPRIATE ORIENTATION AND MENTORING

Novice teachers universally complain that they are overwhelmed and inundated by the sheer quantity of new learning required and the speed at which it must be learned. Further, novice teachers complain that what they really want is just to get into their new classrooms and to get those rooms ready for the first day of school.

A glance at Figure 3.4 shows us that typical orientations (bold box) try to deliver too much information at once. Also, the dotted lines for the best practice in orientation shows the amount of information that is appropriate. Information needs to be reduced and prioritized.

Essentially, initial orientation topics should not be selected because they are important for novice teachers to know. Regardless of how "important" something is, if a novice teacher is struggling to get ready for tomorrow, or if a novice teacher is unaware of the need for the information, it is likely that they honestly *cannot* benefit from the help and information that we offer. Maslow (1987) was right about survival being an obstacle to higher level activity!

So the best practice is a mix of providing just the information needed to get off to a great start, time to put that information to use, time to work at preparation of the classroom, and time with the mentor receiving individualized help and planning initial instruction.

A great model of instruction that should serve as *our model* for the initial orienting and mentoring of novice teachers includes the following steps:

- Assess the prior learning and experience of learners.
- Plan differentiated activities to build on the prior knowledge of learners.

Figure 3.3   Sample Orientation Program Schedule

Sample Orientation Program Schedule	Your Analysis: Mark if this is a good activity.	Whose needs are met by this activity?				
		New Teacher	Mentor	Administrator	District	No one's
Day 1						
8:10–8:25 Greeting from the Superintendent and ice breaker						
8:25–9:10 Video and discussion—"The Effective Teacher"						
9:10–9:30 District mission statement, philosophy, and goals						
9:30–10:15 Characteristics of successful teachers						
10:30–11:20 Video and discussion—"Discipline and Procedures"						
11:20–11:30 County Education Association Welcome						
11:30–12:30 New Teacher Luncheon, with mentors and principals by school						
12:20–12:40 Expectations for the week						
12:40–3:00 Classroom management (by levels)						
3:15–3:45 Introduction of *First Days of School* (Wong)						
3:45–4:00 Daily reflective questioning and evaluation						
Day 2						
8:15–12:30 Curriculum awareness/instructional strategies by levels						
2:00–3:50 Group presentations by levels of "First Days of School"						
3:50–4:00 Daily reflective questioning and evaluation						
Day 3						
8:10–9:15 (Teachers) Video and discussion—"Lesson Mastery" (Mentors) Roles and expectations of mentors and mentoring skills						
9:15–10:00 (Teachers and Mentors) Planning protégé lessons for week one						
10:00–11:30 Work with mentor to develop classroom organization plans						
12:30–4:00 School orientation meeting with your principal and mentor						
Day 4						
8:10–9:00 Establishing successful parent relationships (by level)						
9:00–9:45 Community resources and opportunities						
10:00–10:30 Personal mission statement writing						
10:30–11:30 Q and A panel (by level)						
11:30–12:00 Daily reflective questioning, evaluation (days 3 and 4)						
1:00–4:00 Work in classroom with mentor						

Figure 3.4 How Typical and Exemplary Initial Orientation Supports Protégé Growth on the CBAM Stages of Concern

1. Aware	2. Info	3. Personal	4A. Mechanical Mangement	B. Routine Management	5. Consequence	6. Collaborate
Orientation						

Key: ☐ Typical ⁝⁝ Exemplary

- Assess learning, progress, and readiness during the learning process.
- Provide differentiated support based on the evolving needs of learners.
- Adjust instructional plans based on feedback data.

It is "developmentally inappropriate" to "help" novice teachers by requiring activities that ignore their felt needs (such as to prepare their new classroom) and that inhibit their drive to adequately prepare for the opening of school.

When orientation, mentoring, and training for novice teachers reflect this instructional approach, novice teachers' needs are met, the obstacles to learning at more complex levels are removed, and what *we* know is critical can eventually be learned. When good instructional practices are followed, then learners are able to grow.

SOME ALTERNATIVE ORIENTATION AND MENTORING MODELS

Figure 3.5 provides an example of a developmentally appropriate initial orientation and mentoring system. Notice how this approach attempts to strike a balance between the competing organizational and novice teacher perspectives of what is needed.

This approach is more desirable than the traditional method (Option 1) since

- It provides time for organizational messages and needs in phased chunks that are more easily learned, understood, and used in practice.
- It provides time for mentors to guide novices in application of their learning in practice.
- It provides time for the needs of novice teachers to be addressed and supported, so that those needs can be resolved and novice teachers can turn their attention to other new topics and learning.
- It provides guidance and structure for mentors, ensuring their focus on the highest priority tasks.

The model in Figure 3.5 for novice teacher orientation and mentoring *should overlap and occur simultaneously* with the *following* model in Figure 3.6 for *morning* mentor training and *afternoon* implementation of the mentor training.

Figure 3.5 Option 2: Integrated Orientation and Mentoring—Protégé Part

	Monday Day 1	**Tuesday** Day 2	**Wednesday** Day 3	**Thursday** Day 4	**Friday** Day 5
8:00 a.m.–noon	• Welcome • Information on district and community • Meet key people in district • Information about key programs • District bus tour with stop at the Teacher Center	• Training in the district's improvement initiatives and Model of Best Instructional Practices • Orientation to district teacher evaluation system • Novice teacher requirements	• Orientation to teacher-specific curriculum and grade level, the big picture, the outcomes for the year	• Training in novice teacher need topic A: Classroom Management • Training in novice teacher need topic B: Parent/Family Communication	• Training in novice teacher need topic C: The District Assessment System and Technology
Noon	• Lunch with mentors and principals	• Lunch on your own			
1:00 p.m.	• Report to your school, get key	• Work with your mentor to set up your classroom	• Work with your mentor to outline the curriculum plan for the year by units	• Work with your mentor to set up your classroom rules and consequences	• Work with your mentor to relate district assessment system to first week lessons and develop an assessment plan
1:30 p.m.	• School-level orientation by the principal and other leaders			• Work with mentor to plan lessons and develop materials for week one	• Work with mentor on final room setup
2:30–4:00 p.m.	• Work with your mentor to set up your classroom				

63

Figure 3.6 Option 3: A Model for Mentor Training During Orientation—Mentor Half of Overlap

	Monday Day 1	Tuesday Day 2	Wednesday Day 3	Thursday Day 4	Friday Day 5
8:00 a.m.–noon **Mentor training and debrief of the prior day's work**	• Introductions • Information on District Induction and Mentor Program • Needs of novices • The challenges of effective mentoring • How to assess novice needs and professional growth • Initial checklist and mentor tasks • Plan follow-up for work with protégé this PM	• Problem solve day #1 mentoring • Roles/tasks of effective mentors • The M-P relationship • Effective mentor communication • Plan follow-up for protégé learning on: – District initiatives – District teacher evaluation system – Novice teacher requirements	• Problem solve day #2 mentoring • How mentors promote novice teacher growth • Mentoring styles • The mentoring process, adjusting your mentoring • Mentor growth goals and plan • Suggestions for mentor follow-up for today's protégé learning	• Debrief & problem solve day #3 mentoring • Training in novice teacher coaching for instructional improvement • Coaching practice • Suggestions for mentor follow-up for protégé learning on: > Class management > Parent communication	• Debrief and problem solve previous day mentoring • Mentor pair coaching practice • Suggestions for mentor follow-up for protégé learning on: > The District Assessment System and Technology
Noon	• Lunch with principal & protégé	• Lunch on own			
1:00–4:00 p.m. **Mentor and protégé work and application of AM learning**	• Report to school w/protégé, keys • Protégé at school orientation by principal • Mentors prepare in own rooms • Mentor gives protégé school tour • Help protégé set up classroom →	• Help protégé set up classroom • Mentor follow-up support for protégé's morning training • Build the MP relationship while working together • Follow checklist	• Work with protégé to outline the curriculum plan for the year by units • Finish start of school checklist	• Work with protégé to set up their classroom rules and consequences • Work with protégé to plan lessons and develop materials for Week 1.	• Work with protégé to relate district assessment system to first week lessons and develop an assessment plan • Finalize protégé room setup and prepare for start of school

Implementing such an overlapping model accomplishes several very valuable goals:

1. It ensures that mentors' learning and planning are immediately put to work to benefit protégés. This affirms in mentors' minds the practical value of the training, and it ensures the training is used right away before parts of it are lost to memory.

2. It ensures that mentors have the support and problem solving opportunities they deserve the next morning in their next training.

3. It breaks up a large amount of mentor training into smaller chunks.

4. It creates a context in which mentors can actually learn more because they immediately use what they learn and then can turn their attention to additional new topics and tasks.

However, there are some challenges in implementing such a complex, ideal model. The major challenge is that trainers for mentors and novice teachers are both needed in the morning so mentors and novices can be released for work together each afternoon. Depending on district and program size, these may be the same people, who clearly can't be in two places at once. Here's how to solve this challenge.

If your district has an insufficient number of staff development leaders to run such an integrated and overlapping program, then developing *teacher leaders as staff developers* will become a critical strategy for success with this model.

If sufficient teacher leadership cannot yet be arranged, or there are other limitations, the next best thing to do is to *form a consortium* between your district and a regional service center, university teacher program, a larger district, or several smaller ones. Such a collaborative gives you and your partners the critical mass of talent needed to run such a quality program. Be sure the collaboration is effective for everyone. Often such an approach allows partners to "pool" resources to buy dedicated program leadership time when none of the individual partners can afford it themselves.

PROTÉGÉ TRAINING

On the surface, training of new teachers seems to be a "no brainer." However, again our instincts are not an adequate guide for the task. What about the use of the CBAM to design the training?

What do program evaluations and feedback from program participants tell you? What research and expert practice can give us better understanding of best practice for this important topic? If we want a high impact new teacher training component, there seems to be plenty to examine and learn.

A new teacher cannot learn and understand all that is expected during a few hours in a meeting. After orientation, there is still much that must be learned. Professional development for new teachers requires a carefully orchestrated system of ongoing workshops and seminars, support groups and grade-level groups, supervision, and mentoring all year long.

Training is the best way we know to start improvement of teachers' instructional strategies and skills. Training that accomplishes this goal is designed to offer a series of events targeting the unique and evolving needs of new teachers. The content ranges from strategies for classroom management, parent communications, and assessment to providing structured interaction with curriculum specialists, mentors, and other colleagues for support. Such sessions are also a terrific opportunity for program leaders to monitor the success of beginning teachers and the effectiveness of the induction and mentoring support being provided.

Figure 3.7   A Sample Collaborative New Teacher Seminar Program

Month	Location	Group	Topics
September	University	First-Year Teachers Only	Classroom Management: The Nuts and Bolts Help! I'm Trapped in a Classroom! Working With Mentors
October	Education Service Center	First-Year Teachers Only Second-Year Teachers First- and Second-Year Teachers	Working With Parents: A Whole Team at Work Communicating for Change Assessment of Student Learning
November	University	First- Year Teachers Only Second- Year Teachers First- and Second-Year Teachers	Time and Stress Management Educational Career Questions and Decisions Peaceable Schools: Contemporary Strategies
January	University	First- and Second-Year Teachers	Practical Instructional Strategies That Work!
February	University	First-Year Teachers Only Second-Year Teachers Only First- and Second-Year Teachers	Idea Exchange/Curriculum Planning Valuing Diversity as a Strength Learn From Each Other: Classroom Case Studies
March	Education Service Center	First-Year Teachers Only	Valuing Diversity as a Strength Teacher Learning and Action Research
April	University	First-Year Teachers Only First- and Second-Year Teachers	How to Be Proactive in the System How to Be Proactive in Your Classroom

The program shown in Figure 3.7 was designed and led by the collaborative efforts of a university and regional educational service center. School districts may sign up to participate and are charged based on the number of new teachers that they will enroll. It is a fairly classic model.

One note: while there are some topics reserved just for second-year teachers that could be useful for first-year teachers too, this program has elected to limit the amount of ideas and information given to first-year teachers so they are not overwhelmed. One problem with the model in Figure 3.7 is that it offers no choices for the novice teachers, whose differing needs and levels of experience may make the program ineffective for some of them on some days. In that way, it has missed the opportunity to model and then expect of novices the individualized teaching that is the whole goal of the program! Beginning teacher training will create that desired result only when it is designed to *be* that Vision for Excellent Teaching and Learning that is expected of every professional educator.

An interesting twist to combining orientation and training is the "Great Beginnings" Induction Program of Fairfax County Schools in Virginia. The program pays a small stipend to new teachers to attend the three days of their "Summer Institute," which provides training in

- Organizing your classroom
- Establishing a supportive classroom climate
- Implementing classroom management procedures
- Setting high expectations for all students
- Getting started with the curriculum

Then there are three *additional days of general orientation* following that. The general orientation includes the usual district welcome and introductions, plus an overview of the curriculum, a school-level orientation, and time to prepare classrooms and plan the first week. The program puts new teachers into "collegial peer cohort" *support groups* at that early stage, and they attend meetings of these about once each month. Each protégé is *assigned a mentor* from their local school and is *coached by "coaches"* from a different school.

This approach doesn't just make sense to new teachers. About two years ago, the Virginia Department of Education chose the Fairfax County Induction Program as a model program, the only one in the state and one of three nationally selected for use in grant-funded induction pilots across the state.

If you'd like to review the Great Beginnings Afterschool Seminars content, go to <www.fcps.k12.va.us/DIS/OSDT/GreatBeginnings/syllabi_pdf/b1.pdf>.

Increasing the Impact of Novice Teacher Training

Whether or not you already have a novice teacher training program, here is some tested and proven advice to improve your training component.

- Always design new teacher training with the CBAM structure as the basis, and use CBAM-based data on participant needs to guide your planning.
- In addition to providing training, include *"knowledge building"* activities that capture and celebrate what new teachers are learning about becoming a professional educator. (See the section on support groups for details.)
- Add *peer support activities* to the training and knowledge building agendas.
- Design the required training content to *include regular district improvement initiatives,* but keep these requirements to as small a list as possible (see below).
- Research suggests that offering choices may be the most effective approach because that increases the chances that the participant's needs will be met. (Bartell, 2005)
- Design a series of trainings based on your research data *and* on your own experience. Plan these as *electives* and structure novice teacher requirements for the number of clock hours, not for specific content. The range of prior experiences, new teacher needs, and other factors are better served by requiring the amount of training but allowing participants working with their mentors to *choose* which trainings are the best fit with their needs. Doing this also requires teachers to critically reflect on their strengths and areas where they need to grow, so *two goals are served.*

> Research suggests that offering choices may be the most effective approach because that increases the chances that the participant's needs will be met.

- During each meeting, *collect* appropriate parts of the same *needs assessment items* as you initially assessed to allow you to ascertain and demonstrate protégé growth (or not) and adjust your program to improve its impact.
- *Create an induction website* and place all of the resources provided at the meeting on that site so all can access them *again* at any time.
- *Invite* (don't require) *mentors* to attend protégé trainings or send them a summary.
- *Remind mentors* to help the protégé apply that learning from the meeting in their work with their students.

Figure 3.8   How Typical and Exemplary Protégé Training Supports Protégé Growth on the CBAM Stages of Concern

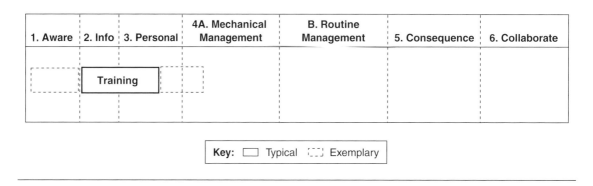

The CBAM diagram in Figure 3.8 shows us that typical protégé training provides information about a topic and often can go so far as to involve participants in (early personal stage) thinking about their own possible uses of the training content.

Best practice training (dotted line) would start by checking (not assuming) the level of the participants' awareness of the topic and their readiness to learn about it. Then best practice training would add near the end:

- Opportunities and support for *individual design* of a plan to implement their learning from the training in their work as teachers (upper personal stage)
- Opportunities with feedback to practice the skills taught in the training (mechanical management stage)

CBAM Planning Strategies

Next are the CBAM planning and assessment strategies I have developed, which have proven effective over years as a staff development and mentor program leader. You may want to consider copying this section from the book as a specific guide for the next staff development program you have to plan and lead. The results will be worth the effort you invest.

1. Preparing to Use the CBAM in Staff Development

Effective staff development takes time. If we need results, we also need to take the time to do it right. Here is advice for getting started.

- Understand that the only way to sustain an intensive and effective approach to doing staff development the right way is to have *local* data, collected across time, that show the effort has been worth it and that staff has grown and improved.
- Start by collecting CBAM Stages of Concern–based data on each of your current new teacher training topics. Establish the baseline using the Stages of Concern for the extent of teacher knowledge and use of each innovation *before* planning your use of the CBAM in design of the staff development.
- People will be cautious about revealing to you what they know and don't know, and do or don't do, in their teaching practice. Therefore, be careful to frame the collection of the data as necessary to
  – seek later school board financial support for more effective staff development
  – plan effective support for the people contributing data
  – identify areas for program improvement
  – clarify that you will report a summary only without individual names

2. Using the CBAM to Plan Your Staff Development Process

Design a sequence of several two- to three-hour trainings with a few weeks between each to allow time for implementation of what has been learned. I call this approach the *train-do-train model*. An example might be to do the following:

- (*Information stage*) Teach best practices in classroom management to first-year teachers in September.
- (*Personal stage*) At the end of that training, ask "teacher to individually develop" their own *plan* to implement learning in their classrooms, but *not* to actually implement their plans. Invite them back for the next meeting two weeks later and have them bring their management plan.
- (*Personal stage*) At the training two weeks later, ask them to use a handout with the numbered best practices in class management and to mark those numbers on their plan where best practices are used. Then put them in small groups to share findings and give each other ideas for how to improve their plans. Finish by providing time to improve their plans. Ask them to implement their plans and bring them to the next meeting.
- (*Mechanical management stage*) Provide individual help with any problems they are having.

> Collect and use needs assessment data for each training topic but use the Stages of Concern to structure collection of it. Identify where your learners are.

Collect and use needs assessment data for each training topic but use the Stages of Concern to *structure* collection of it. Identify where your learners are and the number of participants at each CBAM stage for each topic.

Collect pre-event data by sending the participants, two weeks in advance, a one-page, topic-specific version of the statements from the CBAM. Then plan which content and activities they need. An example of this method and the kinds of results you might receive is found in the box below. Read this carefully—it contains CBAM-based questions framed for the topic and example data you might receive as a result of sending it to (in this case, thirty-one) participants.

Example of CBAM-Based *Pre*-Training Data

"Protégés, when you think about your knowledge and skill in class management, which response below best indicates *your* most immediate concern or need?"

PRE TRG DATA Number of participants = 31

I am not sure what effective class management really is. (aware)	1
I need to know more about the factors that lead to effective class management. (info)	4
How can I plan for more effective class management in my work? (personal)	5
I need help solving class management problems so I can become a more effective classroom leader. (mechanical management)	14
I have good class management skills but I wonder if what I do can be improved so kids can accomplish and improve more. (consequence)	4
I'd like to share what I know and to learn from others who are good at class management. (collaboration)	3

If you were to lead a training on classroom management, and the data given above had been obtained for your training participants, what would you plan to do that would be appropriate for the people at each of these levels?

For example, if most participants already have basic information and are ready to implement it, they are at the personal stage. You could provide time and support for planning implementation and examples of plans for their use. You could ask "routine management" users for testimonies about the innovation and for warnings about pitfalls to avoid. Those advanced level users could work individually or in small groups with those who need to discuss their plans or have them checked.

Don't just think "training!"

Use the Stages of Concern to plan an entire sequence of events. Design content, delivery, and activities for each step in the whole sequence of growth and to ensure adequate implementation support between events. In other words, decide when and how you will provide the information, when to demonstrate exemplary use, guide planning, and expect staff to begin use of the skills. Then provide mentor support for problem solving and adapting to specific settings, and create time for users to meet to share what they've learned, to encourage each other, and to refine to improve consequences. Plan what you will do to guide participants through each Stage of Concern during the process. Simply stated, design the training to "treat individuals individually" and to maintain the Chain of Causes and Effects during the experience.

> Use the Stages of Concern to plan an entire sequence of events. Design content, delivery, and activities for each step in the whole sequence of growth and to ensure adequate implementation support between events.

Begin each subsequent training by answering questions that have arisen since the last meeting and sharing what was learned implementing the material taught in the previous training. If you couldn't assess each person's CBAM stage for the topic, do so right then.

Here's one on-the-spot assessment strategy. Create a set of seven signs, each with the topical statement for each of the CBAM stages. Post the signs around the room. When folks enter and it is time to assess where the learners are, have them stand under the sign that best says how they feel about the topic. Have one person in each group record on their sign how many are in that group. You will see where your learners are and how you should meet their needs as learners. If you decide to use this idea, it is best to come prepared with a training plan that gives you options to guide you when you get the data on the spot.

3. Using the CBAM to Assess Effectiveness of Staff Development Events

Of the two options for assessing effectiveness, this is the first you should consider.

After you have the pre-event needs assessment data, but before doing the event, create a "standard" for use of the new strategy. When you have the pre-event data back, use that knowledge of the participants to estimate the Stage of Concern they are at when they start, and then the stage you want the entire group to attain as a result of the event.

At the end of the session, ask participants to mark the Stage of Concern they feel they are at on the same needs assessment (post data). Compare pre and post data for growth of individuals and for the whole group to see whether *your standard was met.*

The following example shows what the post training data might look like for the same group of thirty-one used above.

Example of CBAM *Post*-Training Data

"Protégés, when you think about your knowledge and skill in class management, which response below best indicates *your* most immediate concerns or needs?"
POST DATA Number of participants = 31

I am not sure what effective class management really is. (aware)	0
I need to know more about the factors that lead to effective class management. (info)	3
How can I plan for more effective class management in my work? (personal)	16
I need help solving class management problems so I can become a more effective classroom leader. (mechanical management)	4
I have good class management skills but I wonder whether what I do can be improved so kids can accomplish and improve more. (consequence)	8
I'd like to share what I know and to learn from others who are good at class management. (collaboration)	0

> Caution: if you expect real, candid data, you must state what you will and will not do with the individual data they give you. Participants must know that their individual responses will be kept confidential and not communicated to others.

Now here is the second option. Sometimes, because of the way you will provide follow-up support, you need to know each *individual's* Stage of Concern to allow for adjusting that support to each individual's new level of needs.

Ask participants to put their initials on the pre- and post-event assessments. Tell them why you need this information. This allows planners to compare individual needs assessment data for Stages of Concern growth and to plan to address each person's needs for follow-up support.

Caution: if you expect real, candid data, you must state what you will and will not do with the individual data they give you. Participants must know that their individual responses will be kept confidential and not communicated to others. Focus primarily on feedback for program improvement.

Another Variation—Action Research

Set up a "treatment" group, such as a training to be planned and conducted using CBAM. Use as a "control" another group that is to be trained by different trainers using the same content but planned and conducted without use of the CBAM. Then collect Stages of Concern data for both groups, pre and post events, and compare the two groups for their growth on the CBAM.

4. Using the CBAM to Plan Follow-up Support

Option 1: Readiness

- Eliminate any training as not worth doing *unless* there is CBAM data and follow-up support for progress on the CBAM for that topic.
- Share the national research (e.g., Joyce, Showers, & Fullan, 2002) and your local data on implementation of current initiatives with the school board. Seek funding to provide teacher time for follow-up support for any training done, or even just for an experimental group.
- Share the CBAM Stages of Concern and the CBAM-based research on lack of implementation with your faculty, administrators, and mentors. Discuss and collaboratively define teacher and administrator roles in helping to decide how follow-up support for every training will be accomplished.

Option 2: Implementation

- Train your teacher trainers and your mentors in the CBAM Stages of Concern. Give them guidance and practice in using this structure for pre-event assessment of learner needs and in developing appropriate training designs in response to those needs.
- Define mentors' roles to include providing follow-up support for district or school-level orientation and training events and for other induction program events such as protégé observations or peer group meetings. This is the "Mentor in the Middle" strategy addressed later in this chapter.
- Provide individual Stages of Concern post-event data to mentors who are trained in the CBAM and prompt them to design and give follow-up support based on these data.

- When a number of event participants have similar needs, you can also give teacher trainers post-event Stages of Concern data and prompt them to design a *later event* just for those people whose needs suggest they would benefit from additional training.
- Use the train-do-train model (see under point 2 above). Ensure that teacher trainers collect and use Stages of Concern data at each step of the staff development

> Provide individual Stages of Concern post-event data to mentors who are trained in the CBAM and prompt them to design and give follow-up support based on these data.

sequence to assess before and after events, plan follow-up support and future events, and track participant progress and development. The more you can do this, the more you will see the wonderful power of this strategy.

5. Using the CBAM to Demonstrate Progress and Implementation

Use the final step under point 4 above, and also track and compare Stages of Concern data for individuals and groups across time. Use CBAM data to show how many stages people have moved and the number of people who have moved from just a knowing or a planning phase to implementation of the training. Also use them to demonstrate the number of participants who have moved to the consequence stage or collaborative stage and who are now focused on student results rather than just their own skills.

Create a database, or at least a chart that shows the *patterns in the data* you are collecting. Make this display public, at least by sharing it with the participants. It is important to demonstrate to staff that you *expect them to implement* training, not just attend meetings. When you do this, you are using the CBAM to hold them individually accountable for following through on their good intentions. As staff "get" this, the implementation of your trainings will improve even more.

6. Using the CBAM to Assess Effectiveness of Program Changes

Over time, you will eventually have CBAM-based data for every step in the staff development sequence. The growth, or lack of growth, you can see at that point will show you exactly where professional development and implementation are *succeeding* or *breaking down.* That will allow you to look at your plan (see under point 2 above) and decide on needed changes in professional growth programming. For example, maybe trainers moved from providing information to implementation and missed providing time and support for planning (personal stage). After making program changes, you'll want to be able to show whether professional growth and implementation of training have improved as a result of your revisions.

Also, compare Stages of Concern data for individuals and groups across the years, before and then after any program changes.

PROTÉGÉ OBSERVATIONS OF EXPERT PRACTITIONERS

To improve the performance of protégés, induction programs often require them to observe experienced teachers at work. This strategy seems to be simply common sense, but in reality the results of observations can be disappointing. However, this need not be the case. This powerful strategy can make the difference between whether or not a protégé is rehired for a second year. Why does "observation" often fail, and what needs to be done to capture the potential of this strategy? Using the following best practices will help ensure that *the goal* of the observation experience is attained.

High Impact Observations, the Challenges, and Best Practices

One would think that new teachers would love to be able to visit and observe experienced colleagues, but making this a *productive* activity is much harder than you might suspect. Here's what you can do to make observation of experts a powerful high impact experience.

Common Problems	*Solutions*
The observation is put off to the end of the year, when it does little good, because novices do not want to leave their own work and are not yet comfortable observing others at work.	• Require protégés to make a half-day visitation each quarter and report on it to their mentor. • Provide a panel presentation or quotations from second-year protégés who say, "I was sorry I put it off and I got great ideas I could have used all year." • Require protégés to *first observe their mentors* during the first month or so.
There is no support for helping protégés to identify what they need to learn or how they need to improve, so *they don't know what* they need to observe. Recent research has found that "teachers will benefit most from observation of others if they are looking for something specific. They should first observe and then discuss what they have learned with their mentor" (Bartell, 2005).	• Prompt mentors to *discuss professional growth goals* with the protégé very early in the first month and then to revise them each month thereafter. • Ask mentors to explain *how to use* the protégé's professional growth goals *when selecting the person to observe*.
The time for the observation is chosen randomly or for the protégé's convenience and is not an appropriate or useful time or event to observe.	• The mentor helps to arrange the observation and speaks in advance to the expert to be observed about *what needs to be observed that will help the protégé's growth area and when* it would be best to observe that.
There is no support for identifying an expert who might be worth observing, so the experienced person who is observed *does not model what the novice teacher needs to see.*	• Organizations should *identify top teacher "performers" in a range of specific strategies.* Create a directory of persons willing to be observed and list the nature of their strengths. • Mentors should suggest people to observe whom they know are great models of just what the protégé needs to learn.
The novice does not understand what the experienced person is demonstrating so the *modeling occurs but the protégé doesn't "get it."*	• Mentors should explicitly help protégés to *plan what will be observed.* • Mentors *go with the protégé* and observe the same event. Bring a writing pad for communicating during the visit. Afterwards, the mentor prompts protégé comparison of what was observed with the protégé's own practices, and then do some goal setting.

Planning the protégé observation component so it is based on the CBAM helps us see that typical observations by novice teachers can only give protégés new information and only prompt their thinking about using what was observed.

Figure 3.9 How Typical and Exemplary Protégé Observations Support Protégé Growth on the CBAM Stages of Concern

1. Aware	2. Info	3. Personal	4A. Mechanical Management	B. Routine Management	5. Consequence	6. Collaborate
	Protégé Observations					

Key: ☐ Typical ⌷⌷⌷ Exemplary

That sounds OK, but look at what best practice observation accomplishes beyond that. The best practice observation ensures that protégés will increase their awareness of areas where growth is needed. Therefore, their readiness to learn in these areas is increased. Figure 3.9 also shows the last step—one that ensures maximum learning from observation. The mentor should meet with the protégé after the observation and ask the protégé to identify ideas observed that the protégé would like to implement. Then, together, they would develop an implementation plan. Mentors would provide data from their own observation of the protégé's efforts. Finally, the mentor would support the protégé's attempts at improvement and skills development.

> The best practice observation ensures that protégés will increase their awareness of areas where growth is needed. Therefore, their readiness to learn in these areas is increased.

PROTÉGÉ PEER SUPPORT

The support of a new teacher peer group has always been a critical opportunity for protégé growth. Some of the discoveries that novice teachers need to make are best learned through peer interactions. However, younger generations of employees have made reliance on the peer group the *primary* source of support. *In some cases, the power of peer influence makes peer support even more important than the mentoring of an experienced person.* The implications for induction and mentoring programs are tremendous. Keep in mind that programs don't need "chat" groups in which the "blind lead the blind." They need new teacher peer support activities *which are carefully structured and skillfully facilitated. This difference is crucial for the success of today's induction programs.*

Opportunities for mentors to work with their protégés *after* peer support activities are crucial. Mentors need to ensure that the learning was practical and useful and, if so, that it has been implemented in the workplace.

> Programs don't need "chat" groups in which the "blind lead the blind." They need new teacher peer support activities that are carefully structured and skillfully facilitated. This difference is crucial for the success of today's induction programs.

Peer support activities are beneficial for participants, but they should also be beneficial for the program. Program leaders face challenges in building and keeping the support of district decision makers, especially for mentoring and induction. Why have some programs struggled with gaining this support? What can increase the positive impact of peer support activity on participants and also help the program?

The necessity of a confidential relationship makes many of the terrific things that happen in a mentoring relationship "invisible" to everyone else. It is critical to capture and celebrate these wonderful experiences but to do so in a way that does not violate confidentiality. This peer support strategy is crucial because the important impact of the induction program can be monitored by program leaders and seen by decision makers who may control resources but who may never have experienced the power of mentoring themselves and who may have no reason to value it. Figure 3.10 presents a diagram and directions that show how this strategy works.

Format for a New Teacher Peer Support Meeting

Each meeting is two hours long, from 4:30 to 6:30 p.m. Snacks are provided and the agendas follow the same pattern.

During the first hour, the "content" of the meeting is addressed. The topics are those in your Beginning Teacher Training Plan.

The second half of the meeting is the peer support portion. One facilitator is responsible for the entire series of meetings and provides the continuity across the various presenters. This facilitator is responsible for leading the discussions and structuring the activities, which basically fit into one of two types of activities: knowledge-base building; and problem solving and support.

Knowledge-Base Building

This process has several steps:

- *Statement of the question*(s) for the discussion. Dialog focuses on carefully crafted questions that prompt novices to think about and grow in needed areas. An example is "It's October 1. What advice would you give to the new teachers we hire next year about how to survive during the first month of school?" The focus is on their *own* experience so their confidential mentoring relationship is protected.
- *Open discussion of the lessons people have learned*, insights they have reached, problems that have occurred, and solutions developed or suggestions offered. Reactions are generated in safe, small table groups. Someone is asked to summarize and share the group's answers. This creates anonymity for individuals, which promotes a willingness to take the risk of publicly sharing a concern.

Figure 3.10   Strategy for Supporting, Capturing, and Celebrating Protégé Growth

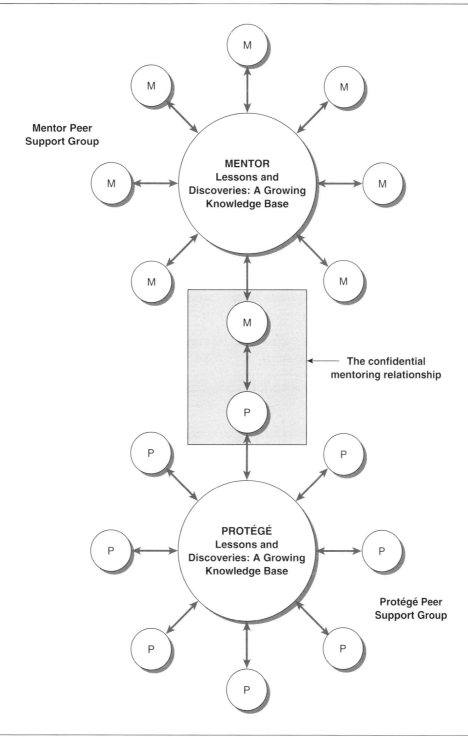

- *Capture the ideas on flip chart paper* as the small groups report their general findings. Flip charts are posted on an easel, and writing is done by the facilitator who clarifies what was said before writing it—a process that helps speakers distill ideas to a gem. If multiple questions are explored, there should be a chart for each question, as the ideas will be expressed in a fairly random pattern. The facilitator just moves to the corresponding chart to record the ideas.

- *Affirmation and celebration* by the facilitator of the increasing wisdom displayed, lessons learned, and accomplishments attained by the new teachers. This can be a simple statement or it can be a ritual that symbolically represents the celebration, such as lighting a candle for each good idea.

- *Request permission from the group to share the ideas* captured with people who are not in the program and who may not have the experience or opportunity we do to value mentoring and induction programming. The strategy works well because ideas are shared in a group (public) setting, so most will not mind sharing the ideas outside of the room. Nevertheless, permission should be sought.

- *Type up the answers later* and *share them* with everyone—for example, in a mentoring program newsletter. Do this often so nonprogram people can value what is being accomplished within the confidential mentoring relationship. Ideas are also used to inform future program improvement decision making, such as when refining the new teacher and mentor training for the next year.

Figure 3.11　How Typical and Exemplary Protégé Peer Support Activities Support Protégé Growth on the CBAM Stages of Concern

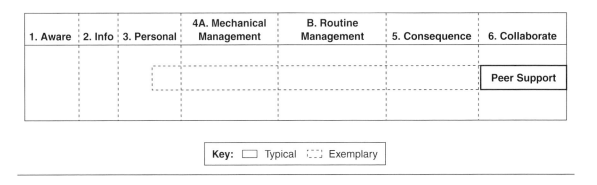

1. Aware	2. Info	3. Personal	4A. Mechanical Management	B. Routine Management	5. Consequence	6. Collaborate
						Peer Support

Key:　☐ Typical　┌┈┐ Exemplary

Problem Solving and Support

The second major purpose of the protégé peer support activity is support for problem solving and sharing among peers. Support is both practical in helping to solve problems, and emotional in affirming others or letting others discover that they are not the only ones who are struggling.

Problem solving can be a difficult challenge for new teachers, especially at the beginning when there may be little risk taking because there is little trust established. To encourage sharing of problems, try the ideas below and work hard to build the quality of these experiences. As you can see in Figure 3.11, this activity can eventually take new teachers to their highest level of professional practice.

- *Facilitators should model* self-disclosure by sharing a challenge they are facing and asking the group to generate solutions. This modeling includes thinking out loud about how the suggestions might work or not, predicting how the students may react, how their own strengths can be used to make the idea work, etc. This approach models the way effective teachers think and helps new teachers to learn and internalize this thinking.

- *The "secret ballot" method* can be used to raise the problems. The facilitator starts the discussion by reminding everyone that all effective teachers are continually learning throughout their careers. Next, facilitators can tell a story about something they have recently learned because they were open to feedback from a peer whom they trust. Then the facilitator passes out one or two index cards to each person and states all persons are to
  - reflect on their recent teaching experience and the challenges they face
  - choose just one or two problems they have experienced
  - write a bit about the problem and the situation on one side of the card
  - write a question about the problem on the other side of the same card

Then the facilitator goes around with a bowl or box and each drops in the question cards. At this point, the facilitator can stir the cards and pull one out for discussion. Repeat this until all cards have been discussed or the time is gone. Another option is to place all the cards on a table, sort them by type of problem, read several similar problems, and deal with them as a whole. The group asks questions that clarify the problem and the situation and then brainstorms possible solutions.

The Value of Peer Support Groups

1. If the activities include "knowledge-building" methods then protégés will learn the importance of "giving something back to their profession" (Sweeny, 1995).

2. Sharing their challenges and experiences helps protégés to discover that these struggles are not unique and that everyone's experience is the same (Sweeny, 1995).

3. The peer support activities provide an opportunity for protégés to gain support and encouragement from each other.

4. Participants gain helpful ideas because of the pooling of all the other protégés' experiences and learning. If *only one protégé learns* an important lesson, the sharing allows all to learn and use it (Sweeny, 1995).

5. By using peer support activities for reflecting on problems and solutions, protégés are led to go beyond their sometimes narrow understandings. This happens only if they are in *structured* reflection in a collaborative setting (Bartell, 2005).

6. Novice teachers are more likely to turn to their equally inexperienced peers for help than they are to go to experienced teachers. Using the peer support activities described here, allow the induction program to "harness" and use this peer pressure for fostering best practices (Sweeny, 2003).

7. Teachers routinely find these support meetings to be useful, but only if *their issues and questions* form the focus of the agendas (Bartell, 2005).

PROTÉGÉ REFLECTIVE PRACTICE AND THE PROFESSIONAL STANDARDS

Perhaps, reaching this section, you are wondering whether you need to read it. After all, novice teachers are kept very busy just getting ready for tomorrow's instruction. You may wonder about suggestions to add components to your induction program focused on teaching reflective practices and documenting professional growth. Bartell (2005) concludes that it is important for induction programs to include the self-initiated issues and concerns about survival that characterized early induction efforts; however, it is vital to do more. She says induction needs to move beyond providing the emotional support and be standard-driven.

Figure 3.12   How Typical and Exemplary Professional Development Goals, Plans, and Portfolios Support Protégé Growth on the CBAM Stages of Concern

1. Aware	2. Info	3. Personal	4A. Mechanical Management	B. Routine Management	5. Consequence	6. Collaborate
			Professional Development Goals and Plans			
			Professional Development Portfolio			

Key: ☐ Typical ⌐⌐ Exemplary

A review of the CBAM Stages of Concern shows professional growth goals, plans, and portfolios serve needs and promote the growth of protégés to a very high level—a level supported only by mentoring itself.

If we wish our new teachers to quickly attain high levels of practice, their development at those stages must be very well supported. Professional growth goals and plans seem important for this reason.

Not all reflection is necessarily productive, because not all reflection leads to learning and professional growth (Calderhead, 1992). Yet reflection is a critical component of professional learning. That professional development and reflection tools—such as those presented in this chapter—are being required at both preservice teacher education and inservice teacher levels is testimony to the critical role that reflection plays in professional learning.

USE OF PROFESSIONAL DEVELOPMENT GOALS AND PLANS

Professional Development Goals and Action Plan

There are several reasons why some induction and mentoring programs ask mentoring pairs to develop professional development goals and action plans. The most common reason is that state-mandated beginning teacher programs require the use of professional development planning. Usually, the requirement exists because the state program is based on a set of teaching standards. In this case, teachers will almost always be assessed or assess themselves against those standards. Also, teachers need a structure when developing plans to address the gap between their current practices and those defined by the standards. This kind of reflective analysis is always beneficial, so even if state requirements for professional development goals do not exist, your induction and mentoring program should require staff to engage in this kind of reflection.

However, Fendler (2003) and Bartell (2005) recommend that programs avoid being overly prescriptive in determining exactly how (the process) protégés should be reflective, what they should reflect on, or what forms must be completed as evidence.

Kilburg (2005) found that mentors play a critical role in guiding protégés through their processes of reflection, and thereby help their protégés to better understand and describe the problems they are experiencing. Research has also found that by helping their protégés to reframe and better understand their problems, mentors actually teach protégés how to diagnose problems and develop alternative solutions for them.

Ellen Moir, Executive Director of the New Teacher Center at the University of California—Santa Cruz, leads one of the most successful induction programs. She believes novice teachers should systematically identify areas for growth and set personal performance goals, then—with help from their mentors—develop the skills required to attain them (Moir, cited in Portner, 2005).

> Mentors can play a vital role in teaching their protégés to reflect on experiences and to identify and then solve problems. Using this approach means that not only do the protégés reflect on and improve their practice, but they also learn a variety of processes for how to do that.

To summarize, mentors can play a vital role in teaching their protégés to reflect on experiences and to identify and then solve problems. Using this approach means that not only do the protégés reflect on and improve their practice, but they also learn a variety of processes for *how to do that.*

Successful professional development planning emphasizes long-term goals that require a semester or more to accomplish. Some induction and mentoring program leaders put off requiring the development of the plan until several weeks after the start of school so professional development planning is based on actual teaching experience and realities.

Contents of a Professional Development Plan

The professional development plan should include the following:

1. A desired result or long-term *goal.*

2. A logical *sequence of questions* about the protégé's learning that should be answered as the teacher is progressing toward the goal.

3. *Criteria that can be used to measure the progress* of the teacher's development. The criteria should focus on what is learned and also on accomplishing a step or completing an activity in the plan.

4. The *initial steps* to be taken and the *intermediate objectives* to be accomplished.

5. The role or *responsibilities* of each of the members of the mentor/protégé pair or mentor team.

(Continued)

(Continued)

> 6. The date or *period of time* during which *each question or step* will be taken. A calendar should be used to maintain and help measure progress, but should not be used to push the developmental process faster than the actual development of the teacher indicates is useful.
>
> 7. The *resources* that are required to accomplish the plan and where they can be obtained.

When a program clearly states that results are expected, the mentoring pair will be required to demonstrate those results, or at least structure their work so it is most likely they will meet expectations. Programs that are less focused on results still may use professional growth plans to get teachers to think more intentionally about their growth. As a result, the type of plan required in any program varies considerably and usually *correlates with the program goals.* For example, programs that focus on developing and assessing *competence* usually provide a detailed structure to direct teachers to create a plan that relates to standards.

Some other methods are far less structured. A district might simply require a plan that details how teachers will implement the school improvement goals in their teaching and what they will need to learn to accomplish this. Of these options, I recommend that beginning teachers who are developing such a plan use a standards-based approach. That way their plan will not only lead them to meet program, local, and self-expectations but will also lead them to satisfy certification requirements as well.

It is critical that this developmental planning process be mediated by the protégé's mentor. Bartell (2005) found that plans were most helpful if the new teacher developed them in close consultation with their mentor.

Building a Professional Development Plan

The creation of a professional development plan usually includes the following steps:

1. The protégé reviews the teaching standards or district model of effective teaching and reflects on their own current professional practices. The protégé selects an area of growth that serves as the focus for observation by the mentor and forms a question that the collected observation data can help answer.

2. The mentor observes the beginning teacher and records the observational data, such as on a checklist of effective teaching behaviors or a rubric that is related to the identified standard that is the protégé's chosen target for growth.

3. Mentoring pairs conduct a conference at which protégés first describe their perception of the lesson relative to the standard. Then the mentor presents and guides the review of the observational data for any patterns it reveals.

4. The mentor asks the protégé reflective questions to prompt comparison of the observational data with the protégé's self-assessment of the lesson. Questions are

also asked to prompt the protégé to set a professional growth goal that includes the protégé's desired performance on the state standard that was the targeted skill.

5. The mentor guides the protégé in the development of a written plan detailing the steps each of them will take individually and together to address the identified goals and improve the protégé's skills. These steps are linked to a time line.

6. The mentor and protégé decide how they will evaluate the success of their respective activities. They decide what criteria will be used to assess whether the protégé's skills have improved and whether the plan was a success. If further improvement is needed, they revise the plan.

Frequently, the requirement of a professional development plan is linked to an expectation for a professional development portfolio that provides evidence related to accomplishing the plan's goals. The portfolio may include a log or journal of the protégé's mentoring activities to document accomplishment of the steps in the plan.

THE PROFESSIONAL DEVELOPMENT PORTFOLIO

There is little doubt that professional growth portfolios can be very useful methods for several goals. It is easy to design the portfolio process to fit your goals but trickier to avoid the pitfalls of requiring portfolios that then become mere compliance activities and are not seen as useful by teachers. Also, portfolios can easily add too much to the already overloaded schedules of novice teachers and negatively affect their instructional planning time and readiness for teaching. This section offers guidance so you can capture the benefits of these tools while avoiding the pitfalls.

Professional
Development
Portfolios

A professional development portfolio is a collection of plans, documentation, reflections on work or experiences, and artifacts that illustrate that the purpose of the portfolio has been accomplished. The purpose of the portfolio is usually related to one or more of the goals of the induction and mentoring program. Whether a portfolio is developed by the mentor, protégé, or both, and who reviews and evaluates the portfolio depend on program goals. The required contents of the portfolio will also vary for each mentoring program, as this will reflect the way the mentoring pairs are expected to carry out the program goals.

Assessments of teacher competency have shifted from sole use of written tests to including methods that demonstrate what teachers can do. For such performance assessment goals, the very best assessment method is actually *watching teachers teach*. However, for most large-scale assessments like state certification processes, portfolios are clearly one of the best and most feasible tools.

When program leaders decide a professional development portfolio is needed, they will usually require it of all beginning teachers and expect it to be maintained across several years until tenure (local) or standard certification (state) is earned.

A school district might require the developing teacher to keep a professional growth portfolio for several reasons.

> When program leaders decide a professional development portfolio is needed, they will usually require it of all beginning teachers and expect it to be maintained across several years until tenure (local) or standard certification (state) is earned.

Generally, these fall into one of two categories: those that focus on assessment of competency and those that emphasize professional development. One is about proving and the other is more about improving. The focus determines the type of portfolio developed, which is usually either an "assessment" or "developmental" portfolio.

The Assessment Portfolio

Programs require an assessment type of portfolio when they perceive a need for evidence of the protégé's professional performance. Such evidence can be focused on involvement in improvement activities and may not be specific regarding any desired results from these activities.

Providing evidence that professional growth has resulted in attainment of a specific, predetermined level of performance is the goal of an assessment-type portfolio. This is particularly true if the program must document the teacher's ability to perform a set of required skills such as those defined by a district model of effective teaching or by a set of teaching standards.

High stakes uses of a portfolio for certification and job retention require great care in the process of interpretation and evaluation of portfolios (Moss, Schultz, & Collins, 1998). Often, when an assessment portfolio is required, other goals are involved such as showing teacher use of student learning standards in instruction. This may mean a prescribed series of items must be included in the portfolio. The list of items typically found in an assessment portfolio is outlined below.

Typical Contents for an Assessment Portfolio

What contents are needed for assessment?

- A *professional development plan* developed by the beginning teacher and the mentor
- Professional development *goals* for the beginning teacher
- A *log or journal* of activities kept by the beginning teacher
- Copies of completed *self-evaluations* by the beginning teacher
- Copies of completed *formative and summative evaluations by the required persons*, such as by a principal or the members of an assessment team
- Copies of notes or of completed instruments as *evidence of coaching* conferences and observations
- Copies of *representative instructional materials* or lesson plans developed by the beginning teacher
- Copies of *instruments that indicate that the beginning teacher has demonstrated* specific skills or competencies
- Evidence of additional *graduate-level course work* and/or attendance at probationary teacher staff development seminars or *workshops related to the teacher's goals*

Developmental Portfolio

Some programs view teacher induction and mentoring as more of a developmental process. Those programs usually prefer to focus on addressing the needs and concerns of the beginning teacher and on determining when to challenge the novice to take on new responsibilities or risk trying new ideas. They use this approach to assess both the stage of maturity of the developing teacher and the developmental readiness of that person for the next learning challenge.

For these programs, a professional development portfolio represents both a record of past growth and accomplishments and a diagnostic tool for better planning and support for further growth. In this approach, the portfolio process and product should try to capture both quantitative and qualitative evidence that portrays the abilities of the beginning teacher. The availability of these two forms of data provides a more complete picture of the protégé's stage of development and readiness to grow.

Developmental portfolios can include the same items as assessment portfolios, but may also focus on evidence of individual growth and improvement.

Typical Contents of a Developmental Portfolio

- A *professional development plan* or a sequence of professional development plans that show work and growth over time toward stated professional growth goals
- *Journals* that record the reflection and thinking of the beginning teacher
- *Analysis of the written record* (journals, plans, etc.) for transitional patterns that show the developmental stages of the beginning teacher and can be used as evidence of progress or development from earlier stages
- *Samples of work* done early in the year and comparative samples of similar work done more recently as evidence of increased skill
- Copies of written *self-evaluations* by the beginning teacher discussing changes in thinking, what has been learned, personal insights, etc.
- Copies of completed instruments as *evidence of coaching* conferences and observations
- Copies of *representative instructional materials* or curriculum developed by the teacher
- Professional *educational philosophy* statements
- Evidence of additional *graduate-level course work* and/or attendance at probationary teacher *workshops or professional conferences related to the teacher's goals.*

We've looked at the theoretical purposes and recommended components of portfolios. To summarize, portfolios can serve as an ongoing record of development and achievement that is worth reviewing and can prompt reflection over the years. Portfolio use can allow teachers to celebrate how far they have come in their teaching, and can help teachers identify important skills that may need further improvement. However, what steps can leaders take to ensure that the positive effects that *can* result from portfolio use are actually *achieved?*

Guidelines: Keeping Goals, Plans, and Portfolios Meaningful

Professional growth does not happen because people are required to complete tasks. No matter how well designed an activity is, or how great an idea may be, they will not automatically produce growth. As someone once said, "The door to change is locked on the inside." For a protégé or mentor to grow, the door must be unlocked from the inside. This means that people must:

- *Understand* something enough to be able to evaluate whether it is likely to be a benefit to them and whether it is worth trying to learn
- *Be aware of a need* to learn something
- *Decide that THEY need* to learn or improve in some way
- *Choose* to do what's necessary to grow
- *Have the time and skills needed* to be able to do what is necessary to grow
- *Accept support and advice* colleagues offer to help them during the process

The Language

The way we talk about things with others is critical to helping them to become ready to do new activities.

1. *Avoid* using "deficit" language like "should," "must," "need to," "ought to," "good enough," "not good enough," and "evaluation."

2. *Try* to use language like "could," "might consider," "may want to," "assessment," and especially "self-assessment."

3. Labels such as "portfolio," "professional growth goals," "professional growth plans," and "journal" can be *loaded* with good or negative feelings from past experience, or because a person never used these approaches and has no basis for valuing them. Therefore, avoid using such labels initially and use the following advice.

> Don't use compliance language that portrays the activity as required, undesirable, a waste of time, or not useful. While you may feel that way, your opportunity to learn otherwise may have been limited.

4. Use language that assumes the best of others and invites them to engage in best practices by asking questions that lead them to do things well.

5. Don't use compliance language that portrays the activity as required, undesirable, a waste of time, or not useful. While you may *feel* that way, your opportunity to learn otherwise may have been limited.

The Process

Think of the process of implementation of portfolios as a learning sequence.

1. It is often too overwhelming and scary to be told you need to "Do a journal and portfolio" or "Set professional growth goals and maintain professional development plan." These sound overwhelming to all of us! Teachers are very busy people. If mentors talk that way, they may be viewed by their protégés as compliance-oriented, rather than protégé-oriented and helpful. That is to be avoided at all costs.

2. Instead of "dumping" an entire process on someone, it is far better for mentors to work with your protégés to *do* the steps of the required activity without labeling it with big scary titles. The best process is to
   • Give the protégé helpful growth-oriented experiences
   • Help the protégé gradually come to value that process as useful and *then* . . .
   • Begin to use labels such as "Professional Growth Plan" or "Portfolio"

Best Practices for Professional Growth Goals, Plans, and Portfolios

Most very experienced teachers spend a part of their day practicing at an automatic and intuitive level because of the extensive routines they have developed. Routines are critical because the unconscious mind can easily handle them, leaving the conscious mind to handle the nonroutine aspects of working with individual students and related tasks.

However, routines can also become a rut if routine tasks are never consciously evaluated or improved upon. The antidote to unexamined routine practice is reflection and self-assessment.

A *reflective practitioner* is one whose routines include taking time to look back on what was done to decide whether it was successful. That practitioner then modifies the routine to make it an even better support for student learning. One would expect that most experienced teachers would naturally be experts at reflection, but that is often not the case. Even experienced teachers can become overwhelmed by just teaching, unable to find the time to reflect except in the summer during vacation. For improvement to occur, reflection must be continual.

High impact mentoring and induction programs often are responding to state, provincial, or accreditation requirements for using these reflective tools, but they should also make sure that the tools are valued and used as helpful, positive supports.

Important opportunities to learn reflective practices could become compliance matters. If mentors have no experience with professional growth goals, plans, or portfolios but are asked to facilitate such processes for their protégés, those mentoring experiences *cannot* all be expected to be positive.

Because teachers are very busy, if a required task does not appear to be helpful, it will be handled as a "do the minimum" compliance activity. To avoid this, ask mentors to complete the same activities before you ask protégés. Mentors need time to learn and find value in these processes. Then mentors will have some experience from which to plan their work with protégés and that work will lead to the desired results.

> Because teachers are very busy, if a required task does not appear to be helpful, it will be handled as a "do the minimum" compliance activity.

Reflection and Professional Growth Goals for the Mentor

At the mentor training, each mentor should use self-reflection and assessment of expected actual mentoring performance versus an Ideal Practices of Effective Mentors checklist. Each mentor should follow that with setting mentoring growth goals and writing an implementation plan for how they will live out their good intentions in their practice.

About three or four times a year, the Mentor of Mentors should meet with the mentor and facilitate reflection on progress on mentor growth goals, reflection, and self-assessment versus the Ideal Practices of Effective Mentors, and revising or setting new goals and writing or revising the implementation plan.

Reflection and Professional Growth Goals for the Protégé

1. *When:* Ongoing during the school year, such as at the end of each quarter.

2. *What:* Mentors facilitate their protégés' reflection and self-assessment comparing models of excellence, data and artifacts, setting professional growth goals, using
   • A district effective teaching model or state teaching standards
   • Protégé observation of expert teachers and of the mentor
   • Data from mentor observation of the protégé on the protégé's priorities
   • Artifacts saved by the protégés based on their professional growth goals

---

Effective Professional Growth Plans Include at Least

• A description of a teacher's knowledge and skills, such as on a check sheet
• Professional growth goals that focus on a specific knowledge or skill
• Indicators to be used to show when each goal was accomplished, such as
  – tasks done, participation
  – knowledge learned or skills mastered
• results achieved, such as growth as mentor/protégé, teaching behaviors, student behaviors, or learning/performance
• Evidence of improvement in the selected indicators
• Steps or activities to be done, in sequence with a time line
• Resources and support needed

Recently, some important lessons have been learned from using portfolios in a variety of ways and situations. Here are the two key points to remember.

1. Reflection on memories is not as powerful for growth as is reflection on "stuff." "Stuff" could include lesson plans, student work, previous reflections, student grades on lessons or units, even videotapes of the teaching.

2. The more the focus is on student learning, the more critical will be the portfolio as a reflection tool to help the teacher improve.

> Reflection on memories is not as powerful for growth as is reflection on "stuff."

However, *a portfolio can easily become developmentally inappropriate for beginning teachers.* This is especially true if a portfolio requirement cuts into the huge amount of time novice teachers need to plan each day's instruction. Try this approach instead.

The "Save Your Stuff" Professional Growth Portfolio

At the opening of school, new teacher orientation novices are told that after the school year gets started their mentors will help them to

- Set professional growth goals
- Develop an action plan to achieve those goals
- Accomplish their action plan and achieve their goals
- Revise goals and the plan as appropriate.

Novice teachers would be also told that they are to *save stuff* that *relates to their work on those professional growth goals.* Anything can be saved that would show what they did and what they accomplished or learned. Protégés are told that, at the end of the school year, the mentor will help them make use of the items that were saved. At no time is a "portfolio" discussed. It is just "save your stuff."

After the initial mentor training, mentors use growth goals and an implementation plan to guide them in "saving any stuff" that relates to work on their mentoring growth goals. Mentors are given guidance for their role in helping protégés learn how to reflect on their teaching, the relevant models of excellence, data, and artifacts.

Mentors use their growth goals and an implementation plan so they will *have personally experienced the same process* through which they must lead their protégés.

> Mentors use their growth goals and an implementation plan so they will have personally experienced the same process through which they must lead their protégés.

During the year, mentors meet periodically with the Mentor of Mentors (MoM), who teaches mentors to reflect on their own teaching and their mentoring, update their goals, and collect artifacts.

At the final mentor support group meeting of the year, mentors are asked to bring and led to reflect on "stuff" they have saved all year that is related to their mentor growth goals. Revised growth goals are developed, along with an action plan. Mentors then discuss with each other how they could lead their protégés through the same process. Questions are answered and advice offered for prompting protégé growth.

After the close of school, the mentor and protégé meet to review the protégé's professional growth goals, action plan, and the artifacts saved by the protégé. The mentor leads the protégé through reflection, comparison of actual to desired practices, goal setting, and action planning to implement those goals. New goals are set for professional growth in the summer and second year.

Only at the end of that process does the mentor explain that what they just did was use the artifacts in a "portfolio" to help their reflection. The mentoring pair also discuss how, during the next school year, the protégé will keep adding to and reflecting on the portfolio and setting and working toward professional growth goals.

Whatever reflects the several aspects of the person's mentoring and teaching responsibilities, their growth experience, and their goals for learning should be placed in the portfolios.

What Should Be Saved in the Portfolio by Protégés?

Protégés should save artifacts related to

- Their professional growth goals for improvement as a teacher
- What they learned as protégés about working with and benefiting from mentors
- The applications in classrooms of the learning from working with their mentors
- The protégé's discoveries about facilitating student learning
- Learning about any of these things gained from interactions with other teachers and other induction program activities

---

What Should Be Saved in the Portfolio by Mentors?

Mentors should save artifacts related to

- Their professional growth goals for improvement as a mentor
- What they are learned as mentors about working with their protégés
- What they have learned from interaction with the Mentor of Mentors
- Their professional growth goals for improvement as a teacher
- The applications in their classrooms of the learning from working as mentors
- The mentors' discoveries about facilitating student learning
- Learning about any of these things gained from interactions with other mentors and other induction program activities

---

THE MENTOR IN THE MIDDLE

Part of the role of mentoring is to provide follow-up support for implementation. To visualize this role, look again at the "puzzle" diagram for induction, Figure 3.1, at the beginning of this chapter. The arrows illustrate the role of the mentor helping the protégé apply in the classroom the learning gained from all of the other six induction program activities. I call this the "bridging" function. To help mentors learn how to effectively fulfill this role, the *preparation* of mentors should include

- Informing mentors that their role includes follow-up support for novice teacher implementation of what was learned at induction programs
- Practice serving as implementation facilitators
- Reviewing the content outlines for novice teacher training, or (not a requirement) attending novice teacher trainings once to learn what it is that protégés should have learned and should be ready to implement

The Best Mentor Follow-Up Practices

How would I train a group of mentors to provide follow-up support? Start by defining follow-up support as a discussion to be held anytime protégés have done something *formal* to learn or to improve their practice. Notice how this facilitated process follows the CBAM Stages of Concern:

1. *Reviewing* what the protégé learned from the activity (information)

2. *Asking questions* to ascertain the extent of the protégé's understanding of what was learned and if a possible need exists for further explanation of the topic by the mentor (information)

3. *Deciding* what aspects of that learning need to be implemented right away (personal)

4. *Setting realistic longer-term goals and shorter-term objectives* for implementing the learning in the work with students (personal)

5. *Planning* the specific steps to implement that learning in the protégé's work, including a time line for the activities and objectives, resources needed, feedback needed, etc. (personal)

6. *Deciding* how the mentor can support the protégé's plan to use the new learning and skills in the protégé's work (to coach the protégé through mechanical management to routine level of practice)

Once the routine level is achieved and learning is implemented, the mentor can coach the protégé to move the new practice to the higher "consequence" level by helping the protégé revise the new activity to increase impact for the protégé's students.

Then the mentor can help the protégé locate and *collaborate* with other staff who use the same strategy but at an even higher level of success.

Figure 3.13 How Typical and Exemplary Mentoring Supports Protégé Growth on the CBAM Stages of Concern

1. Aware	2. Info	3. Personal	4A. Mechanical Management	B. Routine Management	5. Consequence	6. Collaborate
	Mentoring		>	>	Coaching			

Key: ☐ Typical ⌐ ⌐ Exemplary

This process of facilitation works really well because it uses the process (CBAM) that mirrors the way people naturally grow. Figure 3.13 shows this effect.

The original induction activity "plants the learning seed," and the mentor is the "gardener" who tends the development process.

THE MENTORING BRIDGE

Figure 3.14 illustrates the research by Joyce and Showers (1987) and shows that the "waters" of implementation are "shark-infested" and not fertile areas for risk-taking, growth or learning.

Figure 3.14 The Roles of Mentoring and Coaching in Improving Teaching and Learning (Bridge Diagram)

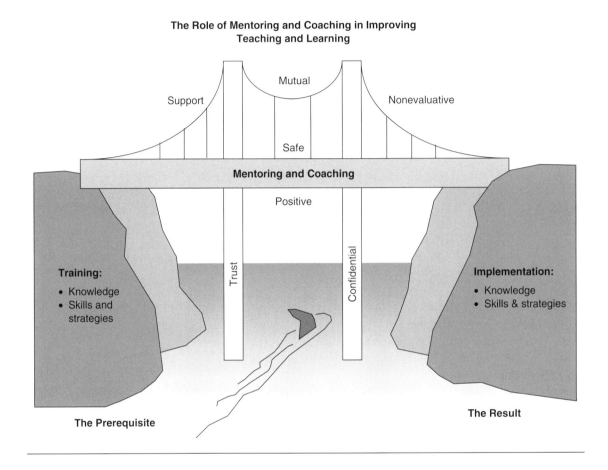

Only when coaching and mentoring are provided is it reasonable to expect that employees will be able to

- Adapt strategies learned in training
- Solve the problems of adoption and fitting new strategies to existing settings and other skills
- Master the new strategies

If mentoring and coaching are designed to support these steps, the protégé's day-to-day practice is improved and the desired results are increased. The implications of this insight are tremendous!

The *only time* we should ever provide any training is *when we will also provide the follow-up support* people deserve to help them implement what they learned.

Otherwise, why waste time and resources providing training we *know* will rarely change practice?

WORKING TOWARD THE IDEAL INDUCTION PROGRAM MODEL

The design of the new teacher induction program *is* a significant task with far-reaching implications. You may not feel ready to put all this to work just yet. If this is the case, use the CBAM Stages of Concern yourself.

   This book has given you essential information. For now, figure out what logically fits your needs (personal stage) and start planning how you will implement what you have learned. Begin in just one or two areas of your program and give yourself time to build your skills (mechanical management) and master the concepts (routine management). In other words, start small but "go for the gold!"

4

Providing the Time for Effective Mentoring

Before implementing a program of support for effective mentoring, we must address the need for the time during the school day to conduct that mentoring. Without consistent and dedicated time, even the most skillful mentors will struggle to help their protégés succeed.

FULL- OR PART-TIME MENTORING?

The most common mentoring structure is assignment of a teacher with a full-time teaching responsibility to serve as a mentor. Essentially, the full-time teacher has assumed an additional, part-time job. In part-time mentoring, the pair must "find" the time to plan, observe, set goals, solve problems, discuss teaching, and so on. Part-time mentors often receive stipends in recognition of the extra time they invest as they try to make this approach work.

Sometimes induction leaders don't have the resources to provide stipends, or don't wish to do so, but they recognize the need for mentoring time—especially if instructional improvement is a goal. In this case, the mentoring pair can be provided with substitute time to use when planning, staff development, observations, or coaching conferences are needed.

In small schools and districts, providing substitutes is often the most practical way to create time for mentoring, but this takes the best teachers away from their own classrooms. This sacrifice can be justified by the many benefits the protégé's current and future students will gain. Still, the arrangement causes instructional inconsistency and other problems (Moir, Glees, & Baron, 1999). Even so, mentors must take time for mentoring from their own classrooms or the additional time must be purchased through stipends or extended contracts.

> A restructuring approach makes finding time for daily professional development and collaboration a greater priority.

A restructuring approach makes finding time for daily professional development and collaboration a greater priority (Moir, 2005). Restructuring is implemented when a district realizes it must provide the tools for people to do the work that is expected, so the use of time is aligned to the expectation that teachers improve their professional practice. Barkley (1999) offers powerful suggestions for making time available for such initiatives.

Larger mentoring programs sometimes have a sufficient number of novice teachers to assign a full-time mentor to protégés for two to three years. Such a configuration is increasingly common, due in part to the successful full-time mentoring model used by the New Teacher Center (NTC) at the University of California—Santa Cruz (Bartell, 2005). Full-time mentoring is also used in Milwaukee, Minneapolis, and Baltimore, where program size enables this approach.

Recently, smaller cities like Yuma, Arizona, and some suburban systems such as Cherry Creek Schools in Colorado have begun to use full-time mentoring too. Despite the added salaries, these districts find ample return on investment, making this a cost-effective option. In Cherry Creek's system, mentors are released from all teaching responsibilities for two to three years and assigned to work intensely with twelve to fifteen protégés at a time. The number varies based on the diverse expectations on the mentor for improving instruction and other goals. Generally, the more complex the assignment, the more time is needed with each protégé to attain the desired results. Consider what Terri Romer (1999), formerly a mentor in the Cherry Creek STAR Mentor Program, says about full-time mentoring (see box).

One tremendous plus as a full-time mentor is not having the responsibilities of a classroom full of children and being able to concentrate on the needs and growth of our mentees, and on development of our own skills as mentors. Also, a secondary administrator recently told us that first-year teachers who had a STAR mentor have grown at a pace that took three or more years for a new teacher without a mentor. This fantastic growth is due to three facts.

1. Full-time mentors can devote all their time to assisting, advising, and coaching the mentees to cause that growth!

2. Full-time mentors can spend in-depth, extended time with mentees as needed. No other commitments get in the way. We get to know our mentees so quickly and "intimately" that individual needs, worries, plans, idiosyncrasies, strengths, etc., can be quickly discovered and acted on. I am able to be a better mentor.

3. The third reason for success is our "data curtain," which represents an imaginary wall around the mentoring relationship, so nothing they discuss is shared outside their relationship. The data curtain protects the confidentiality of the mentoring dialog and ensures mentees will feel free to discuss their real problems and concerns with mentors. Then, we work to remove the obstacles to growth. Great strides can quickly be achieved. Full-time mentoring increases mentee improvement so much (Romer, 1999).

Every educator knows the tensions created by the scarcity of time in schools. The Cherry Creek STAR Mentor Program and other programs that use full-time mentors are providing better support for their new teachers and are achieving outstanding results. The return on investment is delivered by dramatic reduction in new teacher attrition costs.

A successful example that uses full- and part-time release mentors is Prince George's County Schools in Maryland, the seventeenth largest school system in the United States. Their mentor program began in 1997 when the state required that they provide mentors to new teachers in schools with high rates of teacher turnover and/or low-performing schools (Kellaher & Maher, 2003).

Other Benefits of Full-Time Mentoring

- Eliminated costs of mentoring stipends
- Decreased problems with finding and frequency for using substitute teachers
- Decreased costs for substitute teachers
- Eliminated disruptions to instruction
- Accelerated professional growth for both the mentor and protégé
- Decreased costs for recruitment, orientation, and training of new teachers
- Decreased waste of administrative time because of increased teacher retention
- Decrease in administrative time required to supervise and evaluate new teachers

---

Full-time mentoring is effective because the use of time is restructured to match the priority to improve instruction. Dedicated time clarifies for all staff the commitment of the district to student success. It eliminates the conflict between the needs of students in the novice's classroom and the needs of students in the mentor's own classroom. When that conflict is unresolved or increased by placing excessive expectations on part-time mentors, the kids in the mentor's classroom "win," and the mentoring process and the kids in the protégé's classroom "lose" almost every time.

While it may not be an appropriate configuration for every mentoring program, full-time mentoring is a "win–win" situation that most programs should consider.

FINDING AND MAKING TIME FOR MENTORING

Ensuring adequate time for mentoring is a leadership role, not a mentor or protégé responsibility. The effectiveness of mentoring is directly linked to the amount of time the mentor and protégé spend together. In one report, only 38 percent of protégés who are mentored "a few times a year" report substantial improvements in their teaching skills. An impressive 90 percent report big gains if mentored "at least once each week" (Parsad, Lewis, & Farris, 2000). In research on problems in mentor relationships, Kilburg and Hancock (2003) found the "lack of time" for mentor meetings was the greatest of eight reasons for problems and failure. However, mentoring that seeks to improve instruction requires that mentors observe the protégés' classroom work, collect data, and confer with

> High-impact mentoring is labor and time intensive, but it is the best way to achieve the desired results of improved teacher and student performance.

their protégés about what to improve and how to improve it, even as often as once a week (Bartell, 2005).

High-impact mentoring is labor and time intensive, but it is the best way to achieve the desired results of improved teacher and student performance.

Program leaders must understand this work as having two stages, the first being finding and providing time to allow quality mentoring. Also, leaders must press to redefine the use of professional time for everyone. Small fragments of time are never sufficient to dramatically alter practice and student results. Instead, schools must provide time for professional interaction and collaboration during the school day. In an improving school, the time available is shared between teacher and student learning because teaching improvement is a prerequisite to student improvement. Mentoring and induction must not be merely an effort to "help new teachers," but must also support the wider changes needed for increased teacher and student performance.

> Restructuring the use of time is one of the most difficult challenges leaders face, but it may also be one of the most critical contributions they can make.

Clearly, restructuring the use of time is one of the most difficult challenges leaders face, but it may also be one of the most critical contributions they can make. Providing employees with the tools and the time they need to do the job that is expected is a central function of administration and leadership. In most schools, increased results cannot be attained without increased commitment of time and resources (Portner, 2005). One contribution to solving this problem is a very structured approach to mentoring time advocated by Udelhofen and Larson (2003).

To successfully solve the "time challenge," effective leaders use a three-pronged effort. First, think outside the "time box" to find and make time needed for effective induction. Second, conduct induction and mentoring activities using best practices, so the program makes highly effective use of the time available (Portner, 2005). Third, collect local data to show that effective induction and mentoring is cost effective and worth the investment.

FIND TIME "PIECES" BY THINKING CREATIVELY

A quick search of educational literature reveals numerous ideas for finding the time for mentoring. The key to creating the needed professional time for mentoring is to think outside the boundaries of our assumptions and to dream of what might be. Here are some examples.

- At secondary level, eliminate supervision periods, study hall, or hall duty for mentors. Advocate for time and guide decision makers to allocate dollars to provide mentors with lighter teaching assignments. This investment should include clearly established expectations for the use of release time, training in coaching skills, and simple accountability for time use through a tool such as mentoring logs.
- In elementary schools, consider eliminating hall or lunchroom supervision, bus and playground duties, and chaperone times for mentors and protégés. Interns or parents can assume these duties. Other strategies include planning a common lunch, library, or art and PE times for mentors and protégés. Some ideas below also work at elementary level.
- Provide full-time release from teaching and assign mentors to several protégés.

- Provide full-time release from teaching and assign mentors to other staff development duties as well.
- Create year-long district mentoring internships free of any evaluation expectations that could reduce a mentor's effectiveness. This is a great leadership development and succession planning strategy.
- Assign a mentor and beginning teacher to one classroom as a teaching team. This ensures time to model, coach, and facilitate the protégé's growth on a daily basis. It also eliminates any need for mentors to leave the classroom to observe the protégé. Though an expensive option, growth of the mentor and the protégé is increased and disruption to instruction is decreased. The trade-off is well worth it.
- Use recently retired teachers as mentors. They have the time and experience. Involve retired staff in district staff development so they stay "current."
- If you are having trouble getting good retired teachers to substitute, interview a few of them to determine what they want to avoid in subbing, and what they would be willing to do. Then create a system of professional development subs with those features and invite the retired teachers to join. Be sure to market the benefits. Commit to call on them only for professional development reasons that are scheduled in advance.
- Arrange with your local university for administrative interns. Use these interns to undertake routine tasks to free administrators to substitute for new teachers and mentors so they can meet for coaching.
- Utilize grade-level teams of teachers in creative ways. For example, combine the classes of four teachers for activities that three teachers can easily supervise, and free the fourth person to work as a mentor one period a day, or two to three periods a week.
- Provide partial release from the mentor's own class assignment (Bartell, 2005). Although it is expensive to release a teacher a day or half-day each week, that mentor could give quality support to all or most of the new teachers if the school is not too large. Combine this with a Guide for each teacher for their specific curriculum and grade, and that mentor could really focus on coaching novices for improved instruction. An example of this approach is used by the "Great Beginnings" induction program in the Fairfax County Public Schools in Virginia (Auton, Berry, Mullen, & Cochran, 2002).

THE COMMITMENT TO EFFECTIVENESS IN INDUCTION AND MENTORING

Regarding time for effective mentoring, the true problem is often not the lack of time. When the challenge of time for mentoring is discussed, we discover the real problem is often people's unstated or unconscious priorities regarding what they should do with their time. Competition for limited time creates the challenge and explains why a mentor who might profess to value observation, data collection, and coaching for instructional improvement can rarely find the time to provide that support. It may be that the mentor believes in

> When the challenge of time for mentoring is discussed, we discover the real problem is often people's unstated or unconscious priorities regarding what they should do with their time.

instructional coaching, but never received any coaching, and so has never had the opportunity to personally discover the impact of effective coaching. Although the stated support for coaching suggests a priority, the fact that time is not made to engage in coaching indicates that other activities are actually the priority.

There are two approaches for dealing with such conflicts of priorities. The first is to collect and discuss research showing that innovations have greater impact than traditional methods. This approach works well if one can present specific local data. Then follow the research discussion with an invitation and opportunity to try the innovation so that local data can be collected and the innovation proven or disproven in the local setting. The second approach is to provide the mentor with a personal experience of benefiting from the innovation and a facilitated opportunity to debrief what was learned, why it was learned, and how that learning could benefit others and the students.

Both approaches work because they eliminate a person's excuses for not doing the better practice. Success in finding and making time for induction and mentoring depends on a commitment to effectiveness in mentoring and induction program activities rather than to merely conducting those activities. Leaders and trainers should not be content with providing a mentor training. The goal should be the ongoing development and improvement of mentor training, such that mentors are increasingly more effective and report greater success in the use of the limited amount of time they can give to mentoring.

To increase mentor effectiveness and the belief that time invested will be productive, mentor training must

- Train mentors in how to most effectively use the mentoring time they have
- Provide mentors with sufficient time for guided, coached practice of essential mentoring strategies
- Be provided at a time when mentors are ready to learn what is offered
- Include sufficient time for follow-up support and problem-solving activities, in both individual and group contexts

Effectiveness depends on providing the time learning takes and timing the help to fit the developmental readiness of the learner. To do otherwise risks creating the perception that induction and mentoring are not worth the investment. If staff reach that conclusion, then you have lost the commitment and goodwill the program needs to survive.

Conversely, effective practice that provides sufficient time, adequate preparation, and support for effectively using that time, and a model of and training in how to assess the timing for providing support, will result in improvement of practice and results (Portner, 2005).

Sometimes mentors try to schedule time with protégés but protégés are reluctant. Mutchler, Pan, Glover, and Shapley (2000) report this factor and call on mentors to assert leadership even when protégés don't seek assistance.

How does a mentor or program leader learn how to provide what is needed when it is needed? The answer is to plan a program and train trainers and mentors to treat individuals individually. We have previously explored how to use the CBAM Stages of Concern to accomplish this, thus ensuring an efficient use of people's time.

MONITORING MENTORING TIME

A common monitoring tool is a "Time and Activity Log," a one-page chart that mentors complete to log what they do, how often they have done it, and with whom they have done it. The logs are submitted to the program leadership quarterly or at some other interval.

While logs can be valuable data sources, they are often perceived as a demonstration of a leader's mistrust (Sweeny, 2005). Mentors understand the log as an accountability system. If you are considering use of a log, helping everyone value this tool is an important goal. Consider the following questions:

- How could you communicate so that mentors value the log?
- What do mentors need to know and believe to value the logs?
- What could be done to remove the objections mentors might have to logs?
- What does the program do with log data it collects?
- How could those data be used to benefit the program, mentors, and protégés?

Consider the potential of the log and how best to capture that potential to benefit all involved (Sweeny, 2005). If you feel mentors are not giving the time they should to mentoring, and protégés are not getting the support they need, think about the following:

1. Inadequate mentoring time is usually a program problem, not a mentor problem. A lack of mentor time commitment is likely because mentors do not know how to be effective. Teachers don't invest time in activities they feel are ineffective and unproductive. Their time is too precious to waste.

> Teachers don't invest time in activities they feel are ineffective and unproductive. Their time is too precious to waste.

2. If we assume mentors are doing the best they can and only give time to mentoring when they know it will be well spent and productive, then the program needs to ask itself and its mentors what training should include so that mentors are prepared to use mentoring time productively.

3. The program needs to provide Mentoring of Mentors so mentors personally experience effective mentoring. Then support mentor planning for how to apply their learning in their work with protégés.

If your program is going to use a Mentoring Time and Activity Log

- Let mentors know that you understand they can give only limited time to mentoring.
- Explain that the log is not being used due to mistrust or to pressure mentors to give more time to mentoring.
- Instead, confess (it's true, isn't it?) that the district has not yet been able to make available the kind of time that highly effective mentoring probably requires.
- Prompt a mentor discussion of what data might help the district increase mentor time.
- Thank mentors for the time they *can* give to mentoring.
- Inform them that the log data will help the program lobby for better support.
- Let mentors know that log data is to learn what mentors cannot do, given pressures of their other work, as well as to see what mentors can do to make time for mentoring.
- Finally, tell them the data on time that mentors can give and the results that limited mentoring produces will clarify what is reasonable to expect from mentoring when the time is limited.

Your program could present these data and ask the administration and board for increased time to mentor since the results they seek from mentoring require more time than mentors are currently able to give.

An example of an actual "Mentor Log" based on these methods can be found at <http://t2t.fms.k12.nm.us/instforms/forms/home.html>.

5

Designing Components of a High Impact Mentoring Program

Mentoring is the core of the induction program. Once the induction framework has been developed, and time for effective mentoring has been allocated, we are ready to define the specific work mentors do. In addition to defining the work of mentors, this chapter discusses how best to recruit, select, and match mentors with protégés and the most effective ways to support mentors and increase their effectiveness. We also will consider incentives that attract our best staff to mentoring and recognize the wonderful work they do in that role.

DEFINING ROLES AND TASKS OF PARTICIPANTS

Our first step is to define the roles and tasks of each of the participant groups. These include mentors, protégés, and school administrators.

What Makes an Effective Mentor?

When we search the mentoring literature we quickly become convinced that defining a good mentor is a major theme. In "The Good Mentor," Rowley (1999) identifies six categories of "qualities" that are essential. Olsen (1999) offers similar insights. This and other research tells us that mentoring is complex work.

A mentor is the person who assumes the *primary responsibility* to provide mentoring, a process defined earlier. This definition works well with any of several approaches for providing assistance, support, and guidance to beginning teachers. Each approach incorporates a different conception of mentoring and goals for induction.

At the most fundamental level, the mentor is always a role model. Everyone who implements mentoring wants novices to learn from an expert. However, program leaders may have different answers to the question, "What should a mentor model?"

Many mentoring programs at least imply that the mentor is an expert with all the answers who must ensure that novices learn those answers. I refer to this as the "mentor cloning model." This cloning approach is less than professional and out of sync with current ideas about learning and teaching. The mentors we want today must be models of continual learning, not people who have "all the answers." Your Vision for Excellent Teaching and Learning cannot be internalized by new teachers if their induction focuses on observing leaders and mentors who act like the "sage on the stage."

Do you remember the attitude that must be expressed at every link in the Chain of Causes and Effects?

- *Mentors* must openly model an excitement for learning every day. Mentors must be driven to find ever better ways to help their students and colleagues succeed.
- This kind of mentoring will help *new teachers* become models of continual learning, whose passion is finding ever more effective ways to ensure student success.
- Developing this kind of new teacher is the best way to grow *students* who are lifelong learners and collaborative workers and who will continually search for more effective ways to achieve their own goals.

Clarifying what we want mentors to model is crucial in developing a mentoring program that actually improves teaching and student success. This ensures that the mentor link in the Chain of Causes and Effects is aligned with the rest of the links. Once you have clarified what you want mentors to model, then you can move on to plan the other structures in your mentoring program.

Characteristics of Effective Mentors

A list of the characteristics of effective mentors is an essential *first step* for assuring that the best possible mentoring occurs. All programs should adopt or develop their own list of effective mentor characteristics. Those characteristics are needed to guide you in determining the *roles and tasks* of effective mentors that you will use to plan the remaining parts of your program.

Before designing roles and tasks for mentors, we must apply what we said earlier about the importance of the mentor as a continual learner. Program leaders cannot focus exclusively on high standards when what they really want is to support professional growth. The characteristics of effective mentors should be used flexibly as a target to work toward. *Growth is the goal, not perfection.* Rarely does an individual exist who has all the characteristics of an effective mentor. In fact, finding someone who matches all the characteristics *may not be practical or even necessary.* Instead, the goal should be to find people who have as many of the characteristics as possible *and* demonstrate the attitude of a continual learner. In fact, anyone claiming to have all the

> Program leaders cannot focus exclusively on high standards when what they really want is to support professional growth.

answers should probably *not be selected* to mentor because they won't model continual learning. Such a person may also be out of touch with the movement toward constructivist, brain-compatible teaching methods that show there is not one right way to teach or to learn.

In addition, any list of "perfect" mentoring characteristics must always be flexible since the varying needs of different protégés should dictate what mentors need to do to be effective. The characteristics necessary to be effective in one specific situation will likely not be *the same* as those required in another situation.

WHAT TO DO WITH THE LIST OF CHARACTERISTICS OF EFFECTIVE MENTORS

Characteristics are often a mix of "fuzzy" and "clear" descriptors, which means that such a list has minimal value in program planning, training, or program evaluation and improvement. However, the list should be used to identify and define mentor roles and tasks. These roles and tasks will effectively inform your program.

A role is a broadly stated function that describes the *relationship* of the mentor to the protégé (friend, advocate, teacher, etc.), while a *task* is a specific behavior that can be observed.

Figure 5.1   Using Characteristics to Define Mentor Roles and Tasks

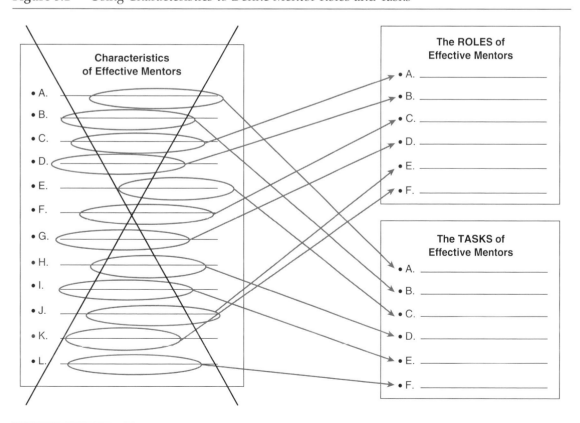

To make the transition from characteristics to roles and tasks of effective mentors

1. Analyze the characteristics to see which of the two above categories they fit.

2. After sorting your characteristics, develop a list of the roles you want your mentors to fulfill and a list of the tasks you want to see the mentors doing. Of course, some characteristics suggest more than one mentor task. For example, if a characteristic of effective mentors is to empathize with their protégé, the role might be "active listener" and tasks might be to set aside a regular time to confer with the protégé and use active listening skills. As you develop these two lists, be sure to include the following three statements on each list:
   - The roles (or tasks) are of the *ideal* mentor.
   - Actual mentoring is determined more by the *specific needs of the protégé* than a generalized list of ideals. Not every protégé needs a mentor to be all the things on the general list.
   - The idealized lists of roles and tasks are *designed to prompt mentor self-assessment, reflection, goal setting, and professional development.*

ROLES AND TASKS OF THE IDEAL MENTOR

The following describes the kind of mentors who will be effective with multiple protégés.

Possible Roles for Teacher Mentors

The ideal mentor would be

1. *A* helper *by being a*
   - *Resource*—of knowledge and experience with teaching methods, strategies and options, and of ways to learn these methods and improve them
   - *Linker*—accessing the resources and experiences in the school, district, and community
   - *Giver* of time, energy, encouragement, and support

2. *A* colleague *by being*
   - *An advocate* for improving student learning, the protégé, and the profession
   - *A listener*—caring about the protégé and their ideas, dreams, needs, and concerns
   - *A confidante*—establishing and maintaining the mutual respect and trust needed for necessary risk taking
   - *A sharing friend*—helping the protégé feel like part of the team
   - *A celebrant*—recognizing protégé accomplishments and building professional self-confidence

3. *A* model *by being*
   - *A visionary* with a dream for teaching and learning by both adults and students
   - *A reflective thinker*—using self-analysis, diagnosis, problem solving, and planning to improve

---

- *A career-long learner*—observing, listening to, and discussing ideas of others, giving and seeking feedback, and interested in becoming the best educator they can be
- *Integrative*—building on current knowledge and skills by integrating best practices and research
- *A facilitator*—meeting the needs of others and enabling their growth
- *A situational leader*—providing guidance as needed by being
  - *A teacher*—helping develop options for better teaching and assessment
  - *A motivator*—challenging, encouraging, and promoting the discovery and development of the unique potential of the protégé
  - *A leader*—self-directed, appropriately motivated, and worth following
  - *A needs assessor* who recognizes stages of development and who diagnoses obstacles to growth and readiness for learning
  - *Flexible*—adapting responses to the needs of the setting and goals

Note: There is *no* ideal mentor. This list exists to facilitate goal setting and mentor growth.

Using the Ideal Mentor Roles

Use the mentor roles to develop processes and criteria for mentor *recruitment, selection,* and mentor-protégé *matching*. During recruitment and training, *inform* people about the roles, and explain that mentor candidates should be these kinds of people, but do *not* try to *train* for these. People can learn new roles, but only through learning specific behaviors (tasks).

A different approach has been developed by Hall (2003), who suggests a three-tiered model for mentoring roles. One role is the "Beginning Level" for new inexperienced mentors, a second role is the "Advanced Level" for more experienced mentors, and a third level comprises experienced mentors who will also be "Mentor Trainers." Being a "Mentor of Mentors" could also be added to the third level.

Ideal Mentoring Tasks

Tasks are what effective mentors *do*. These are behaviors that can be modeled, observed, practiced, learned, and assessed. Note, however, that although protégés can learn a great deal by observing expert teachers at work, analyzing, weighing, and making choices are *internal* processes that *cannot be observed*. Helping protégés learn about these internal processes will be discussed in Chapter 6.

The following provides an example of mentoring tasks.

The Tasks of a Mentor

This list includes the kinds of activities in which mentors should be involved. However, the specific needs and prior experience of the protégé may indicate that some of these activities will not be included or that other unlisted tasks should be included.

(Continued)

(Continued)

If assigned at the start of employment, the mentor will

1. Communicate *in advance* of meeting, such as by phone or e-mail, to answer the protégé's questions and to schedule a formal meeting time and place

2. Assist the protégé in selecting from *among orientation event options*

3. Work with the protégé to prepare the workplace and plan class management and the first student assignment

All mentors will

1. Meet with the protégé for introductions and to schedule their work

2. Provide the protégé with *orientation* to the
   - Organization and its community and expectations
   - Building layout, resources, and key district and school staff
   - Community and other district sites such as a teacher store and meeting sites

3. Inform the protégé of local *procedures and expectations* of employees
   - In the organization
   - In the department or grade level

4. Help the protégé *locate* needed resources, equipment, and services

5. Meet regularly with the protégé during and after work to talk about their joint work, the students, the protégé's reactions to the work, and to plan and to share ideas

6. Develop plans, assign tasks, and *set goals* for their work together

7. Set boundaries for access to the partners, such as how late at night, how early in the morning, weekends, and holidays

8. *Demonstrate strategies* for increasing the effectiveness and efficiency of work

9. *Facilitate* the development of the protégé by helping to
   - *Analyze and evaluate* ideas and experiences
   - *Develop and test out* solutions to problems, collecting data on the experience
   - Encourage *self-assessment, analysis of data for patterns*, and increased understanding
   - Promote protégé *self-confidence* and learning

10. Discuss current relevant *research and theories*, model a desire to learn more about them and to improve use of them in their work to increase their effectiveness

11. *Model effective practices and openness* to feedback about your work and its impact on results

12. Demonstrate a willingness to be *flexible* and to adjust as appropriate

13. *Arrange other experiences* for the protégé, such as
    - Visits with those who model effective practices that the protégé needs to learn
    - Attendance at appropriate trainings or at committee meetings
    - Research on topics relevant to work and growth goals

14. Use observation, data collection, and conferences to coach the protégé to develop
    - Interpersonal and communication skills
    - Skillful use of observation and need assessment
    - More effective plans
    - More flexible and realistic use of strategies to implement plans

15. Set goals and implement plans for their own professional *growth as a mentor*

16. Support the work and growth of *other mentors* and their protégés

17. *Evaluate the mentor program* and offer improvement suggestions

Using the List of Mentoring Tasks

The list of mentoring tasks is useful in developing mentoring checklists, both of the "First Week of School" type and the monthly reminders type. I have published elementary and secondary versions of such reminder (Sweeny, 1996), as has Jonson (2002). Such lists help mentors recall the many things they know and prioritize those things so as to provide what protégés need in a timely manner and avoid overwhelming them. Other uses for the Mentoring Tasks Lists are to

- Identify and use *selection* criteria that ensure *partners* have a basic *minimum* ability to do these tasks. A minimum is all that is needed *if* mentors understand that they will be growing their abilities as mentors and *if* the program supports that professional growth.
- Use guided *self*-assessment during trainings to help individuals see their need to grow in these abilities. Be sure to keep the focus off "can you do these?" and on "to what extent are you likely to do these things without a reminder?"
- Provide time during trainings and guide each individual to use the data from his or her self-assessment to set goals and develop a plan for professional growth.
- Prompt mentoring partners to share their growth goals and discuss and plan how they can support each other in living out their good intentions.
- Ask each mentoring pair to share their goals and plans with the program leaders as data to guide planning for future training and support activities like Mentoring of Mentors.
- Plan mentoring *training* and *support* activities to remind participants of the ideal tasks and their goals and commitments to grow and to support that growth.

To ensure that mentoring is an effective link in the Chain of Causes and Effects, these role and task definitions should reflect the program's Vision for Excellent Teaching and Learning. This means mentoring must include treating individuals individually.

To provide a mentor to every new teacher in your district, regardless of prior experience, models "batch processing," not individualized "instruction," and breaks the Chain of Causes and Effects.

MATCHING ASSISTANCE TO PROTÉGÉ NEEDS

Mentor roles and tasks should provide different levels of support to protégés who have different levels of experience. In the program I coordinated (1987–92), we defined two functions: the *mentor*, for protégés with a year or less of recent experience, and the *guide*, assigned to protégés with more than a year of recent experience. We developed these two levels because we found that experienced new hires did not require the same intensive support, guidance, or accelerated professional development as the beginners. These two mentoring roles allowed flexibility and efficiency because we did not have to train, support, or pay the same stipends to people who served in the less intensive guide role, and their assistance was just what their more experienced protégés needed.

An example of the "Mentor and Guide Policy" at Poudre School District in Fort Collins, Colorado, can be found at <http://www.psd.k12.co.us/programs/mentoring/mentoring.aspx>. I recommend that you develop a similar approach to complement your mentoring. The orientation tasks assigned to guides are identical to those of mentors. However, mentors support protégés whose needs continue well beyond orientation.

Guides offer other benefits. Your program will have increased flexibility when matching mentors and protégés. Consider, for example, a new band teacher at the *middle school*. There is no other band teacher in the school to mentor this person. The *high school* band teacher could be the mentor, but that person probably does not know the school, the middle level, the grade level team structure, or other site-specific topics.

However, guides can appropriately support such specialists. The high school band teacher can mentor and help with curriculum. A guide at the middle school helps with local site issues. All the needs of the new band teacher will be met by this team approach and division of tasks.

Example: The Guide Application Process

In April every year, the Program Coordinator provides applications for service as a guide. All staff interested in serving as a guide should complete and return the form to the Program Coordinator by May 1.

A list of guide *applicants* will be maintained, and those persons will be invited to the next guide training session. Although guide trainings can be held at any time, at least one training should be scheduled during May.

Each June, the Program Coordinator supplies principals with a current list of staff who are trained as guides. The list indicates staff members who have previously served as a guide, their most recent year of service, and their previous guide assignments.

The Guide–New Employee Matching Process

Principals and supervisors have usually participated in interviews with new employees, and so are best positioned to know the strengths and needs of new staff. Principals and supervisors know most of the strengths and limitations of the current staff who might serve as guides or mentors. However, the coordinator of the mentor and guide programs has experience with and insights into experienced guides and mentors that other administrators do

Figure 5.2   Guidelines for Choosing a Guide or a Mentor: Providing Assistance That Is Matched to Need

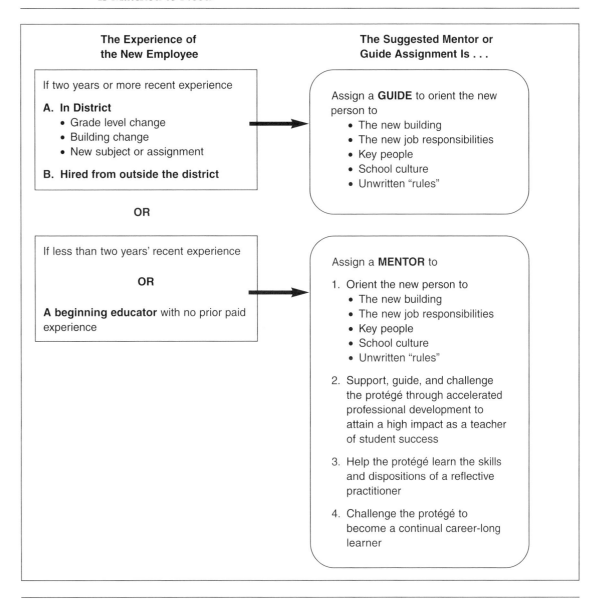

not have. Therefore, the coordinator should consult with the principal or supervisor to determine the most suitable person to serve as a guide. The decision can be informed by

- The level of experience and need of the new employee
- The policy for assignment of a mentor or a guide
- The job assignment of the new staff member
- A determination as to who is the best available guide, mentor, or combination thereof

An untrained person may be selected as a guide or a mentor if

- The guide or mentor has applied for the position
- The guide or mentor meets all other qualifications
- The guide or mentor can be trained within two weeks of the start of school

ROLES AND TASKS OF PROTÉGÉS

Some programs don't define protégé expectations. Others have protégé roles and tasks spelled out, but these typically do not reflect an essential concept. Mentoring is a partnership. I recommend that after defining roles and tasks for mentors, you do the same for protégés, checking that both lists complement each other.

Sometimes, mentoring partners must have the same characteristic, such as being an active listener. At other times, each of the partners needs complementary but opposite characteristics for the partnership to work. This means that the pair can be highly effective as long as one partner has a strength the pair needs and the other partner recognizes and benefits from the partner's gifts.

Two steps should be taken to make the partnership effective.

First, the program needs to change its language so that "mentoring" is redefined as a more inclusive process. Try not to use the word "mentor" unless you specifically mean to exclude the protégé from something. Try to use the word "mentoring" as much as possible to place the emphasis on what the pair does together, not just what one partner does.

Second, the partners need to openly talk about the challenge of being partners when their experience levels and individual strengths may be very different. They need to determine how they might best work together to be an effective mentoring *pair* in which they each contribute to the other's growth. If one partner is more task oriented and the other more relationship oriented, the *pair* can still be highly effective if they recognize, honor, and defer to each other's strengths. The ultimate benefit is the celebration of the diverse strengths and increased learning of both partners.

ROLES AND TASKS OF SITE ADMINISTRATORS

Often building administrators are left out of the loop regarding mentoring and induction. This is usually just an oversight. Building level administrators should be included in the program beyond simply sharing program information with them. When you define the roles and tasks for them, use the title of this section so it is inclusive and addresses principals, assistant or vice principals, deans, and other supervisors of beginning and experienced educators (Brewster & Railsback, 2001).

One common reason administrators often have no role in induction and mentoring is their required role as evaluators. Induction leaders want mentoring to be separate from evaluation. This vital distinction needn't be a big concern. Site administrators have a vested interest in the success of new teachers:

> One common reason administrators often have no role in induction and mentoring is their required role as evaluators. Induction leaders want mentoring to be separate from evaluation.

- Most extend more support and guidance than their legal role requires.
- As the instructional leader, the principal is concerned about the students and the extent to which novices are becoming effective teachers.

Figure 5.3   Complementary Characteristics of Effective Mentors and Protégés

An effective MENTOR is	An effective PROTÉGÉ is
1. Willing to serve as a mentor and to be approachable	1. Willing to approach the mentor and others for help
2. Foresighted, anticipating problems and preparing solutions in advance	2. Respectful of the other time commitments the mentor has made to his or her own teaching and other responsibilities
3. An excellent role model of a professional educator	3. Responsive to the role modeling of excellent educators
4. Sensitive to the evolving developmental needs, feelings, and skills of others	4. Understanding of the developmental nature of learning to be an effective teacher
5. Candid, but also positive, patient, encouraging, and helpful	5. Candid, but also positive, patient, and responsive
6. Committed to the success of their protégé	6. Committed to the success of their students and mentor
7. Discrete, confidential, and astute in what is said and not said	7. Discrete, confidential, and astute in what is said and not said
8. Nurturing, caring, and accepting	8. Nurturing, caring, and accepting
9. A dedicated, enthusiastic, experienced, effective, and reflective teacher	9. Actively seeking to become a dedicated, enthusiastic, effective, and reflective teacher
10. Emotionally stable, trustworthy, reliable, and self-confident	10. Emotionally stable, trustworthy, reliable, and self-confident
11. A continual learner, open to the views and feedback of others and a risk taker	11. A continual learner, open to the views and feedback of others and a risk taker
12. Team-oriented, seeing diversity as a strength	12. Team-oriented, seeing diversity as a strength
13. Adept at balancing maintenance of relationships and accomplishment of tasks	13. Adept at balancing maintenance of relationships and accomplishment of tasks
14. Knowledgable about the organization and its culture, mission, and values	14. Actively seeking to understand the organization and its culture, mission, and values
15. An effective listener and communicator	15. An effective listener and communicator
16. Respected by others	16. Respectful of others' diverse experiences, views, and styles
17. An effective leader and facilitator of both adults and students	17. Responsive to the experience and leadership of their colleagues
18. Able to articulate his or her own decision-making process and rationale for behaviors	18. Actively learning to articulate his or her own decision-making process and rationale for behaviors

- Building administrators don't want to lose a new hire at the end of the year and negate all they have invested in that person's success.
- They don't want to interrupt momentum in school improvement, curricular initiatives, or staff development.

Building administrators have a role in new teacher induction and mentoring. As the legal supervisor and evaluator of new teachers, site administrators have an interest in their success. However, building administrators' *effectiveness in that role varies considerably* for several reasons. We need to ask the following questions:

- Are administrators adequately trained to function as staff developers?
- Are administrators adequately informed about the mentoring program, the roles and tasks mentors do and should perform, the roles and tasks administrators need to perform, and the mentoring strategies that will help administrators to be effective in supervision of novice teachers?
- How well coordinated is the work of new teacher orientation and support by administrators with that of mentors?

An example of a program's definition of the "Responsibilities of the School Administrator" is online in the Mentoring Program Plan for the Farmington, New Mexico, Public Schools starting on page 7 at <http://t2t.fms.k12.nm.us/instforms/forms/pdf/FMS MentorPlan.pdf>.

How Site Administrators Should Support Protégés

Getting people to enter the teaching profession is not easy, but the real challenge is *keeping* new teachers in this career. Research suggests that, while salary level is a factor, new teacher retention is impacted more by whether novices feel they are successful as teachers and their relationships with their supervisor.

As instructional leaders, site administrators have a responsibility and an opportunity. They can do a lot to support their new staff and also provide the leadership needed to enhance the whole school faculty and culture. However, site administrators are even more isolated than teachers. As a result, they often have little opportunity to reach their potential in the mentoring and induction effort. This section provides practical strategies for administrator support of new teachers.

Realistic Assignments for New Teachers

Many protégés are stunned by what they find at their school.

Typical New Teacher Assignments

Typical new teacher assignments include

- The most preparations, which require a large amount of planning time
- Multiple school sites
- Multiple classrooms

- Classrooms stripped of resources
- The most difficult and challenging students
- Teaching assignments that include subjects for which they are not prepared or certified
- Multiple extra duty assignments like clubs, supervision, chaperoning, and coaching sports
- Requirements for graduate coursework in the teacher's first and second year

This kind of job assignment is completely unrealistic for novices and is one of the biggest reasons for our huge teacher attrition problem. Novices accept these challenges because they need a job. Some even seek such extra duties because of a love for athletics or other reasons, but if you check with them after a month or two you will hear a lot of misgivings. Once the reality of their task as new teachers hits them, they know they have taken on too much, but it is too late. They feel trapped, overwhelmed, and even incapable of learning to be effective teachers. No wonder so many choose to leave the profession!

Before they assume full responsibility for the classroom, novices cannot understand what a teacher's workload is like, and school leaders must not take advantage of this. Building administrators perceive that they have limited options too, and in some cases they cannot avoid this problem. However, there are more options available than you may think. Most administrators would relish some clarity about their role in induction and mentoring and would appreciate and use advice about what administrators can do to better support their new staff.

Throughout the world, *other countries* routinely ensure that new teachers

- Gradually assume their new duties and don't become overwhelmed
- Have the time and guidance needed to learn how to teach effectively
- Have a reasonable opportunity to succeed

Some North American administrators are adopting models used in other countries and are creating more realistic conditions for new teacher success. For example, as early as 1998 while on an ASCD video production team (Sweeny & Johnson, 1999), I saw schools in Minneapolis, Minnesota, in which novices had reasonable work assignments that gradually increased in intensity and that provided daily time for peer, administrative, and mentoring support early in their experience. These novice teachers' development was dramatically accelerated, and their chances of success were greatly increased.

When realistic novice assignments cannot be arranged, an effective administrator reduces *other* demands on novices and provides added support to increase their opportunity for success (Sweeny, 2002a). Effective professional learning and collaborative work take time. An adjusted work expectation for protégés is especially helpful during the initial year of a new assignment when the district has increased expectations for protégé orientation and training. Site administrators should also consider adjusting the other professional expectations for both the protégé and the mentor, especially those that do not directly relate to the protégé learning the new job. Such extra duty assignments can include supervision, chaperone or activity sponsorships and athletic coaching, workshops and distant meeting attendance, or some trainings.

> Effective administrators with high teacher retention rates do what they can to help create success conditions for the protégé, mentor, and the mentoring process.

Effective administrators with high teacher retention rates do what they can to help create success conditions for the protégé, mentor, and the mentoring process.

Administrators can reduce the teaching load, reduce the number of preparations, reduce the number of students with known discipline problems, and reduce the extent of supervisory and noninstructional duties. Tell new teachers that you are doing this to increase the time they have for mentoring and that you support their frequent and regular use of this time. Also tell them you know they might use it for teaching preparation and other related work, especially *if* they use their plan or lunch period for mentoring work. Give them some control and flexibility, while maintaining expectations for the effective use of that added time. Administrators can also assign new teachers to team-teaching situations with the mentor and structure daily common planning time and lunch for protégés and their mentor.

Although these suggestions seem simple, they involve changes for current staff too. Rather than just making changes to help the protégés and mentors, site administrators should explain in advance to all the staff how the changes will positively impact the school. They can acknowledge that these changes will mean veteran staff will assume a bit more of the overall work of the school but that it makes sense for them to want to help the newer members of their profession. In addition, they are the most likely staff to successfully handle the challenges.

Such support for novices will lead to protégé success, increased student success, school success, and reduced attrition of new teachers. Once the novices have settled in and grown, responsibilities can be revised to share challenges more equitably. The site administrator's persuasive skills are critical in helping staff perceive this as a "win-win" situation for all.

Help Create a Plan for Coordinated Protégé Support

Site administrators need to initiate a meeting with mentors to review induction program checklists. Mentors have ideas about how to support the protégés, but site administrators do too. Both need to discuss and agree on one plan. Site administrators should make time before or very early in the school year to ensure that "who does what" is mapped out, that each person who provides protégé support knows their tasks, and that the plan makes sense as a whole (see Figures 5.4A and B).

This checklist is provided to help ensure that new teachers do not "fall through the cracks." The priority for now is to confirm that critical orientation tasks are being covered by someone (see Figure 5.5).

Provide Technology Support for Novices

Begin by checking that the new teacher has a well-equipped room with appropriate technology. Ensure that protégés have e-mail immediately and are trained in its effective use. No doubt they can use it for regular correspondence, but what about e-mail journals and other possible induction and mentoring uses? The mentor or the site administrator should show the protégé ways to use e-mail to stay connected with key resource people.

Ask your technology coordinator to create a special section on the district's website for the induction and mentoring program and "stock" it with new hire resources, most of which already "reside" on computers throughout the district and only need simple conversion to html.

Assign Protégés Rooms Near Their Mentors

Administrators have very few ways of saying "thanks" to veteran staff who have served the school long and well. One option is to assign a veteran a classroom that is well positioned and nicely sized and laid out. However, this approach can conflict with the goal of providing a protégé with a room near their mentor. This is especially challenging if an administrator has used the first approach for years and then decides to adopt the second approach to better support new teachers. To minimize ill feeling, I recommend a collaborative decision-making process.

Begin by discussing with all staff what can be done to make the school more supportive of new teachers' success. Ask questions that help the staff to think of and then offer closer room assignments and other such ideas. If most staff members like the idea, some subtle social pressure will be

> Begin by discussing with all staff what can be done to make the school more supportive of new teachers' success.

brought to bear on those whose rooms may need to be changed to help a novice. When changing rooms, alert new teachers to the sacrifice veterans have made for them. Ask the novice to thank those veterans for their sacrifice and offer to help the veteran pack and move.

Use Positive Language

Be cautious about the symbolic implications of your word choice when discussing new teachers, mentoring, and other requirements or any changes. For example, new teachers *need* lots of help, but saying they *deserve* that support is more positive. Also, instead of informing staff of requirements to attend trainings, and so on, frame these as support and opportunities to grow. For example, if the district offers mandatory training for a new elementary math text, express your pleasure that the district is supporting *our* teachers and kids with the best, most current materials and opportunities to learn from teachers experienced with the series. In addition, using *collective and inclusive* words, such as *our* new teachers, *our* school, *our* challenges seems subtle, but can begin to alter the whole tone of the school. Such word choices include and challenge everyone to be more collaborative and supportive. Conversely, saying (as the principal) "my school" or "my faculty" allows others to think "not my problem, not my students" and contributes to a sense of fragmentation in the school and faculty.

Welcome Ideas

Designate someone—perhaps the assigned mentors—to provide a school orientation and tour. You could also request a school parent group to provide a "welcome new teachers" luncheon or snack time to get to know the new teachers and help them meet community or parent leaders. Finally, have the school secretary and other willing staff purchase an appropriate number of medium-sized baskets at garage sales, add a big bow to each basket's handle, and fill the basket with supplies such as a stapler, staples, chalk, pens and pencils, Post-its, thumb tacks, grade book, note pad, legal pad, box of "thank you" cards, a coupon to the "teacher store," and a small book with new teacher survival tips. Write "Welcome from all of us!" on the pad and give the basket at the orientation or "welcome" luncheon.

Figure 5.4A   Who Does What Before School Starts?

New Teacher Orientation	By Mentor	By Principal	Other
BUILDING TOUR:			
___ general school layout and floor plan/site map			
___ washrooms			
___ faculty lounge			
___ school office			
___ supply room			
___ custodian			
___ Learning Center/Library and AV equipment storage			
___ bus entrance and teacher parking			
___ rooms for specialists, nurse, social worker, psychologist, music/art/Title I			
___ other?			
TOUR OF OTHER IMPORTANT PLACES:			
___ the School Service Center (SSC—admin. building)			
___ location and time of first day Institute activities			
___ the district's Teacher Center (hours, services, equipment)			
___ local "teacher store"			
___ good lunch spots			
___ other?			
BUILDING PROCEDURES:			
___ hours for teachers, building use at other times			
___ extra duties, bus, clubs, activities, chaperoning			
___ attendance			
___ school improvement processes and responsibilities			
___ movement of children, entry/exit from building, going to washrooms, lunch, etc.			
___ student and teacher "dress code"			
___ fire-disaster drills, security alarms, warning and other such announcement codes, and "lock downs"			
___ lunch supervision, eating arrangements			
___ homework, testing policies			
___ student accidents, emergencies			
___ pullout programs and the need for flexibility			
___ other?			

Figure 5.4B   Who Does What Before School Starts?

New Teacher Orientation	By Mentor	By Principal	Other
Access to Resources:			
____ classroom and teaching supply requisitions, budget process			
____ AV equipment requests and operation			
____ shared equipment and materials (with other staff)			
____ textbooks, supplemental materials			
____ other?			
Student Discipline:			
____ behavior expectations for hallway, lunch, washroom			
____ establishing classroom behavior expectations			
____ what works with the range and diversity of our children?			
____ consequences for extreme behavior, parent? referral?			
____ expected staff supervision outside of classroom			
____ accessing administrative support for discipline problems			
____ referral process for students with special needs			
____ other?			
Curriculum and Instruction:			
____ the curriculum guides/manuals			
____ the district curriculum goals and expectations for teachers			
____ the central office staff in Curriculum (Dept. of Instruction)			
____ management of curriculum "demands" and pacing of learning			
____ introduction to texts and available supplemental materials			
____ lesson plan procedure, expectations			
____ subject matter and strategy experts on the building staff			
____ opening day schedule, administrative details			
____ curriculum "flow," overview of units throughout the year			
____ a plan for the first week's lessons			
____ other?			
Organizing the Classroom:			
____ options for room arrangement, effect on teaching, learning			
____ storage and access to materials			
____ student access to texts, equipment, teaching centers			
____ other?			
Decisions and Procedures:			
____ calling in sick, and personal or professional days			
____ expectations sharing with and support of colleagues, what others can do for you and to help you			
____ we appreciate you for who you are, be your personal best			
____ make time for yourself and the adjustment to a new job			
____ other?			

Figure 5.5   Who Does What During the First Week?

New Teacher Orientation	By Mentor	By Principal	Other
HOW IS IT GOING?			
___ don't wait, ask about concerns, new ideas, proud moments			
___ share your experiences too (we all work at the same issues)			
___ how can I help and when? I'm open @ . . . , let's work on . . .			
___ provide praise, be enthusiastic for their successes, suggest celebrations, such as first week, parent call, grading			
___ give feedback or "options" if 1 right way or got permission			
___ give them permission to "blow the whistle" if they are about to over load on too much info sharing at any time			
___ other?			
BUILDING AND DISTRICT REQUIREMENTS:			
___ sub folder, lesson plans, requests for specific subs			
___ faculty meetings, schedule			
___ the school calendar for the year			
___ progress reports procedure			
___ report card process			
___ professional staff evaluation process			
___ contractual requirements for nontenured staff			
___ other?			
HELPING CHILDREN WITH SPECIAL NEEDS:			
___ special education service and staffings procedure			
___ cumulative records and the issue of confidentiality			
___ avoiding compromising situations, touching, rides, etc.			
___ introductions to support staff—gifted, reading, LAP, LD/BD, speech, social worker, psychologist, nurse, and guidance			
___ other?			
PERSONAL AND PROFESSIONAL TOPICS:			
___ insurance procedures, forms, access, completing, and timing			
___ opportunities to attend professional meetings/workshops out of district, registration, permission, costs, grad. credit			
___ importance of attending all meetings for new teachers			
___ get the new teacher and colleagues away from the building for a social gathering to begin building friendships			
___ explain guide/mentor teacher's class schedule, availability, and if the mentor minds calls at home? Hours?			
___ accountability—certificate, portfolios, documents, reflection			
___ school improvement planning, participation, and timing			
___ state assessment schedule and preparations			
___ other?			

HOW ADMINISTRATORS SHOULD SUPPORT MENTORS

Although the mentors in your school are veterans, they still need your support. Further, if you don't demonstrate support for them they *will* notice it. Try some of the following.

Create the Time for Effective Mentoring

Mentoring requires a major time commitment. Site administrators need to consider adjusting the normal work responsibilities of and demands on mentors. This helps create the time necessary for the mentor to be successful in the mentoring task and gives the mentor flexibility in adjusting his or her own schedule to create time to work with the protégé. If work expectations are not adjusted, the mentor's own motivation and desire to do it all *and* also to be a mentor can actually create serious problems. Both the normal work activities and mentoring may suffer. The protégé may not receive the needed level of support, and the organization may not realize the anticipated benefits of the program. After all, the goals of the mentoring program extend beyond assigning mentors to providing effective mentoring that impacts the protégé's performance and, as a result, also impacts student performance. Mentors need sufficient time to learn, practice, and refine their mentoring skills and to invest in the protégé's learning and growth.

Help Mentors Feel Accountable for Effective Mentoring

Mentors may become overwhelmed and reduce the amount of time and effort invested in the protégé. Site administrators can counter this by occasionally talking with the mentor, even in brief informal moments. Start by stating that you remember the need for confidentiality in the pair and that your interest is in the mentor's experiences, not the protégé's. Discuss your expectations for a sincere, consistent mentoring effort and eventual development of the needed skills and strategies by the protégé. This accountability need not be formal or forceful, but should be more a friendly reminder that you acknowledge a mentor's efforts and care about the desired results of the process. This helps mentors balance their work and mentoring. Attending mentor training positions you to regularly ask mentors about the specifics of their own mentoring growth.

Help Mentors to Grow as Mentors

Every step in mentor improvement is also a step toward better teaching for both the protégé and the mentor. You help this happen when you attend mentor training and participate as if you were becoming a mentor yourself. Watch for strategies you can use to make your supervision a more powerful force for professional development. In addition, you can ask mentors about their own growth goals and help them feel accountable for implementing their training in practice. Though mentors are some of the best employees, part of the mentor responsibility is to model continual learning and growing to become even better mentors and teachers. That's challenging enough, especially since a mentor must do it in front of a colleague. Still, that's how mentors teach their protégés. Many mentors have never been responsible for facilitating the professional growth of another adult. Mentor training should prepare them for this complex process. Mentors will finish training with one or two goals for their improvement as mentors. The next step is *implementing* that training in their mentoring practice. Site administrator inquiries about and support for their growth as a mentor—even statements of expectation for that growth—are helpful.

Due to a protégé's specific needs, effective mentoring of one protégé may require only some of the characteristics of effective mentors. When working with a different protégé, new skills and mentor growth will be called for. Mentoring of more than one protégé over a period of time helps mentors realize they need to develop the skills of the ideal mentor. When administrators talk with mentors about the learning they experience as mentors, the questions prompt the mentors to reflect on, adjust, and apply the skills learned with their earlier protégés to benefit the protégé they are currently mentoring. In addition, you can prompt mentors to consider how their mentor learning could be applied to their teaching practice. A comparison of principles of adult learning with principles of engaged learning indicates that the skills of mentoring *are* the skills of great teaching. Supervisors who are trying to incorporate mentoring strategies into their own supervisory practice are excellent resources for such conversations with mentors. Both are trying to grow in the same skills and strategies, and the different contexts make for a very interesting contrast in experiences. Each can share mentoring insights and learn from the other. A key point to note when having such dialogue is to refrain from mentioning specific staff names and focus on your own insights and growth.

Honor and Recognize Informal Mentoring Too!

A pitfall of formal mentoring occurs when all the informal ways in which good employees help each other are limited or even stopped. Effective mentoring should lead to an increase, not a decrease, in staff collaboration! The presence of a mentoring program can actually reduce assistance for and support of new teachers *if* everyone assumes the new teacher's needs are being met by the assigned mentor. The decrease in informal support happens when peers of formal mentors wonder if informally helping others is *still needed.* Informal mentoring may also be limited because peers of the mentor do not want to "step on the mentor's toes." To ensure that this does not occur, site administrators and mentors need to reinforce the value of informal mentoring. During the faculty meeting at the end of each year, recognize *all* staff for how they supported the school's novices. Honor their informal mentoring as a sign of professionalism and commitment to the school and its students' success. In addition, acknowledge *all forms* of individual teacher leadership as necessary to meet the challenges of a diverse school and reach the high expectations *we* share for *our* work together. These first two steps make it more likely that the next step will be accepted and not viewed as divisive. Finally, recognize individual mentors who have willingly given of their time at school and home to help the school's new teachers. Perhaps provide them with a certificate, thank-you pin, or other symbolic token.

Mentor Support for Administrators' Agendas

> The explosion of management and leadership tasks, changes in expectations, and the complexity of leadership all clarify why it is probable that leadership by just one person is inadequate.

The issue of informal and formal employee leadership may be hard for supervisors to understand, or at least affirm. You are responsible for the effectiveness of the department or school and for the results on the bottom line. However, the explosion of management and leadership tasks, changes in expectations, and the complexity of leadership all clarify why it is probable that leadership by just one person is inadequate. Almost every leadership guru has clarified the necessity of empowering and sharing leadership with employees.

In fact, developing the leadership skills of your subordinates is expected of some supervisors. Mentors appreciate your support of their role. If they have been appropriately trained, they will support your instructional leadership as well as district initiatives and will help advance the improvement of performance and results. They will also communicate any serious concerns to you.

If you have identified a problem area for a specific protégé, and if that protégé *is open to mentoring assistance*, the mentor would like to know your concerns and to be an additional support for that person's improvement. The mentor's approach will be *positive and not remedial*, and mentors won't assume the responsibility to make a change happen since that is a *choice* only the protégé can make. Although you know the protégé's performance appraisal is confidential, *mentors may not realize that*, so site administrators will need to work carefully with protégés to determine how best to include the mentor as a part of the support team for the protégé.

MENTOR RECRUITMENT

One would hope that the noble responsibility of the mentor and the motivation to serve one's colleagues and profession are sufficient to generate all the mentors you will need. Typically, these factors play a role, but they are insufficient. We usually have to plan specific activities to market the program and recruit sufficient mentors.

> We usually have to plan specific activities to market the program and recruit sufficient mentors.

The Recruitment Brochure

The first exposure veterans may have to the formal mentor program is the program brochure. The brochure should briefly

- Define mentor roles and tasks
- Explain the benefits of mentoring
- Clarify the expectations of mentors
- Outline the steps in the mentor recruitment, selection and matching process

Another option is to include three written, named, and positive quotations from

- A beginning teacher whose statement affirms the value of mentoring
- A mentor whose statement includes the value discovered by mentors
- A site administrator who has seen program impact on the novice teachers and students

An alternative to testimonies is to cite research about the benefits for mentors. For example, Bartell (2005) found that mentors gain as much as protégés in their growth, that the effectiveness of their teaching practice increases, and that mentors learn from each other.

Mentoring Information and Recruitment Meeting

Consider this meeting an orientation and a recruitment meeting, but *advertise it* as only a "Mentoring Information Meeting." Otherwise you might scare off possible mentors before they have an opportunity to learn why they might choose to be a mentor.

Provide timely, brief informational meetings of less than one hour in length, and require them for any person considering becoming a mentor. Use the meetings to present a realistic definition of what is expected of mentors. While one goal of the meetings is to recruit new mentors, another goal is to provide information that will cause those less likely to succeed as mentors to eliminate themselves. The following three statements are helpful in accomplishing the latter result:

- Mentors must open their own teaching practices to evaluation by less experienced staff. If that makes teachers uncomfortable, they should not become mentors.
- Mentors experience an intensive relationship in which they are the helper, friend, and confidante. Teachers who feel that is inappropriate should not become a mentor.
- Mentors should recognize that their own teaching is not fine "as it is" and must welcome learning new strategies while under the microscope. Teachers who are not comfortable with this should not be mentors.

Ensuring that a program has enough mentors available is a continual concern for leaders and protégés. That is why a program should maintain a "pool" of previously trained and available mentors. Also, every mentoring program should hold two to three mentoring information meetings each year.

Goals for the Informational Meeting

The information meeting is both a presentation and discussion. Goals for the information meetings are

- To recruit new mentors for the program
- To ensure understanding of what is expected of effective mentors so recruits make an informed choice about assuming the role
- To ensure that mentors understand the process and criteria for selection, matching, dealing with mismatches, mentor training, and serving as mentors
- To ensure that persons who should *not* be mentors choose *not* to be candidates for the position

Reread those suggested goals. Pay attention to any underlying assumptions you may detect. Notice that the first goal—an adequate number of mentors—could be in conflict with other goals. Some leaders do not explain fully what is expected of mentors at an initial informational meeting because they need more mentors and are afraid they may "scare off" prospects. This is the wrong approach.

Be careful that, if you want mentoring "in the worst way," you don't get it that way. You should present the expectations of mentors carefully and realistically and, because of the fourth goal, you must be candid with mentoring prospects about what effective mentoring requires.

This approach requires mentor candidates to analyze and weigh options, to reflect on themselves and their tendencies, and to examine whether learning and improvement really are their priorities. This approach uses "constructivist" methods, the same ones we want to see used in classrooms with

> (The final goal is) to ensure that persons who should not be mentors choose not to be candidates for the position.

> Be careful that, if you want mentoring "in the worst way," you don't get it that way. You should present the expectations of mentors carefully and realistically.

students. By using this method at this step, those who become mentors are practicing the desired methods, thereby maintaining the crucial Chain of Causes and Effects.

Think proactively about processes and criteria for selection, matching, and mismatches. Then plan what you can do *now* at the information meeting to set up these future mentors for success later as they go through those other processes, including a possible mismatch.

Creating the Information Meeting Agenda

As you complete this next step, pay attention to the process as well as the content you are producing. The process is a great model for any task design that must serve strategic goals.

Make a planning matrix that is set up and used as follows:

1. Create five vertical columns and about twelve to fifteen horizontal rows.

2. Title the first vertical column on the left "Agenda Items."

3. Title the remaining four vertical columns, each with one of the meeting goals.

4. In the first column, list the topics you want to include in the agenda.

5. Compare your list to the items in the recruitment flyer. Is anything important missing?

6. Compare the agenda items and the goals, checking off the strongest connections, to ensure that
   • Each goal has two to three agenda items. Any with fewer than this risks *not* achieving the goal.
   • Each agenda item has at least one goal it addresses very well.

7. Remove or rework any agenda item not clearly connected to at least one goal.

The practical and powerful process outlined above is quick and easy, yet it ensures that your goals are attained. At a later date, when you decide to transfer to your best mentor pair the task of leading mentor information meetings, you can give them the matrix, which helps them understand and accomplish the goals for the activity.

One effective option is to include a panel of two or three experienced mentors to address some of the content and answer questions along with the leader. As peers, their testimonies and explanations will be very welcome and seen as credible.

Designing a Mentor Application

Creating a mentor application seems straightforward, but this actually requires more complex thinking than may at first be apparent. There are three aspects to working in this area:

1. Mentor roles and tasks lists that guide your design and use of mentor statements

2. Statements mentors might make *before* becoming a mentor, like a mentor application

3. Statements mentors make to clarify their commitments, like a mentoring contract

The major use for a mentor job description and application is to begin mentor selection, which needs to be as objective as possible. Therefore, use the mentor roles and tasks statements developed earlier to design your job descriptions, applications, and mentoring contract.

If you use the *roles* of effective mentors as a guide for developing a mentoring application, the selection process could be fairly subjective. For example, one mentor role is "friend." How can we determine whether an applicant is friendly? If we simply ask the applicants, what is the likelihood that any will say that they are unfriendly? Yet some mentors are very businesslike and do not *act* like friends of their protégé. This is why focusing only on the roles is not particularly helpful.

All mentoring and induction programs need to define and inform potential mentors of "the roles of ideal mentors." However, in order to make applications useful for guiding decisions, we need something more concrete and observable. By using the "tasks of effective mentors" as the basis for an application, more objective information can be collected. The focus is on whether or not an applicant has done the tasks. Just keep in mind that tasks are the *behavioral expression of roles*.

The Mentor Application

Applications help potential mentors learn more about what is required to be an effective mentor and prompt them to reflect on how likely they are to become an effective mentor. In addition, applications affirm that we want effective mentoring to happen and we are clear about what that effective mentoring looks like. If mentor candidates can't "see" themselves doing those specific things, or at least *committing to learn* to do them, then they should not become mentors. An example of such a form is available for viewing on the "Transitions to Teaching" website at <http://t2t.fms.k12.nm.us/instforms/forms/home.html>.

A good application is based on, and helps candidates reflect on, the mentor job description. For example, if the mentoring roles require a person who is a good listener, empathic, and interested in the welfare of others, then the application needs to ask something specific like, "Describe a situation in which you were involved with another adult and which demonstrates that you are a good listener, empathic, and that you promote the welfare of others."

The mentor application may also need other items, since the process and criteria for mentor selection often require certain qualifications. In such a case, the application should also ask the mentor candidate to provide specific information and even "certify" certain qualifications.

- If the mentoring job requires someone with a master's degree, the application should ask when that degree was earned, in what area, and at what university.
- If the mentoring job requires attendance at a prior informational meeting, the application should ask the date of the meeting attended so that attendance can be confirmed in program records.
- If the principal must sign the mentor's application, there should be a place for that and a statement such as, "The principal's signature verifies that the principal knows the candidate has applied to serve as a mentor."

This kind of simple signature statement allows a principal to avoid adding stress to his or her ongoing relationship with the teacher, yet still alert the program in some other way if there is a concern. A slightly different approach to the principal's signature can be seen in the online copy of the Mentoring Program Plan for the Farmington, New Mexico,

Public Schools, at the bottom of page 5 at <http://t2t .fms.k12.nm.us/instforms/forms/pdf/FMSMentorPlan .pdf>.

Do not make principals the "bad guys" who have to tell a staff member he or she can't be a mentor. You may need to explain to applicants that some documentation is already in the district's possession, but since the documentation is confidential, it cannot be accessed by the program.

> Do not make principals the "bad guys" who have to tell a staff member he or she can't be a mentor.

Don't make the application an essay test. If there are complex issues to include, there are at least two alternatives to asking a mentor candidate to write an essay about a topic.

The first involves developing, field testing, and then refining a limited set of questions that will reveal what you need to know without requiring extensive writing. For example, we know that mentors must be able to effectively promote the growth of another adult. That's a skill not often learned in a classroom with children. Revealing a candidate's ability to lead adults could be cumbersome, but here is a question that reveals what is needed without an extensive essay: "What previous experience have you had in leading other adults and what did you learn from that experience about effectively leading adult activities?"

If an application requires more than a brief written answer, or if interaction is needed to answer or clarify an answer, it's probably better that there be an interview where dialogue and interaction can occur. Interviews are certainly more personal too.

MENTOR SELECTION AND MENTOR-PROTÉGÉ MATCHING

The next topics, mentor selection and mentor-protégé matching, are the two biggest sources of program problems! Giving these topics careful and thoughtful attention will help ensure mentoring pairs and mentoring that successfully attain your program goals and will help avoid disastrous results that could end your program.

> Mentor selection and mentor-protégé matching are the two biggest sources of program problems!

Align Recruitment, Selection, and Matching to Your Program Goals

As you design each part of the program, it is essential to align what you *say* you want *long term* with what you *do short term.* Program goals should be used to evaluate every decision and component, including the processes and criteria for recruitment, selection, and matching.

Plan Recruitment, Selection, and Matching as One Integrated Process

Designing the processes and criteria for the mentor recruitment, selection, and mentor-protégé matching components of a system is crucial. This will ensure that they work as one continuous (although staged) process that is consistent with the program's goals. To express it another way, recruitment, selection, and matching must be designed and conducted so they are experiences that maintain the links in the Chain of Causes and Effects.

For example, if you desire constructivist learning when you peek at students working in their classrooms, then the links we call recruitment, selection, and matching must be experienced by participants as constructivist processes.

Selection and matching are filled with a number of pitfalls, leading many programs to unknowingly create obstacles to attaining their own goals. The following guidance can help you avoid those dangers. Although recruitment, selection, and matching need to function as one, we will start by looking at each separately and then integrate them into one system.

The Mentor Selection Process

A high impact induction program includes both selection *criteria* and a selection *process,* although they will quickly become intertwined. There are three methods for mentor selection, the "inclusive," the "exclusive," and the "balanced" approaches. I advocate a "balanced" approach that blends the best aspects of each method and tries to avoid the problems of each.

The program leadership group must thoroughly discuss the method to be used and consider the ramifications and appropriateness of each option for your school culture and staff. The approach selected should be consistent with the purpose and goals of the program. If improvement of teacher and student performance is your purpose and your Vision for Excellent Teaching and Learning is of individualized, engaged instruction, the balanced method is the choice to make. However, don't make that choice without first understanding all three approaches. Otherwise you may be tempted to try some parts of them without insight into problems.

The "Exclusive" Approach to Mentor Selection

The motto of this method is, "Mentors must be the best available models of the best practice." This approach assumes the following:

- The technical skills of teachers are highly valued.
- The best models of excellent instructional practice are selected as mentors.
- Many other experienced staff are rejected as "not good enough."
- As a result, mentors may be seen as the "elite," which is divisive and restricts whole-staff collaboration.
- A higher degree of stress accompanies mentor status since they are viewed as "special."
- The mentor's job is to ensure that the protégé reaches a minimal skill level.
- Mentors may be called on to "evaluate" the protégé to see whether they are "good enough."
- The approach implies an assumption that "mentors should have all the answers."

The Reality of the "Exclusive" Approach

If you place too much emphasis on mentors as models of best practice, you can create the impression that mentoring is a club to which most need not apply, and you risk saying "no" to candidates who might succeed in certain situations. You definitely want to avoid criteria which will cause your program to be perceived as saying to a mentor candidate, "Sorry, you're not good enough." You will struggle to recruit enough mentors because no one wants to be seen as a "know-it-all." In fact, even if you start off with enough mentors, you are likely to find their ranks dwindling over time.

An exclusive approach can create problems, especially in a collaborative or egalitarian culture, and can actually be counter to the collaborative culture that mentoring tries to establish. As we have discussed, it is not necessary or even desirable for mentors to be "the best" employees, if you want to *build* a highly effective mentor program and *develop* highly qualified new teachers. I recommend that you avoid an "exclusive" approach to mentor selection.

The "Inclusive" Mentor Selection Process

The inclusive motto is, "Anyone willing to try can be a mentor." Characteristics are

- A desire to model inclusiveness and openness
- An assumption the current quality of teaching by good teachers is good enough
- An assumption that good teachers will naturally be good mentors
- The assumption that new teachers need to be as good as the school's best teachers are now
- The demonstration of an unstated intent to "clone" the good teachers

The Reality of the "Inclusive" Approach

Inclusiveness sounds terrific for legitimate reasons of diversity and equity. However, if you take this approach you risk creating the impression that mentoring is an insignificant role requiring no special skills, experience, or personal qualities and that anyone can be a mentor. This position comes close to accepting new teachers as they are and thinking that they are good enough too. This approach leads to acceptance of anything as OK. In teaching, this is a disaster. The inclusive approach sounds nice, but it should also be avoided.

The "Balanced" Mentor Selection Process

The motto of the balanced approach is, "The best mentors are models of continual, visible learning, an openness to feedback, and the daily, career-long struggle to be the best educators they can be."

I recommend the balanced selection process because it effectively helps mentoring and induction programs transform teacher performance for everyone, and improves student achievement as a result. The balanced selection method is the best way to continue the transfer of the vision of individualized, engaged teaching and student learning down the Chain of Causes and Effects. It does this because the balanced approach

- Highly values reflective, collaborative, continually improving teachers as learners
- Defines the mentor's primary job as a model of continual learning and growth
- Believes most veteran teachers can be mentors because the commitment is *not* to *be* the perfect teacher and mentor. Rather, it is to work at *becoming* an even better teacher and mentor every day.
- Lowers levels of stress as everyone will learn together
- Requires ongoing training and support due to the expectation that mentors and protégés will continually grow

- Requires anticipating and proactively checking for problems and dealing with challenges as they arise. Participants are trained in conflict resolution and are encouraged to value their differences as strengths for the pair (Weeks, 1992).

The balanced approach reflects the desire to be a learning community that supports everyone's development.

HOW DOES A BALANCED SELECTION AND MATCHING PROCESS WORK?

There are several strategies that together make the balanced approach so effective.

Design a phased process with several steps and criteria for each

Do not make selection a one time "do or die" process. Figure 5.6 shows how this process works. Suggested steps in the process are

1. Application to be a mentor (the "threshold")

2. Attending the initial mentor training

3. Being called "mentor" and joining the mentor "pool"

4. Being matched with a protégé

5. Remaining matched with the protégé

6. Working a second year with the same protégé

Notice that the method places mentor training within selection and matching, not at the end as many programs have done. Read on to see why this is a good approach.

At each step, add more detailed education about what it means to be an effective mentor

Instead of thinking of mentor training as a one-time event, think of it is a gradual process delivered at each step of the recruitment, selection, and matching process and continuing as long as mentoring does. At each step of mentors' development, their training gives them just what they need at that level and readies them for successful learning and work at the next level. For example, the mentoring information meeting gives a broad outline of just what a person needs to know to make an educated choice about whether to apply to be a mentor and to decide whether they want to take the step of attending the mentor training. No more information than that is provided at this point.

During mentor training, each candidate learns about and then practices effective mentoring strategies. While they are not yet called "mentor," by the end of the training they are much better informed about what being a mentor entails and can then make a good decision about whether to move to the next step of the process.

Figure 5.6   A Recommended Mentor Selection and Matching Process Map

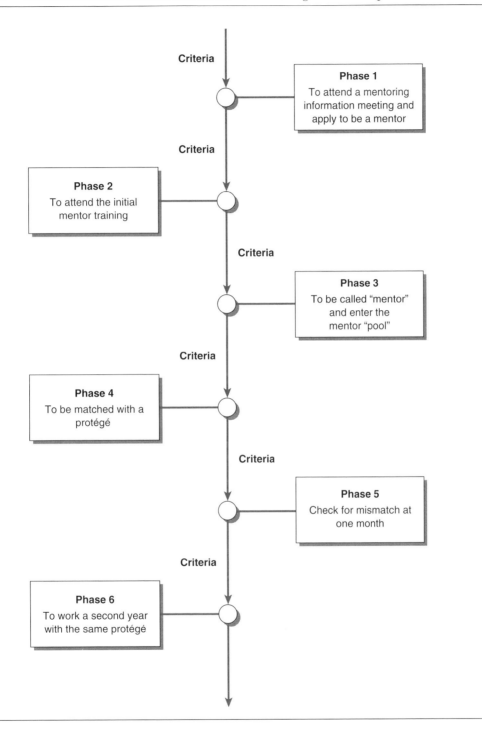

Make the criteria for moving from one step to the next the likelihood of success at that next level

The education at each step in the process should be just what people at that step need and should prepare them to be successful at the next step if they choose to take it. This process is based on the CBAM Stages of Concern (covered in Chapter 1), the way people naturally learn and grow. Look at Figure 5.7.

Figure 5.7 Correlating Recruitment, Selection, and Matching With the CBAM

The Recruitment, Selection, and Matching Process	CBAM Stages of Concern	Questions Asked
Phase 1—In recruitment flyer and at the mentor information meeting	1. Awareness	What does an effective mentor do?
Phase 1—In recruitment flyer and at the mentor information meeting	2. Information	How do selection, matching, and training work?
Phase 1—mentor information meeting	3. Personal	• Should I be a mentor? • I'm ready to complete an application.
Phase 2—At mentor training *Phase 3—Becomes a "mentor" and enters mentor "pool"* *Phase 4—Matched to a protégé and starts work as a new mentor*	4. Mechanical management	• Can I learn and demonstrate the skills? • Where do I need to grow? • What goal to improve should I have?
Phases 4 and 5—Matched to a protégé and keeps working as a new mentor	5. Routine management	I'm doing well. How else must I grow?
Phases 5 and 6—Assigned to work with same protégé the second year	6. Consequence	• Is my protégé growing? • Are the protégé's students improving? • How can I increase the results I want?

Using CBAM as a structure for design of recruitment, selection, and matching works because it helps potential candidates learn and move through the process as they are ready. Focusing on individual candidate readiness is the best way to ensure growth, to ensure that mentor recruitment, selection, and matching will help mentors best accomplish their jobs, *and* to gain mentors support for the Vision for Excellent Teaching and Learning.

Define more challenging criteria at each step in the process

Meeting a specific criterion is less of an obstacle to a candidate if done *after* the mentor training when the candidate has learned what that specific criterion really looks like and why it is important. The basic concept here is to ask candidates to commit when they are informed enough to make a wise choice. Asking a person to be a mentor and then making them one before they really know what's involved makes little sense and leads to numerous, needless problems.

Include "safety checks" at each step in the process

Plan opportunities at each step of the process when a poor mentor candidate may be counseled to withdraw and exit the program in a face-saving manner. For instance, when you candidly present the challenges of the roles and tasks of the mentor, the expectation of modeling one's own learning in front of others, the time required, and the need for openness to protégé questions, some will choose to exit the system. They may be unwilling to let a novice teacher question their practice, but they will probably use the excuse of "I can't give that much time." Thank candidates for considering mentoring and being willing to help others, and then excuse them.

Candidates may say they understand expectations and will meet them, but when mentor training comes and they must practice and demonstrate these skills, they may act passively and refuse to participate, saying, "I hate role playing." Simply state, "I'm sorry you are uncomfortable with these strategies that mentors must be able to do. Just because you chose to try out mentor training does not mean you have to stay here when you don't like it. We understand that and thank you for coming to find out more. Just slip out during the next break."

Figures 5.8A and 5.8B provide much greater details than the basic "phased model." The same six stages are there. However, this figure gives examples of the criteria at each phase that provide the gradual process. Also shown in the far right column on each page of this figure are the "safeguards" for each phase to help unprepared candidates opt out of the process at that time. As critical as these safeguards are, your program will not need to use them very often, especially after the program has been implemented for a while and becomes better known to nonparticipants. When you need the safeguards, you'll be glad they are in place because they help prevent

- Unqualified or inappropriate people from becoming active mentors
- Embarrassing mentor candidates who are inappropriate
- Placing yourself in a position to say *"no"* to very many candidates

You should take the time needed to read and understand this figure. Then use it in your program design, or design your own version of a phased process for recruitment, selection, and matching.

Consider calling a person a "mentor" *after* they are trained, but *before* they are assigned to work with a protégé

This timing creates several benefits:

- Calling a person a "mentor" affirms a candidate's professionalism and desire to grow while helping others. Doing this after defining this valued role, such as at the mentor training, makes it a more significant and meaningful title to earn and to "wear."
- Calling a person a "mentor" *after* they are trained also places mentors into ongoing training, mentor meetings, and peer support groups, perhaps even before they are assigned to help a protégé. Unassigned or less capable mentors can learn from their assigned colleagues, the more experienced mentors. In the case where a person is a "mentor" but is not really as strong as a protégé may need, they can have the recognition as a mentor, but not be assigned to a situation where the match might fail. However, requiring such a person to continue participating in mentoring meetings ensures that they will continue to improve as mentors by vicariously learning through their peers' experience and examples.
- Poor candidates may persist and slip through even a very careful selection process. Labeling persons as "mentor" after their training but before assignment to a

Figure 5.8A   A Selection Process With Staged Criteria and Safeguards—Part A

Selection Criteria Steps	Staged Criteria	Safeguards
1. Application to be a mentor	**Threshold Criteria:** • Five years' experience in similar job and at that location • Rated "Excellent" on most own most recent evaluation **Application Criteria:** • Attended a Mentor Program Information Meeting out of interest in learning about what mentoring is all about and the expectations • Submitted complete application • Supervisor's signature on application **If met, attend mentor training**	• Some mentor candidates will "self-select" out when they learn what is expected and are counseled to opt out by the meeting leader • Supervisor may privately share concerns about the candidate with the Mentor Program Coordinator • Criteria and process help to screen candidates to ensure those who continue in the process are likely to succeed
2. Attend the initial mentor training	**Training Completion Criteria:** • Active participation in mentor training • Self-assesses against ideal mentor criteria and sets goals for growth to be more effective • Agreement between candidate and trainer that the candidate is likely to succeed as a mentor **If met, becomes a mentor and enters "pool"**	• Mentor Program Coordinator or trainer observes candidate during training and can counsel out disengaged candidates
3. Enter the mentor "pool" and be called "mentor"	**Mentor Designation Criteria:** • Actively participates in quarterly mentor support meetings • Accepts support and accountability for ongoing growth as a mentor in relationship with the Mentor of Mentors • Continues growing as a mentor	• Allows ongoing monitoring of the mentor as a continual learner and in interaction with peers by the Mentor Program Leader • Allows the mentor to continue to learn and grow as a mentor through interaction with experienced mentors and with the Mentor of Mentors (MoM)

protégé is a "safety net" in that the program does not have to assign the mentor to a protégé until the mentor's strengths are known to fit the needs of a protégé and the mentoring pair is likely to succeed. That means that a "mentor" with limited skills may still be assigned when a protégé who is strong and needs only limited help comes along. In other words, if the mentor's few skills fit well with a strong protégé's needs, it is still a good match.

• You can avoid making promises about what attending mentor training means. People should understand that being trained as a mentor is the next step in a *process* and *does not* mean they will automatically be assigned to work with a protégé.

Figure 5.8B   A Selection Process With Staged Criteria and Safeguards—Part B

Selection Criteria Steps	Staged Criteria	Safeguards
4. Be matched with a protégé	**Matching Criteria:** • Is more experienced than the protégé in the same assignment • Mentor Program Leader and supervisor see mentor's strengths as matching protégé's needs for growth • Is in close proximity to protégé for access and so both formal and informal mentoring can occur • Is available and willing to serve as a mentor right now **If met, is assigned as a mentor**	• Matching criteria and process help to screen candidates • The best match may never be found for any specific poor mentor who slipped through • Emphasis on "mentor's strengths" matching protégé's needs increases likelihood of an effective match • Mentor Program Leader's ongoing interaction with mentor pair allows monitoring and prompting toward best practice
5. Remain matched with the protégé	**Ongoing Match Criteria:** • Information available from first year's experience in mentoring & observations by the Mentor Program Leader confirm appropriateness of the match **If met, remains assigned as a mentor**	• Emphasis on "mentor's strengths" maintains dignity of mentor if a mismatch occurs • Automatic mentor-protégé mismatch check is acceptable since it is done with all pairs • Automatic mentor-protégé mismatch check allows for mentor reassignment if conflict resolution is unsuccessful
6. Work a second year with the same protégé	• Information available from first year's experience in mentoring and observations by the Mentor Program Leader and protégé's supervisor confirm the appropriateness of continuing the match **If met, remains a mentor**	• Is essentially another automatic mentor-protégé mismatch check • Ensures that the protégé has not outgrown the strengths of the assigned mentor

MAKING THE DECISION ABOUT ASSIGNING MENTORS TO THE MENTOR "POOL"

Of the six phases in the balanced selection process, this phase poses the most challenges. When the mentor training is completed, you must make the "mentor or not?" decision. Simply attending mentor training does not ensure that a person will be an effective mentor. Instead, during the training the program leader needs to actually see each person using the strategies of and behaving like an effective mentor. This is why using criteria at this phase and making a decision *after* the training are so important.

> When the mentor training is completed you must make the "mentor or not?" decision.

If a trained person is to be called a *mentor* and placed in the pool, you are agreeing that you believe this person can be an effective mentor. There should be very few exceptions. If a trained person does not appear to be ready to be an effective mentor, they should not be called a *mentor*, nor should they be placed in the pool.

Being in the mentor pool means a person is trained and ready for assignment to a protégé. When a program is new, it's likely that all your mentors will be assigned. However, it is important to develop a reservoir of talent in your mentoring pool as soon as possible. Happily, some folks will volunteer to be trained as mentors just because they want to do it, and they will likely be the first persons in the pool. The pool is crucial because nothing ever goes according to plan. Here are two examples of when you will need to "dip into the pool."

- In October, an assigned mentor becomes sick, or for some reason resigns the position. You have no mentor training planned, so who can replace the mentor who resigned?
- In September, after mentor trainings are completed, a principal calls to say that enrollment required splitting a class and a novice teacher has just been hired. Who can mentor her?

Criteria for Selecting for the Mentor "Pool"

These criteria should be used after the mentor training, ensuring that the candidates are aware of the criteria and know exactly what is required of mentors.

- *The candidate has actively participated in mentor training.* Willingness to practice mentoring skills and allow observation by a trainer or program leader is essential. If a trainee does not actively participate, find out why. Consider counseling that person out of the process.

- *The candidate has set goals and planned for his or her own growth as a mentor.* Training should include self-assessments describing what effective mentors do (tasks) and what effective mentoring relationships are like and a mentoring styles assessment (ability to shift task and relationship orientations throughout the mentoring process). Each mentor should analyze the self-assessment results and write one to two goals and a plan for professional growth.

- *The candidate is willing to work with the district-assigned "Mentor of Mentors."* By mentoring the mentor on his or her goals, the Mentor of Mentors demonstrates effective mentoring. This first-hand experience increases the mentor's ability to be effective.

- *The candidate is willing to support the professional growth of other mentors.* Positive peer pressure increases the likelihood that mentors will learn from each other. Meetings build knowledge and capture emerging best practices. All mentors can learn from what one of them discovers.

- *The candidate is an effective leader and facilitator.* Training should be carefully designed and used for candidate observation and assessment. For example, leadership roles during small-group activities can be rotated, giving the trainer an opportunity to evaluate whether a candidate effectively facilitates or just tells and directs. Mentors should be selected for their ability to work with other adults and treat them as adult learners, not children (Bartell, 2005).

- *The candidate has demonstrated effective mentoring practice.* I consider this optional, preferring to use an inclusive approach based on demonstrated *willingness* to work at *becoming* an effective mentor. Also, mentor trainings are too short to allow adequate practice of all the skills in which candidates are trained, such as observation, coaching, and questioning skills. If you use this criterion, be sure you define the skills of an effective mentor and be aware that training time is used to teach, practice, and observe those skills.

Who Decides Whether the Various Criteria are Met?

We are trying to incorporate some elements of an inclusive approach to mentor selection and matching, using safeguards. That is why we must identify *both* candidate and program responsibilities for deciding if the various criteria are met. A candidate who participates in the decision-making process and is excluded from mentoring will have a greater basis for understanding and accepting the decision than one who has had no part in the process.

> A candidate who participates in the decision-making process and is excluded from mentoring will have a greater basis for understanding and accepting the decision than one who has had no part in the process.

While this approach further complicates an already complex process, taking this added step *avoids* the complications that result when a rejected person does not accept the decision. This also helps prevent the likelihood of union or administrative concerns being raised.

Self-Selection Roles

- Clearly define what is needed for success at each stage.
- Counsel candidates through self-assessment against the criteria at each stage.
- Clarify what it means to move to the next stage of the selection and matching process.
- Ask whether the candidate feels that they can succeed at the next stage.
- Make decisions a matter of timing, so that a "no" at some point allows for possible future involvement: "Maybe now isn't the right time for you to be a mentor."

Program Selection Roles

- Invite the supervisor of the new teacher to share unique information and give input during the mentor selection and matching processes.
- Invite mentor trainers, program coordinators, and a program committee to share unique information about the mentor and give input at the appropriate phases. For example, at the end of phase three, the mentor trainer can offer input regarding whether or not the candidate demonstrates the needed mentoring attitudes and skills.
- Use language that honors each candidate and protégé and does not suggest a person has made mistakes or is not "good enough." Instead of saying, "You don't have the qualities that this protégé needs," you might say, "Your strengths are not what this novice needs."

MATCHING OF MENTORS AND PROTÉGÉS

Once a person becomes a mentor and joins the pool, the next step is matching a specific protégé's strengths and needs with the strengths of an appropriate mentor. This decision should be guided by criteria and a defined process.

Choosing Criteria for Matching

Two basic approaches are used by most programs when developing criteria for matching mentors and protégés:

- Criteria that consider *characteristics of people,* such as personality, educational philosophy, learning or teaching styles, or other conceptual types
- Criteria that consider *characteristics of working conditions* needed for success in the work of teaching and of mentoring

> I recommend using criteria that focus on success in the work rather than criteria that focus on the people.

I recommend using criteria that focus on *success in the work* rather than criteria that focus on *the people.*

In reviewing programs using personality or other forms of people-focused matching schemes, I have found good mentoring relationships, people who enjoyed working with each other and were very supportive and understanding of each other, yet who had little basis for learning from each other. I believe this is because little learning occurs when people who think similarly and make the same assumptions are matched together. Instead, I recommend that characteristics of people be used to *select* mentors, but *not for matching* to protégés. My experience in hundreds of mentoring programs shows that learning is accelerated when people see things differently, question each other's viewpoints and check each other's assumptions. While assigning as partners two people who see things differently does create potential conflicts, this does not have to be an obstacle to success.

Mentoring should be preparation for the reality of teaching. The reality is that we do not assign teachers to schools or to supervisors based on styles, nor do we assign students to teachers in such a manner. In fact, matching for personality characteristics suggests that you are *not expected* to get along with people who are different from you. In real life, diverse people are expected to work together and achieve defined goals. Mentoring partners should emphasize the discovery and celebration of the diverse strengths they bring to their work. This is accomplished by assessing and planning the use of those strengths *as a team.* You may also wish to offer training in effective communication and conflict resolution. Also, mentors must be trained in quick strategies for assessing and addressing protégé needs.

Criteria for Matching Mentors and Protégés

Criteria for matching should be based on *what best meets the needs of the protégé.* This goal should guide everything you do regarding matching. You should explain this goal to mentors and protégés and should also keep this goal in mind when resolving a mentor-protégé mismatch.

Specific criteria must be set up to help us create the system of support most likely to meet the goal of addressing the protégé's individual needs. Meeting those needs removes the obstacles to the protégé's growth.

I offer an important caution here. You may occasionally discover that your own focus, or that of an administrator or mentor, has shifted to make *meeting the criteria* the goal. This is logical since standards are an important focus today. But, standards are about "proving," not "*im*proving," and as such they are the wrong focus for your matching process. You must refocus on the correct goal—the needs of the learner. This ensures that the matching process maintains the Chain of Causes and Effects.

Here are my suggested ideal matching priorities:

- The *highest priority* is *close proximity* of mentor and protégé work areas or classrooms. In the daily press of activities, consistent and frequent mentoring can happen only if they are near one another. Otherwise, protégés will often look close by to find another person to be their "mentor," whether that person is trained and capable or not.
- The next priority is to match mentors who have or recently have had a *similar job* assignment to that of the protégé. This is helpful, since curriculum and related work tasks are very big areas for protégé learning.

Other common matching factors include

- A common planning or lunch period
- Seeking *age* differences of a few (up to five or more) years
- An *experience* difference, which is even more important than age

Determining how to use a mix of such diverse criteria can be challenging. In practice, the best match for a protégé isn't always possible. The best mentor may be unavailable due to other commitments or personal situations, or there may not be an appropriate mentor for new teachers in smaller schools, smaller departments in a secondary school, or in unique positions. For example, who mentors the sole art teacher or counselor in a school?

When faced with these problems, the program leader will try to do the best he or she can. However, if the mentor is unable to meet the protégé's needs, the Chain of Causes and Effects will be broken.

To ensure adequate support for every protégé, effective programs integrate matching criteria and processes, define these in "cascading" sets of criteria to structure the matching process, and *adjust the amount of added support* as needed.

To create your cascading criteria, list sets of criteria in priority order with most desired and obvious combination of criteria first. When matching, examine each level starting at the top and work down until an approach can be made to work in the specific situation. Below is an example of cascading criteria written from the district's perspective. Note that bold criteria indicate *what is lost at each level* as you *read down* or what is *new* at each level if you *read bottom up.*

An Example of "Cascading" Mentor Matching Criteria

Mentor assignments with protégés will be made using the highest possible option:

1. *The best possible choice*—Mentor holds at least a standard certificate and also
   - has completed or will shortly complete mentor training;
   - is currently at the same assignment as the protégé or was within the last two years;
   - **has at least two years' experience at a job assignment similar to the protégé's;**
   - works in close proximity to the protégé;
   - shares a common break period and/or lunch period with the protégé;

(Continued)

(Continued)

- has personal and professional strengths to address the apparent needs of the protégé; and
- is a caring, supportive, positive, and insightful person.

What's missing in these criteria? Hopefully nothing. The protégé's needs are met.

2. Mentor holds at least a standard certificate and also
   - has completed or will shortly complete mentor training;
   - currently has the same assignment as the protégé, or did within the last two years;
   - works in close proximity to the protégé;
   - **shares a common break period and/or lunch period with the protégé;**
   - has personal and professional strengths to address the apparent needs of the protégé; and
   - is a caring, supportive, positive, and insightful person;

What's missing? The mentor could have only a year or less experience in the job assignment, which may not have allowed time to build enough experience. If this is the case, what other support could be added to cover that weakness?

3. Mentor holds at least a standard certificate and also
   - has completed or will shortly complete mentor training;
   - currently is at the same assignment as the protégé, or was within the last two years;
   - **works in close proximity to the protégé and has released time for mentoring;**
   - has personal and professional strengths to address the apparent needs of the protégé; and
   - is a caring, supportive, positive, and insightful person;

What's missing? The mentor and protégé do not share a common time during every work day. However, the mentor's access to released time will help create occasional times when they can get together to work and for support, so this solution can also work. Just be sure the mentor understands this stipulation for the use of that released time.

4. The mentor is *from another district site*, holds at least a standard certificate and also
   - has completed or will shortly complete mentor training;
   - **currently works at the same assignment as the protégé, or did within the last two years;**
   - has personal and professional strengths to address the apparent needs of the protégé;
   - is a caring, supportive, positive, and insightful person;
   - mentor and protégé are trained in and have access to e-mail; and
   - a guide at the protégé's site is also assigned to orient the protégé to that setting.

What's missing? The mentor and protégé do not work at the same location, and so getting together will be a challenge. However, they both have e-mail access and there is also a "guide" assigned at the protégé's site who can help with local procedures and so on that the protégé needs to learn but that the mentor will not know. This mix of criteria and support should work well to meet the protégé's learning needs.

5. The mentor is from the protégé's site but has a different assignment and holds at least a standard certificate. Also
   - **another mentor from another school has the same assignment so is assigned to mentor this protégé;**
   - both mentors and the protégé have e-mail access;
   - both mentors have completed or will shortly complete mentor training;
   - both mentors have some strengths that together address the needs of the protégé; and
   - both mentors are caring, supportive, positive, and insightful persons.

What's missing? The *local* mentor can help the protégé grow as a professional because of a knowledge of pedagogy and the local students, but does not know the job the protégé has to learn. The *remote* mentor can help the protégé learn the job but will be able to help only when appointments and time away from work can be made, or via e-mail and phone. The *local* mentor should be charged with assuring that the combination of assistance is adequately addressing the protégé's needs. If both mentors are willing to coordinate their assistance, this arrangement can still work fine. The program coordinator has to monitor the arrangement.

DEALING WITH A MENTOR-PROTÉGÉ MISMATCH

Mismatches are awkward and stressful, so we must have a strategy for dealing with them. However, if you have educated partners for their work together and carefully matched them, the occurrence of mismatches is rare.

There are several strategies for avoiding and reducing the occurrence of mismatches and also for dealing with them in as positive a way as possible when they occur. One example of a mismatch policy can be seen in the online copy of the Mentoring Program Plan for the Farmington, New Mexico, Public Schools, at the bottom of page 8 at <http://t2t.fms.k12.nm.us/instforms/forms/pdf/FMSMentorPlan.pdf>.

The *usual* method for dealing with mismatches is the "reactive" approach, in which solutions are developed after a problem arises and in response to it. I do not recommend this approach.

The Challenge of a *Reactive* Approach to Mismatches

In a reactive approach, mentor and protégé matching is viewed as unrelated to mentor and protégé training. If a mismatch occurs, the solution is presented in an emotionally charged setting and the individuals feel singled out and think *they* are the problem. That is *not* the best time to decide what to do. Every strategy you offer for resolution, every question you ask, will be taken personally by one or both of the partners. To solve the mismatch at this stage, you must do the following:

1. Research the problem, probably with each person separately.

2. Try to resolve the problem if you think it can be fixed, like a misunderstanding.

3. Assume that everyone is doing the best they know how to do.

4. Use positive language that dignifies people.

5. Restate and keep the focus on the goal of matching to meet the needs of the protégé.

6. Place "blame" for problems on the *program*, not people. Here is an example of this. When discussing the mismatch, use that specific term, "*mis*match," as it places the responsibility for the problem in the rightful place—which is on the program. Do not use terms such as "bad match," or "poor match." These terms can be perceived as placing the blame on *people*. Instead, explain the following:

> When discussing the mismatch, use that specific term, "mismatch," as it places the responsibility for the problem in the rightful place which is on the program.

- Matches are made as early as possible after an employee is hired to ensure that new employees quickly receive the support they deserve.
- This means that matches are made with available, but sometimes inadequate, information.
- Matches attempt to fit the mentor's strengths to a new employee's potential needs.
- When it is discovered that the program has mismatched a pair, we step in to try to resolve the problem. If that is not possible, we will dissolve the match and make a new one.
- Second matches usually work better because they are built on a more complete understanding of what the specific protégé needs.
- Always explain that conflicts are a natural result of putting diverse people together to work as partners. If a mentoring pair can work through conflicts by valuing how diverse they are, the richness of their different viewpoints, background and experience, then they can learn a great deal more from each other, *precisely because they are not thinking the same way.* Seen from this perspective, *differences are a strength rather than a weakness* of any relationship.

By using statements and language such as this, you diffuse the situation and allow *both parties* to mentally excuse themselves and "save face." Don't use a mismatch discussion to deal with a stubborn, reluctant protégé, or an inadequate mentor. Deal with those situations individually.

The risks in taking a reactive approach are that your program will have more mismatches to dissolve, the dissolutions may be unpleasant, and mentors and protégés may tell colleagues that "mentoring doesn't work." For these reasons, you should adopt a *proactive* method of matching.

Using a *Proactive* Matching Approach

The best time to decide what to do about mismatches is *before* concerns arise and before they become emotional. To do this, you need to anticipate possible challenges and plan strategies for dealing with them.

Your goals for dealing with mismatches should be to ensure that the resolution process is an affirming, dignifying one, and that the protégé's needs are met. As you read the steps below, notice how the proactive and reactive approaches are similar and different.

> The best time to decide what to do about mismatches is before concerns arise and before they become emotional. To do this, you need to anticipate possible challenges and plan strategies for dealing with them.

Define a Mentor-Protégé Mismatch Policy

Such a policy should include the following criteria:

- Matches are made as early as possible to provide the support new employees deserve.
- Matches are based on a new employee's potential needs and the mentor's strengths.
- Matches are made with inadequate information.
- The program assumes that a few of the matches will be inappropriate.
- By October 1, *each* partner will be separately asked whether the mentoring match is OK.
- Additional support and guidance are provided to help resolve any concerns discovered.
- It is unfair to a *protégé* to assign a mentor whose strengths don't fit a protégé's needs.
- It is unfair to a *mentor* if the mentor's strengths are not needed by a protégé.
- A new match will be arranged if there is a mismatch and concerns cannot be addressed.

The mismatch policy should be explained and provided in writing at an early date, such as at new teacher orientation for protégés and at the initial mentor information and recruitment meetings and trainings for mentors. In Figure 5.9, the capital M refers to a mentor and the capital P represents the protégé. If you use a mismatch process such as this, you will uncover and resolve almost all the problems before they become serious enough to threaten the match, and you can educate the pair to improve their partnership and results.

Try to Resolve Conflicts as They Surface

When a mentor and protégé are not working well together, it is not necessarily time to dissolve and remake a match. Conflicts can be productive opportunities and lead to terrific spurts of learning for the partners *if* they are handled very carefully.

Basically, a conflict is a disagreement and not every disagreement will be fatal to a mentor-protégé relationship. Also, *learning* how to better resolve conflicts is a valuable process in itself. Although a supervisor may become involved, the lead should be taken by a mentoring program coordinator who should *use effective mentoring strategies* to try to facilitate resolution of the problem(s). That way, the problems may be resolved and the pair can be prompted afterwards to debrief the process used, learn the process, and better understand how to be more effective mentoring partners.

Plan a Mismatch Check About One Month After Mentoring Starts

About a month after mentoring starts, separately ask every mentor and protégé whether they feel their mentoring match is effective. Also ask

- Have any problems occurred?
- What has been done to resolve the problem?

Figure 5.9 Mismatch Approaches

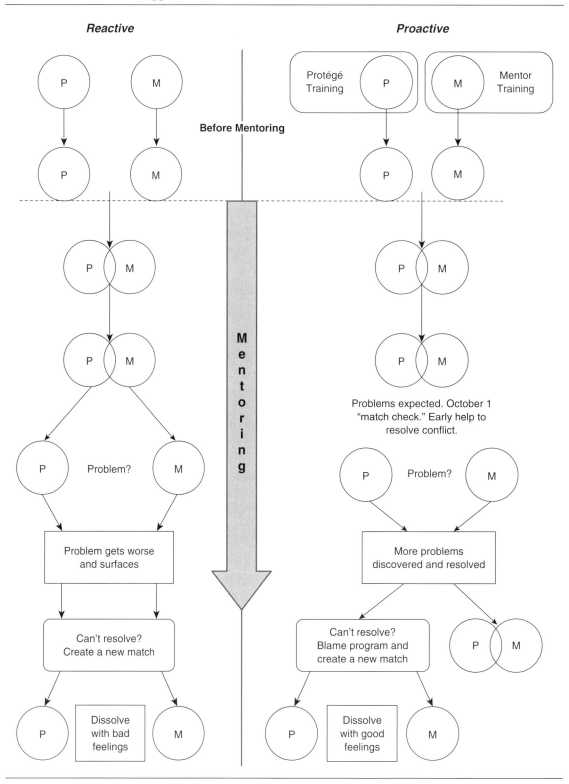

- Has the problem been resolved?
- If not, can the problem be resolved?
- What can the program do to facilitate resolution of the problem?

Ask the protégé first, but if there's a problem don't assume it's time for a change and don't create an expectation for a specific kind of solution. Promise to quickly investigate the situation and to facilitate a "resolution." Then check with the mentor, first asking for feedback about the usefulness of the match *before* sharing any protégé concerns. When one member of the pair says the match is not working, explore the reasons and decide whether the problem can be resolved—or at least that an attempt to resolve it is needed—or whether a new match is required.

An Example: Dealing With A Specific Mismatch

Decide whether a three-way dialogue could identify problems; establish the need for additional direction, support, or training; and get the pair back on track. The focus should be on clarifying that mentoring is not a one-way flow, but that each person is a partner with responsibilities to make it work. If appropriate, you may wish to use the Effective Protégé Characteristics list from this book (see Figure 5.3). If possible, encourage the protégé to specifically define *his* or *her* need, rather than detail what the mentor should do. The program can determine what the appropriate mentor strengths should then be. If that mentor has those strengths, or agrees to work to develop those strengths, then the current match can be sustained and monitored.

In some situations, the mentor's strengths may only partially address the protégé's needs. If this is the case, consider adding to the mentoring team another person who has the needed strengths. Keep in mind that the goal is not for one mentor to do it all, but to provide whatever support is needed to meet the learner's needs.

Discussing the Possibility of a Mismatch

Repeat the basic message ("program fault") when first discussing mismatches. Repeat it *again* just before inquiring if the match is working, and then *again* when you decide that a match must be dissolved and a new match made. Your goal is to teach both the mentor and the protégé that the growth and success of a learner are the priority.

> Your goal is to teach both the mentor and the protégé that the growth and success of a learner is the priority.

MENTOR SUPPORT AFTER TRAINING

Just as we need to provide follow-up support for new teachers to ensure the implementation in practice of their training, so we must also provide follow-up support for mentors. Not only do we want to provide support that mentors need and deserve, but we also want to help mentors perceive it as supportive. This is valuable, since mentors may not think of a mentor training, peer support group, or other program components as supportive *unless we describe it that way* to them.

Recommended Mentor Support Activities

Let's look at some specific methods for supporting the mentors. Some of these are essential and *should* be provided. Others are optional and *might* be offered. Some of the optional methods *should be done*, but which of them are offered is the program's choice.

Ongoing support for mentors should include

- Initial and ongoing training for their work as mentors (this will be discussed in Chapter 6)
- Mentor peer support groups that are carefully structured and facilitated so mentors can mentor each other. These meet approximately once a quarter.
- A Mentor of Mentors role that is fulfilled by a program coordinator
- Release from extra duty assignments, chaperoning, study hall, hallway, bus, or other supervision. This helps ensure time to mentor and minimizes interruptions to instructional time with their own students.

These essential support activities help each mentor learn more about how to effectively develop the protégé. The following support strategies target the same goal but are considered optional.

Ongoing support for mentors might also include

- Substitute teacher release to allow time for collaborative work that models effective practice, joint planning, conferences, and observations of the protégé
- Placement of the mentor in a team-teaching assignment with the protégé. This allows continuous instructional modeling by the mentor, observation of and feedback to the protégé, daily joint planning, and critiques of every lesson.
- A small budget for materials and supplies related to mentoring, such as materials to support the protégé's professional growth goal
- Paying for mentors and protégés to go together to one or two workshops that address the protégé's professional growth goals
- Allowing flexibility in finding the time to mentor. For example, do not insist that mentoring be done outside of school time. This is counterproductive. Even when paid a stipend, mentors who are mentoring during a plan period, for example, will still have to do their planning on their own time.

Mentor Peer Support Groups

Most of what was provided in Chapter 3 on peer support group meetings for *protégés* applies to *mentors* as well. The same structures and strategies should be provided for mentors. However, there are a few distinctions between the protégé and mentor model:

- If initial mentor *training was substantial* (such as two or three days), and focused primarily on effective mentoring strategies, the only remaining need for a full training session may be for coaching models and skills. Other mentor learning needs can be addressed through mentor peer support group activities.
- If initial and ongoing *mentor training is substantial*, support groups for mentors should only be held approximately once a quarter. More frequent meetings are not all that helpful and can even infringe upon time for mentoring.

- If mentor *training is a day or less,* mentor peer support groups should be held as frequently as once a month so training and support are ongoing. Some incentive should be offered for the additional time this requires of mentors.

> Periodic mentor support group meetings are not only helpful for mentors, but can also serve organizational needs by helping to hold mentors accountable for their commitments to each other and to program expectations.

- Periodic mentor support group meetings are not only helpful for mentors, but can also serve organizational needs by helping to hold mentors accountable for their commitments to each other and to program expectations.
- Peer support groups for mentors also provide excellent opportunities for leaders to monitor mentoring activities, mentor needs, mentor perceptions of their protégés' needs, and so forth. Informal or formal needs assessments can be helpful for planning future meetings and trainings or for ascertaining needs for intervention.
- Both protégé and mentor trainings and support activities should offer opportunities for developing supportive relationships with peers. Meetings should include time for pair and small-group conversation relative to the meeting's topics, informational interaction, and strategies, examples, and storytelling that show how people can use their peers for emotional support, to develop ideas, or to solve problems.
- *Unassigned,* but trained, mentors should be requested to participate in peer support groups and future mentor and coaching trainings. Send them copies of program announcements and newsletters to keep them informed about significant lessons learned by other mentors and updated about changes in the program expectations.

Figure 5.10 How Typical and Exemplary Peer Support Activities Support Mentor Growth on the CBAM Stages of Concern

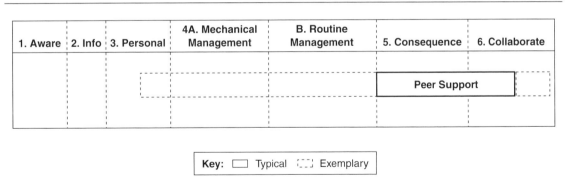

Simply putting mentors together for a "chat" with their peers will likely lead to some gains in student achievement. However, as Figure 5.10 shows, the potential of peer support is so much more. If the recommendations given above are followed, peer support activities will help mentors integrate much of their learning. They will also help mentors to move through most of the CBAM Stages of Concern by planning, skill building, internalizing best practices, and improving performance so it has a strong positive effect on student learning.

MENTORING OF MENTORS: PROGRAM LEADER SUPPORT OF INDIVIDUAL MENTORS

Providing each mentor with a Mentor of Mentors is critical. We know that, without support, the skills novices learn in training will rarely be implemented and applied in practice, which is why we provide new employees with mentors. The same truth applies to mentors. They need—even deserve—follow-up support in order to succeed. It is surprising that anyone would expect mentors to be highly effective with just training alone. In addition to mentor training, of all the strategies a program might use to achieve high-impact mentoring, the "Mentoring of Mentors" (MoM) strategy is *the most powerful*. It provides individualized support and accountability for mentors to implement what they have learned in their training and other learning experiences. It treats individual mentors individually.

The effectiveness of this strategy has been confirmed by both my own experience as a mentor program coordinator and a Mentor of Mentors and the feedback I received from mentors in dozens of mentoring programs. The Mentor of Mentors role is essential to ensure that mentoring actually improves performance and results.

Most mentors have never had a formal mentor who used a model of mentoring at the level of quality and productivity needed today. Attending training on effective mentoring skills is one step; however, applying those skills effectively while mentoring is the next, vastly different, step. The Mentor of Mentors is needed to gently but firmly hold mentors accountable for increasing use and mastery of the mentoring skills in which they have been trained, and to provide support for the mentor's ongoing learning and implementation process.

Figure 5.11   How Typical and Exemplary Mentoring of Mentors Supports Mentor Growth on the CBAM Stages of Concern

1. Aware	2. Info	3. Personal	4A. Mechanical Management	B. Routine Management	5. Consequence	6. Collaborate
			Mentoring of Mentors			

Key: ☐ Typical ⌐⌐ Exemplary

As Figure 5.11 shows, the Mentor of Mentors (MoM) role includes functions that cut across the entire CBAM Stages of Concern. The accountability to and support of the Mentor of Mentors helps ensure that mentors consistently implement their training and that the desired effects on teaching and student learning are achieved.

I offer the following guidelines for the Mentor of Mentors:

- Like all other mentors, the Mentor of Mentors must build trusting relationships with those being mentored, so that the candid discussion of problems is possible and the risk taking necessary for learning can occur.

- Like other mentors, the Mentor of Mentors must remain a positive and supportive force that is focused on the mentor's own goals for improvement and perceptions of need.
- The Mentor of Mentors must be an effective model, able to demonstrate the desired mentoring behaviors and model the required attitudes of openness to feedback and learning from others.

> The accountability to and support of the Mentor of Mentors helps ensure that mentors consistently implement their training and that the desired effects on teaching and student learning are achieved.

- Finally, the Mentor of Mentors is a technical coach who provides mentors with feedback about their use of effective mentoring strategies and support as mentors seek to improve their use of those effective strategies.
- Providing a Mentor of Mentors usually requires additional budget allocations. As a result, many consider this an optional role. I believe that, along with providing mentors and training them appropriately, the role of the MoM is the most important factor in ensuring that mentoring will lead to improved performance for teachers and students. The MoM role is the only method we have to ensure that what was taught in mentor training is used in practice. The MoM role will pay for itself in increased results.

MENTOR INCENTIVES AND RECOGNITION

Incentives, support and recognition are important to your program in two ways. First, they can be important to your program's *success* when *they are provided* and actually motivate mentors to do an even better job of mentoring than they might normally do. Second, incentives can also be a factor in program *failure* when *they are not provided* and mentors feel taken for granted because their hard work and sacrifices are not recognized. Such mentors may decide to never mentor again, and they may tell their colleagues exactly why. You cannot provide a mentoring program—especially one with high expectations—unless you can recruit and re-recruit mentors. Even if you have a good supply of new eligible mentors, your program needs *experienced* mentors to cause significant improvements.

Providing incentives, support, and recognition for mentoring can make or break your program, which makes them worth careful examination. Even if you feel it is inappropriate to provide mentors a stipend, there are other options to consider. The point is *not* "Do we need to provide a stipend?" Rather, you *must* provide a *balanced mix* of incentives, support, and recognition to attract and retain sufficient mentors.

Balanced Incentives, Support, and Recognition

These three topics can confuse people, in part because leaders are not sure how they are related. Also, the strong egalitarian culture of schools causes leaders to be wary of singling out individuals for something extra that others do not receive. The solution to this concern is establishing specific guidelines for working with incentives, support, and recognition. We'll begin by defining these terms.

Incentives

Incentives are motivations that are generally provided *before* something occurs, in an effort to influence others to carry out the desired action. Most well-established programs provide some form of mentor compensation, based on program annual budgets

(Bartell, 2005). Some districts have rewritten their new teacher contracts to include activities such as required orientation meetings, beginning staff development, and work with a mentor. These almost always include compensation.

The additional time required to mentor is not a part of the typical district teaching contract, so a stipend or other incentive makes sense. Also, you want experienced teachers to volunteer to be mentors. Incentives are offered to encourage these very busy teachers to make room in their lives to serve as mentors. If everyone could be a mentor, incentives would probably not be necessary. However, it is a seller's market in which the mentors needed are a special group of teachers. An example of an "Honorarium Policy" can be found at <http://www.ertconline.org>, the web page for the East Ramapo New York Mentoring Program.

Anything you can provide to potential mentors that encourages them to volunteer acts as an incentive. This includes such options such as

- A stipend
- Release from supervision duty, such as hall or recess duty
- Reduced class sizes, number of teaching preparations, or number of classes
- Tuition payment for graduate classes
- Graduate credit for mentor trainings
- Tickets to a sporting or a cultural event
- Allowing use of personal days immediately before or after vacations or holidays

Generally speaking, a rule of thumb for incentives is to provide some element of choice so that each person can find something that is motivating, thus making the incentives attractive to most people.

Support

Support is the provision of the things *during* the activities, which participants *perceive they deserve* because they are needed to do the job well. An example might be staff development for mentors in effective mentoring strategies. Mentors will appreciate and be able to use such support, but they will also perceive it as what the district should do to support their work as mentors. Unless a district is very sophisticated in explaining the provision of mentor training, few mentors will perceive mentor training as an incentive to become a mentor. For this reason, most districts offer the incentive of paying mentors for their time while they attend an initial mentor training before school starts.

> Support is the provision of the things during the activities, which participants perceive they deserve because they are needed to do the job well.

Effective leaders should be aware of some vital lessons about supporting mentors. Some support activities always work well, some work well only when done in specific ways, and some "support" activities are not really supportive at all. The support of mentors is generally provided by nonmentors and is based on the leader's perception of what mentors seem to need. However, some activities that are framed as mentor support really address program needs and not mentor needs and thus may not be very supportive of mentors. Peer support activities could easily fall into this category, since they may not be well led or not facilitated at all, and may be focused on organizational needs without considering mentor concerns. These, of course, would not be viewed by mentors as "supportive."

Recognition

Recognition is a reinforcement that is generally provided *after* something desirable has occurred. An example of this is an end-of-year mentor recognition dinner during which mentors' contributions are collectively affirmed and celebrated. This could include testimonies by high-level district leaders about the value of mentoring, as well as other activities. During the evening, each mentor should be individually recognized and given a token of appreciation.

Recognition can also be provided *during* a general staff activity. For example, a principal might recognize new mentors at the first faculty meeting of the school year. However, such a situation must be handled with care. In the example of the mentor recognition dinner, the audience primarily comprises those involved in the program, so there is no concern about nonmentor teachers feeling overlooked. When giving recognition at a general faculty meeting, it is possible that some teachers may feel overlooked. To avoid this, an effective leader can

- Create other events to recognize different teachers' contributions
- Remind the whole staff of other recognition times by saying, "In the past we have recognized all of you who have. . . . Today we honor those of you who are serving as mentors."
- Point out that the role of the teacher has changed to where the honored title of "teacher" hardly captures all that is expected of a professional educator. Affirm how much more demanding and challenging education has become since most of the staff began to teach. Explain the expectation that every staff member contributes to the welfare of students, each other, and the school, that this professionalism demonstrates staff dedication, and that it is appreciated.
- Look for ways to personally thank individuals for their extra efforts

Possible Forms of Mentor Recognition

The goal is to provide a variety of opportunities for recognition if you can't do something big. General recognition of teachers can include showing a *video segment* that affirms *teachers* and the difference one person can make in the lives of others. Examples include scenes from movies like *Mr. Holland's Opus* or *Stand and Deliver*. Segments from *Finding Forrester* or *The Karate Kid* can affirm *mentors* as a group and the value of mentoring.

Individual mentor recognition can include

- Gifts of significance, such as an engraved clock for a retiring teacher who has served as a mentor, a school bell with an engraved plaque for a mentor who has served three times, a framed photograph of all the mentors for each mentor, or a jacket embroidered with the name of the person and the word "mentor"
- Tokens of appreciation like a "gold" mentor pin, a brass door plaque with the teacher's name and the title "mentor," a framed "mentor" certificate, a wooden plaque of recognition for mentoring, or a golden "apple" engraved with the word "mentor" and their name and the date
- Testimonies, such as written new teacher testimonies of the value of their mentors, administrator, and board representatives affirming the value of mentoring, reading a poem or short story that illustrates the importance of mentoring, mentors telling

a few stories of their own most significant learning or experiences, students telling what it means to see their teachers as continual learners, or parents affirming mentors who ensure the success of new teachers and their students

Incentives, Support, and Recognition as Motivation

However useful these ideas and categories may be, avoid rigid thinking about them. They are each related to each other like the overlapping circles in a Venn diagram. That means there are times when an activity or item intended as an incentive is also perceived as a recognition or a form of support. A good example of this is providing mentors a reduced number of classes to teach, a reduction in the number of preparations, or release from other duties. These are seen as supportive because they provide valuable time, and they might also be an incentive or be perceived as recognition for the task of mentoring.

Here are some rules of thumb for providing incentives, support, and recognition:

- The most important of the three categories is the support you provide to employees. Do everything you can to ensure they have all they need to perform at a high level. That means you *must* do several things within the support category. For the categories of incentives and recognition, I suggest doing at least two things in each category.
- If finances or other factors limit what you can or are willing to do in any one of these categories, do one or two additional things in the remaining two categories.
- If you set high expectations for performance and results, what is most important is that people feel their work is acknowledged, appreciated, and not taken for granted. People must feel they have the tools, skills, and information they need to be effective. Otherwise, they will not volunteer for tasks beyond the minimum—or, worse, they will quit.

If one of your program goals is retention of teachers or increasing teaching performance and student achievement, this advice on balanced incentives, support, and recognition should be strictly and consistently followed. Without this, all other efforts to create a quality induction and mentoring program may not be sufficient. Incentives, support, and recognition are that important.

The ways in which we do or don't provide incentives, support, and recognition for *teaching* create the larger environment in which *mentoring* occurs. It is possible that an unsupportive teaching environment will negatively impact the degree to which teachers are attracted to mentoring, *even if good mentoring incentives, support, and recognition are in place.* In that case, larger systemic flaws must be addressed.

6

Designing a High Impact Mentor Training

In many ways, mentor training is just as critical as beginning teacher training. By increasing the skills of mentors, leaders not only prepare mentors to have a greater impact on the thousands of students who will be affected by the protégé, they also prepare mentors to have a greater impact on the learning of their own students.

Training mentors for their roles is the induction and mentoring program feature most frequently recommended by experienced mentors and coordinators. In fact, research indicates that mentor training is the single most important variable contributing to the success of mentoring (Sweeny, 1995). Gordon (1991) found that poor mentor training and support were major factors in ineffective mentoring programs.

> Training mentors for their roles is the induction and mentoring program feature most frequently recommended by experienced mentors and coordinators.

Mentor training is where all our previous efforts converge and "bear fruit." All your work to recruit, select, and match mentors with the right protégés leads up to the training. You've selected the right people with the right dispositions and skills. The orientation, training, observation, support activities, and professional growth strategies for protégés require effective mentoring to ensure that protégés implement their learning in the classroom. In both cases, the effectiveness of the mentor training ensures improved teaching and student learning.

There are at least four questions to consider and answer when designing a high impact mentor training:

- Who should lead your mentor training?
- What themes should move through an effective training?
- What should be the content and activities in the training?
- What follow-up support is needed to ensure mentor implementation of their training?

153

WHO SHOULD LEAD MENTOR TRAINING?

Ideally, mentor trainers should

- Be experienced staff developers skilled in leading adult learning
- Be experienced and outstanding mentors
- Be knowledgeable about the contents of this book and help design the mentor training
- Be known as teachers who use the methods described in your program's Vision for Excellent Teaching and Learning. Whether in their classrooms or while leading the training, they must model the instructional strategies and methods you wish to see all participants adopt.

There should be three mentor trainers, even if only two of these assume the major leadership roles. This ensures that at least one or two experienced trainers will be available if one trainer is unable to continue for some reason. This will also allow you greater flexibility in the future. For example, with two trainers you could operate a new mentor training and an experienced mentor training simultaneously.

There are four options to consider as you decide who will lead your mentor training. Notice the "?" icon, which will always signal when you have options from which to choose.

1. *You, or the person who designs the training, could also lead that training.* The designers know best how the design is expected to deliver what is needed. If the person(s) are trained staff developers, this is a good option. However, if the designer is initially uncomfortable in the leadership role, or seems incapable right now of successfully leading the training, consider allowing this person to assist while building skills and confidence. If this person will lead the training, select two other people to observe and help as needed. This will help build the training leadership capacity for the future.

2. *Your best mentor or mentors might lead the training.* Of course, this is not a good option for a new program. This solution works if the program has been active for a while and you have had opportunities to see mentors in action. I suggest that you assemble a small group of three to four experienced and outstanding mentors and show them the training design—or, even better, involve them in establishing the design. Then lead this small group to assess their own strengths as staff developers and see whether two or three grow into the leadership role. Selecting more than three leaders could result in fragmented training. However, choosing only one or two leaders means that you will need to go through the same selection process again when one of them leaves the role. Three allows for transfer of responsibilities over time.

A variation of this approach to delivering mentor training was developed by Janice Hall of Utah State University while working with a local school system. She uses a beginning level of training for new mentors, an advanced level of training for more experienced mentors, and a third level of training for very experienced and effective mentors who serve as the mentor trainers for the other two levels. This "grow your own" concept has been very effective (Hall, 2003.)

3. *An outside mentoring expert can lead your training.* An outside expert may or may not incorporate the best practices recommended in this book, so this option poses risks. Each mentoring expert has his or her own experiences, conclusions, and preferences, many of which may not align with your program. If the "expert" has been a mentor, or even a

mentor program coordinator, in only one other program, his or her perspective may be too narrow to meet your program's needs. In addition, hiring an outside expert to lead your training might negatively impact your district's capacity to develop its own program leaders. Ask the expert you consider about the next option.

4. *An outside mentoring expert can lead your first training while mentoring you or your best mentors to take the role of future mentor trainers.* If you have a brand new mentoring program or have previously provided training that was inadequate, I believe this is the best option.

The "training of trainers" approach provides you with multiple benefits. Your program can access the experience and modeling of a proven mentor trainer as well as begin development of your own mentor training experts, who will have seen effective training modeled. Effective mentors require ongoing support, coaching, and periodic training, all of which are best supplied by your own trainers. In-house mentor trainers will become even better mentors themselves. In-house mentor trainers will work to implement the training in their own mentoring and that process will improve their effectiveness as trainers.

WHAT ARE THE THEMES FOR HIGH IMPACT MENTOR TRAINING?

When designing the mentor training, remember to use your Vision for Excellent Teaching and Learning. This will ensure that this next program "link" models and teaches that this vision and the Chain of Causes and Effects result in effective mentoring. Since our Vision for Excellent Teaching and Learning is "individualization for maximum learner success," the mentor training must be designed to meet each mentor's individual needs and promote the maximum development of each mentor.

Maximizing mentor development means that every one of the mentor's experiences in the program is designed to develop the mentor. Will mentors find their individual needs are anticipated and met during training? Will mentors learn information they can apply later as they experience other components of the program? Will mentors see models of effective mentoring during training? If the mentor training is to serve the goals of the program, then the Vision for Excellent Teaching and Learning will drive every design decision, will be modeled in every activity during training, and the impact of that experience will be transferred down through the Chain of Causes and Effects. The goal is to ensure that every mentor's development *is* maximized by the training.

Should We Start With a Needs Assessment?

If the focus is on meeting individual mentor needs, you might assume that you should complete a needs assessment of your mentors before you design your mentor training. This approach offers some benefits; however, remember that *people can tell you only about the needs of which they are aware.* Needs of which mentors are *not* aware will not be revealed in a needs assessment.

So how can you design an effective mentor training? What data are available to inform your planning? I recommend that you use the data that I have collected and the mentor training design I have developed, at least initially.

> Needs of which mentors are not aware will not be revealed in a needs assessment.

I led my first mentor training in 1987. At that time, a major instructional improvement effort was student learning styles. At the same time, I was in a graduate program in supervision and curriculum development, during which we studied management and leadership theory. That dual frame of mind led me to search for information and research on the process of facilitating another's professional development. I used that research base to develop a model of the mentoring process and a mentoring styles assessment that I incorporated into my first mentoring training. The impact was powerful!

Since that time, I have led hundreds of mentor trainings and continued to use and refine the same mentoring process model and mentoring styles assessment. I gradually developed the instructions needed to ensure validity in the assessment results. During an eleven-year period, I collected and analyzed the data this instrument provided. Eventually, I stopped collecting and analyzing the data from that assessment, although I continued to use the mentoring styles assessment. I stopped collecting data because the same patterns kept repeating. Originally, that made me suspicious of the assessment. However, I found that I could create alternative forms of the assessment for many diverse applications and that, as long as mentors were volunteers, I still saw results that showed the same patterns had generalized across these many settings. Generalizability is one of the best tests of an assessment. Since learning that, I have never had any doubt about these data patterns.

One alternative note: Lipton and Wellman (2001) advocate a different structure in the transitions during mentoring. Theirs involves similar vocabulary but a different structure for mentors to learn it. I take affirmation from their structure but suggest you adhere to my training approach until you have more experience as a mentor trainer.

The patterns I found in my mentor styles assessment are extremely predictable—so much so that I have designed my mentor training around those data patterns. The data I will provide here and the mentor training design I offer are trustworthy. You will get the same positive results when you use this assessment and mentor training model.

The Mentoring Process Model

The general mentoring process model I use has four stages (see Figure 6.10 later in this chapter): the direct stage, the explain stage, the collaborate stage, and the letting go stage.

The Direct Stage

This stage occurs early in a mentoring relationship when the mentor has lots to tell the protégé, even if the protégé has not yet asked for the information. Many of the earliest things the protégé must learn are basic procedural items that must be completed "one right way" and are not a matter of choice—for example, deadlines, schedules, expectations, and traditional do and don't procedures. These are the things we place on our checklists. Protégés need to learn this information as soon as possible. However, providing this information can be tricky since, in addition to having lots to learn, protégés must set up their classrooms and prepare for students. There is no time for a gradual process of analysis and discovery.

The Explain Stage

Many of the "one right way" procedures are very straightforward and truly represent one right way. However, some procedures are handled differently at different schools, so those are "one right way *here*" situations. A protégé who is not informed about these things may make decisions that are out of sync with the school culture. Protégés may think that these are issues in which there are choices to make and may feel free to decide what they think is best. They are unaware of past decisions in which the faculty decided, "Here, we will do this one specific way." To effectively prepare protégés for the school culture, mentors need to go *beyond just telling to fully explaining* why things are as they are here. This helps a protégé understand enough to join the consensus instead of asserting their own judgment.

The Collaborate Stage

After a while, protégés learn what they need to know about "the lay of the land" and they also have become more competent as teachers. Others begin to treat them as peers, and their mentoring relationships change. Due to the egalitarian culture of schools, many educators try to get to this stage as fast as possible, sometimes sooner than is appropriate.

At this stage, mentors know protégés have learned most of the basics and that they can handle their own deadlines, procedures, and other such essentials. As a result, mentors feel less responsibility for ensuring protégés get these tasks done and begin to focus more on building collaborative relationships with their protégés. This is a "testing" time in which mentors watch to see the extent to which protégés can function independently. When mentors see that their protégés are more self-sufficient, it is time to move to the last stage.

The Letting Go Stage

The goal of mentoring is to quickly develop protégés into self-sufficient but interdependent educators who work well as part of a team. At this point, formal mentoring is no longer needed. In fact, hanging on to a mentoring relationship past this point may create a dependency, a result that should be avoided.

However, we also know from the CBAM Stages of Concern that the highest level of professional practice is the Collaborate stage. That tells us that as mentors, when we back away from the formal support and guidance of a protégé, we must still remain informally involved in each other's work and we must continue our mutual search for best practices for our classrooms. In other words, the protégé has reached a level of independence, but best practice reminds us to continue a relationship of interdependence in which we keep learning from and supporting each other's development.

What the Mentor Styles Assessment Data Tell Us

It makes sense that educators as a whole would generally be a similar type of people. After all, teachers are motivated to help students grow, gain increased knowledge and understanding, and succeed in life. The public notion of what teachers are like and what they do leads to a self-selection process that produces millions of educators who fit this "helping others" profile.

Consider, then, what happens when from that self-selected group we ask those who are best at helping others to succeed to also become our mentors. The pattern of "helping others" is even stronger in this group. Mentors are not just motivated to help others succeed, they are *driven.* These and other characteristics are fairly predictable in teachers and even more predictable of mentors. *Knowing* the characteristics *can help us design trainings* in three ways:

1. If *we know* where mentors *may not be strong*, we need to help mentors *discover* where they are *not* naturally strong and create a desire in them to improve themselves

there. In reality, most mentors can do all the things they need to do. The real issue is that their tendencies lead them to miss when they need to do some things. They need to give special attention to such an area when they are trained to be mentors.

2. If we know where mentors are *already strong*, we needn't train them to do those things.

3. If we know where mentors are already strong, we need to guide them to examine whether or not those *strengths might sometimes be taken to excess* and become inappropriate. An example is a person who prides himself on being good at explaining things, but whom others see as never willing to listen. We need to be sure our mentors discover these tendencies too and plan for appropriate behaviors when working with others.

Essentially, accomplishing these three tasks is the primary agenda of my mentor training. How do I know with certainty that this is what is needed? The mentoring styles assessment data I have collected consistently tell me so. The data will tell us and the mentors whether they are stronger or need to proceed cautiously at any of the four stages of the mentoring process. Specifically, my research shows that

- About 70 percent of *teachers* are strongest in the middle two styles. They enjoy explaining things to others and they work very well with their peers and others.
- About 98 percent of *mentors* tend to be strongest in the middle two styles. They love to explain things to and collaborate with their colleagues. In fact, in more than half of my mentor trainings, 100 percent of those present raise their hands for the middle two styles when I inquire about the styles in which participants are strongest. This pattern also indicates that the first stage of "Direct" and the last stage of "Letting Go" are weaker areas for almost all mentors, which means they will not naturally do these things when they are needed. This prevalent pattern informs us as we approach training design. However, we must observe two cautions:
  - *Don't "dump" these data patterns on mentors too quickly.* They must individually and gradually be led up to the point where they are ready to learn this information, then led to discover it for themselves and, based on that new learning, begin to rethink their tendencies and develop new skills.
  - You will find a few people who do not identify themselves as being *"strongest in the middle two styles."* You must note who these people are and determine which of the following applies to them. Since their strengths are not in the middle two areas, they are probably weak in those two areas and stronger in the Direct and Letting Go phases. In that case, you need to remember who they are and adapt the training to their different needs.

At this point in the training, it is important to point out that we don't have to be strong in the middle two styles to be great mentors. The *ideal* is to be about equal in each of the four styles so we naturally do what's needed at each phase of the mentoring process. However, few of us are equally balanced in our mentoring style.

These striking patterns are very helpful to us when we plan mentor trainings. However, even more significant are the conclusions these patterns lead us to form regarding our mentor training design.

Mentor Styles to Address When Planning Mentor Training

To effectively use these data to inform our planning, we need to answer two questions:

- Given these data, what conclusions can we draw?
- What do these data and conclusions suggest are the implications for design of mentor training?

---

1. The Direct Stage

General Mentor Pattern: Discomfort and a tendency to not be direct

Conclusion: Early in their careers, protégés need to learn a great deal, but most mentors tend to avoid telling other adults what they must do.

Implications: Training must help mentors who are weak in this style to understand their tendencies.

- Affirm mentors' feelings of wanting to avoid acting like know-it-alls and their desire to allow the protégés to show what they can do.
- Teach mentors that "Directing means that when others don't know what it is they *need* to do, they should be directed to do those things."
- Teach mentors how to discern when they should *not give* a protégé information or answers.
- Teach mentors *when they should be telling* and why it is important that they do so. For example, in their early weeks, new protégés usually are at the CBAM Stages of Awareness and Information. When protégés are at the Information Stage, mentors should give them the information they need.
- Teach mentors how to know *when to stop telling*. Mentors can ask protégés if they would like more ideas or information, or if they are ready to develop a plan of action (Personal Stage, the next stage of the CBAM).

Given this guidance, mentors who are weak in this style should be capable of doing what is needed when it is appropriate.

---

2. The Explain Stage

General Mentor Pattern: Strength and comfort at this stage

Conclusions: Most mentors are likely to naturally do very well at this stage; however, some mentors will take their strengths in explaining to an extreme.

Implications: Training must help mentors with this style understand their tendencies.

(Continued)

(Continued)

- Affirm mentors' strengths in explaining and emphasize the importance of doing so.
- Review with mentors the concept of "one right answer here," the need to realize what these issues are, and the need to develop and use a checklist for mentor guidance.
- Teach mentors to use the CBAM stages to determine a protégé's level of development, which helps mentors identify when they should and should not give explanations to protégés.
- Teach mentors how to know when to stop explaining—for example, by asking protégés whether they understand and whether they are ready to develop a plan of action (Personal Stage of the CBAM).

Given this guidance, mentors who are strong explainers should know how to decide when explaining is or is not an appropriate mentor response.

3. The Collaborate Stage

General Mentor Pattern: Considerable strength and comfort at this stage

Conclusions: Most mentors are likely to naturally do very well at this stage. However, most mentors will tend to begin collaborating too early, while protégés still have lots to learn, and continue collaborating long past the time that protégés are ready for independence.

Implications: Training must help mentors with this style understand their tendencies.

- Affirm mentors' strengths in collaboration and the importance of that stage.
- Teach mentors to use the CBAM Stages to determine a protégé's level of development, which helps mentors know when they should and should not treat protégés as peers, when to collaborate with protégés, and when to stop teaching them.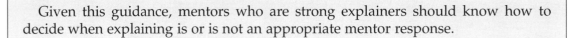
- Teach mentors how to know when to *start* collaborating—for example, by asking the protégé whether they feel ready to work together, or if there are things the mentor still needs to help the protégé understand.
- Teach mentors how to know when to *stop* collaborating—for example, by asking the protégé whether he or she feels ready to work independently.

4. The Letting Go Stage

General mentor pattern: Weakness and discomfort at this stage

Conclusion: Most mentors are not likely to let go or encourage independence as their protégés mature and their mentoring relationships near the end.

Implications: Training must help mentors with this style understand their tendencies.

- Teach these mentors to use the CBAM to assess when a protégé is at the collaborate or refocusing Stage of Concern and to help protégés at that level increasingly connect with others from whom they can learn and gain support. Then mentors need to get out of the way.
- Teach mentors to ask their protégés whether they would like further help (collaboration) in accomplishing the next task or whether they feel they can *do it fine on their own* (let go). Mentors might say, for example, "It seems like you have mastered this strategy, but do you want more help?"
- Teach mentors how to *transition to a more informal relationship* when it is time to let go, by saying for example, "You seem fine with this. Let me know anytime if we need to talk."

Conclusion

Remember the small percentage of mentors who are not strongest in the center two areas? If those mentors are strongest in the Direct and Letting Go phases, this means they are inclined to "tell" protégés what they feel protégés must know and then disappear. Although well intentioned, these mentors might skip explaining and collaboration, the stages at which mentors and their protégés typically need to spend the most time.

Implications

Even though there may be just a few mentors like this, your training must provide for their needs and improvement. Training needs to give these mentors guidance and practice in knowing *when it is necessary to further explain* a topic and *when to use shared work* (collaboration) to assess the protégé's skills, need for further support, or readiness for independence.

Use humor to discuss this mentoring tendency. For example, say "If I was strongest in the Direct and Letting Go styles, my mentoring might look like this . . . " Then walk out the training room door, turn around and stick just your head back in the door and say, "Hi, remember me? I'm your mentor. I just wanted to remind you to get your grades in to the office by Friday. OK? If you need anything else, I'm in room 212. Bye." Then pull your head back into the hallway. Images like this "stick" in people's memory, everyone enjoys it, and it will help to counter the tendencies of this style.

All mentors need to be taught to use the CBAM to assess the developmental levels of their protégés and then to plan their mentoring to help meet their protégés' needs. Be sure to help mentors understand that there will be times when the styles that they are *not* strong in are the ones that are needed.

Something for Every Mentoring Style: Making Menus

Sometimes, mentors have difficulty identifying a protégé's CBAM Stage of Concern. Protégés may struggle just to define their problem, much less to ask for specific help. When this happens, mentors need to know how to form two or three options using the protégé's "problem," with each option framed at a *different* Stage of Concern. This allows the protégé, by the choice of an option, to specifically indicate the stage of need. Here is an example (see box).

The protégé says, "I need help with my grade book. It's a disaster!"

Although it seems the protégé is using a grade book, the first step is to make sure this is the case. If it is, the protégé's stage might be mechanical management, but we are not sure. We do not want to automatically provide help building skills at that stage and later find the assistance wasn't what was needed. The mentor should frame two or three choices, *one at the stage* where the mentor thinks the protégé might be, and another one or two choices *at lower stages*. If the protégé could be at mechanical management, the mentor should frame one choice at that stage, one at personal (plan) and one at information.

The mentor says in response, " Let me think about that for a moment" (to plan the choices). Then the mentor could say, "Which would be more helpful?

"Reading and discussing some suggestions for laying out grade books? (information),

"Planning your grade book using that written guidance? (Personal stage), or . . .

"Looking through your grade book to see if we can discover and solve the problems?" (mechanical management)

When the protégé makes the choice, the mentor knows clearly whether the protégé needs information, a plan, or help in problem solving.

Summary

We have seen that mentor training should focus on two core concepts and their application in the mentoring relationship:

1. *Understanding one's own mentoring style* and the tendencies (helpful or not) likely to impact how each mentor behaves. Mentors must be led to discover their natural tendencies and to analyze whether or not these will always be helpful. Then mentors must use this information to set goals and plan how to use their strengths to advantage while avoiding pitfalls. Training could include the use of case studies, activity scenarios, or viewing and responding to a video to address these issues.

2. *Using the CBAM Stages of Concern to assess and then address protégé needs.* This mentor strategy is used throughout the mentoring process. Practice must include both identifying the protégé's level of need and planning an appropriate mentor response. Internalizing this skill set also takes considerable practice so a carefully planned learning sequence during the training is needed.

Even though the mentor styles and use of the CBAM are the central themes of the mentor training, there are many other elements needed in the training as well. However, to avoid a fragmented training, these other elements should be *linked to the two themes* whenever possible.

WHAT IS THE SEQUENCE FOR CONTENT AND ACTIVITIES IN MENTOR TRAINING?

Considering all the advice given above, how must the initial mentor training be structured? Of course, there are numerous options for sequencing the many themes and elements we have discussed. Over the years, it seems to me I must have tried them all! No need for you to have to try them all too to discover what works best. What follows is the High Impact Mentor Training agenda I use in my own work. It is for three days, since I assume you will need to train mentors in high impact strategies *and* get them off to a good start in coaching each other. Here's my rationale for this decision.

This three-day agenda is enough training all at the one time. To add more time and content does not mean mentors can absorb and apply much more. I have found that even adding more practice at this point can be counterproductive. Mentors need to implement in real relationships what they have learned before they will be capable of learning and using more content, skills, and practice. That's why I often call this training the "initial" mentor training. Therefore, you also need to plan follow-up training, usually about five to six months later.

I save most of the coaching experiences for a later training because coaching increases the intensity of mentoring. In most cases, I suggest that mentors *not* make coaching visits for the first two or three months. However, an *introduction* to coaching *is* provided here because some pairs will be ready for and choose to do coaching earlier than others. Of course, this approach is intended for a multiyear induction program whose goals include instructional improvement and where there is extended time for mentoring.

Finally, as Figure 6.1 shows, the mentor training should ideally utilize all the Stages of Concern from the CBAM up through routine management. This means that mentors' needs can be anticipated and addressing those needs must be built into the training sequence. The agenda provided here does exactly that. It will take mentors at least to the level of routine management, where their use of the mentoring strategies taught and practiced in the training are comfortable to them and starting to work well. It would be further work with a Mentor of Mentors, which helps mentors grow to even higher levels of practice than a training can assure.

Figure 6.1   How Typical and Exemplary Mentor Recruitment and Training Support Mentor Growth on the CBAM Stages of Concern

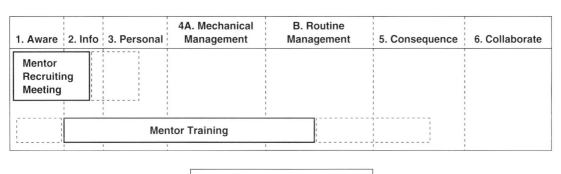

A Suggested Training Agenda

The general agenda for a three-day mentor training is provided first as an overall perspective on the training sequence. Please note that a "day" is assumed to be about seven hours of actual work time, such as from 8:30 a.m. to 4:30 p.m., less an hour for lunch and two fifteen-minute breaks. At the end of Day 3, times are not given since options affect timing. Following this agenda, there will be specific activity directions and explanations provided so you can lead the sequence successfully the first time.

Agenda for Three-Day "High Impact Mentoring and Coaching Strategies Training"

Day 1

8:30 • Presenter and table introductions, training objectives

8:40 • Self-assessment of participant knowledge and skills in high impact mentoring topics

8:50 • Option—information on the District Induction and Mentoring Program

• Option—the value of supporting new teachers

Aligning Visions for Excellence in Mentoring and Teaching

9:00 • Defining our desired Vision for Excellent Teaching and Learning

9:15 • Do good teachers always make good mentors?

9:30 • 75 percent OK, but 25 percent caution! Critical mentoring strategies you didn't learn from students.

9:35 • Principles of "adult" learning and their implications

9:55 • Great mentoring IS great teaching

10:00 • Mentoring ideal—a model of what?

10:05 • Fifteen-minute break

An Initial Glimpse of Our Mentoring Styles

10:20 • "Optical Illusion" mentoring

10:30 • The twenty-three ways mentors can help

11:30 • What do the data tell you about your mentoring tendencies as a group?

11:40 • The problem with too much "telling"

11:55 • Advice for when it's OK to "tell"

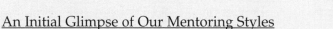

12:00 • Lunch—one hour

1:00 • Your individual mentoring style self-assessment

1:10 • The four phases of the mentoring process

1:20 • Integrating the mentoring process and your mentoring style—insights, goals, and plans

Challenges of Mentoring New Teachers

1:50 • Poem from an unknown new teacher

2:00 • Tom Gordon's model—Transitions in Awareness

2:25 • Break for fifteen minutes

2:40 • CBAM—a system for assessing and addressing new teacher needs

3:25 • Practicing the CBAM

Closing, Reflection on Day 1 and Sharing

4:20 • Insights or discoveries made today you want to remember to use as a mentor

4:30 • Adjourn for the day

Day 2

Strategies for Assessing New Teacher Needs

8:30 • Option—Sharing as a review

8:30 • Test of memory—CBAM Stages of Concern

8:45 • Test of memory—Gordon's Model

8:55 • Compare and integrate Gordon's Model and the CBAM

9:15 • Fifteen-minute break

9:30 • What's a mentor to do at each CBAM stage?

10:00 • A CBAM refinement—make menus, not mandates

Effective Communication and Questioning Strategies

10:15 • Trust-building strategies

10:25 • Confidentiality and information flow suggestions

11:00 • Effective communication strategies

11:30 • Lunch for one hour

(Continued)

(Continued)

12:30 • Capturing the potential of open-ended questions

1:00 • The problem-solving mentoring process—power of questions

1:10 • Pronoun power

1:25 • The three debriefing questions

1:35 • Practice of the three debriefing questions

2:35 • Fifteen-minute break

Experienced Mentor Panel Discussion

2:50 • Panel discussion

4:25 • Insights and discoveries made today that you want to remember to use as a mentor

4:30 • Reminder of focus for tomorrow, adjourn for day

Day 3: High impact coaching for instructional improvement
8:30 • Overview of the day's activities

Pair demonstration—an example, not a "model"

8:35 • *Coaching cycle #1* (total time about one and a half hours). Format: The trainer is the "teacher" and a volunteer is the "coach." The whole group collects data for the "teacher."

10:00 • Fifteen-minute break

Group Coaching Practice

10:15 • *Coaching cycle #2* (total time is one hour and fifteen minutes). Format: Either the trainer plays the role of a new teacher being coached by a mentor, or the whole group serves as the coach.

11:25 • Group assessment. The objective of this step is to assess participant readiness for implementation to begin after lunch.
 – *Step 1:* Advance preparation for trainer
 – *Step 2:* CBAM connections—assessment for trainer planning

11:30 • Dismiss for lunch for one hour—trainer choices for planning during lunch

Small-group Mentoring of Mentors practice

12:30 • *Coaching cycle #3* (takes one hour)
  – *Format A:* The training group is broken into small groups of five to ten participants.
  – *Format B:* One mentor will be coached by another mentor.
  – *Format C:* The rest of the small group fill the role of the Mentor of Mentors (MoM) by observing the pair, collecting data, and offering feedback.

Alternating Independent Pair Coaching Practice

• *Coaching Cycle #4:* The training group is broken into pairs. Each pair does two complete coaching cycles. Partners switch roles for the two cycles:
  – *Cycle A*—teacher to be coached = person A, mentor = person B
  – *Cycle B*—teacher to be coached = person B, mentor = person A
  – The focus of the pair conferences and observations will be scenarios that are based on videos of actual teaching segments, to be viewed later.

Closing Activity: A Final Reflection on the Training and Planning
for Mentoring of Mentors

• The *objective* of this section is to prepare trainees for an ongoing, formal support and accountability relationship with the program leader, who serves as the Mentor of Mentors.
– Expectations for mentors about program-level communication
– Sharing mentoring goals with the MoM and a final needs assessment

A Big Send-Off

• Graduation

• A Parting Thought

DETAILED TRAINING ACTIVITIES AND DIRECTIONS

	Day 1
As participants enter: Self-assessment of participant knowledge and skills in high impact mentoring topics, done before the training starts	"Your Mentoring Knowledge and Skills Self-Assessment" (Use Figure 6.2 at the end of this chapter.) *In Advance*—I use this self-assessment at the start of all my mentor trainings to tell me what my learners *think* they need in the training. It also serves to alert them right away to the possibility that what they think and the reality may be different. Before the training, I take this page to a commercial copy shop and enlarge it to 400 percent, which is 3 by 4 feet. The expense is well worth it since this also serves as a post assessment and is used to collect data for future comparisons. I hang that poster near the door and provide sticky "dots" of *one color* (like for garage sale pricing) so participants can each place a dot on each continuum and create an easy-to-see "bar graph." I refer to this at the start and throughout the training to decide how to allocate time to each training topic and how to adjust my plans given the learners' awareness of their need to know about and do a topic. At the end of the training, I give out a different colored set of dots and each participant repeats the assessment. This gives me a great pre- and post-test of mentor growth and helps me see what steps are needed to further support mentor growth. Also, when I teach the CBAM later during the training, I explain how this self-assessment has used the CBAM Stages of Concern.
8:30 • Introductions	Presenter and table introductions, training objectives
8:50 • Option (if many new mentors)	Information on the District Induction and Mentoring Program. See the end of chapter for a list. *Option—"Preaching to the choir?"* The value of supporting new teachers. Experienced mentors and new mentors who were recently protégés already know this information. However, if the bulk of trainees are new mentors and if administrators will be present, don't make many assumptions. Include about fifteen minutes on this topic. I recommend comparison of Simon Veenman's (1985) study of the needs of (unsupported) beginning teachers with the Sandra Odell (1986) meta-analysis on needs of supported beginning teachers. The difference even minimal support makes is amazing and affirming. (Note that the use of any options requires adjustments to the time schedule.)
	Aligning Visions of Excellence in Mentoring and Teaching
9:00 • Defining our desired Vision for Excellent Teaching	• Point out our need to clarify the end goal of effective mentoring. • For each table group, provide copies of district effective teaching expectations or evaluation models (content, not process), state or provincial standards, and board or strategic plan goals that *summarize* the qualities of excellent teaching. Look for key words like engaged, active learning, differentiation, meeting student needs, etc. • Give the group the following goal and fifteen minutes for the task. Each table group is to look for common threads across the documents and create a bulleted list with no more than four or five items, on a large flip chart page. To ensure visibility, provide dark-colored markers and request that recorders print the answers. • Post each completed chart next to the others on the wall. • Select two or three people to develop a final, poster-size, one-page list that summarizes the Vision for Excellent Teaching. They will do this while the others move on to the next steps. This final list will be used later during the training.
9:15 • Do good teachers always make good mentors?	The objective here is to clarify that excellent mentoring is identical to excellent teaching of students, and we all have lots to learn about this. • Present the question. Give each table five minutes to discuss it and reach consensus. Have each table group appoint a reporter. • Call on each table group, asking for their report.

	Discuss. The leader relates the "vision" to the question, stating even the best teachers (mentors?) still challenge themselves to become better each day. Also, while old styles of teaching students don't work with adults, "Principles of Adult Learning" (see Figure 6.3) engage learners of every age. (Don't distribute the "Principles" yet.)
9:30 • 75 percent OK, but 25 percent caution!	There are critical mentoring strategies you didn't learn from your work with students. Yet, having once been beginning teachers, we all tend to rely on our own intuition about what novices need and how to help them. Often these instincts for helping will be right, but about one-quarter of the time, those instincts will lead us to engage in useless or even harmful behaviors. This happens because of our mentoring styles.
9:35 • Principles of "adult" learning and their implications	Distribute one copy of Figure 6.3 ("Principles of Adult Learning," found at the end of this chapter) to each person. • Assign one principle to each table and ask the groups to discuss whether it would be OK to do with students too. Allow three to five minutes. • Ask table reporters to report to the whole group. Keep a tally on a poster sized version or overhead of the "Principles." Allow about five minutes for reporting and tallying. • What is the conclusion, allowing for developmentally appropriate adaptations? Typically, people confirm that all "Principles" should also be used with students (two to three minutes). • Now look at the summary "Vision for Excellent Teaching" developed earlier. Discuss the extent to which this homegrown vision matches the research-based Principles of Adult Learning. They very likely will be an excellent match. • Final conclusion? Our discussions and this comparison help us realize that effective mentoring is a practical example of desired teaching models.
9:55 • Great mentoring is great teaching.	The leader offers: • If the Principles of Adult Learning should be used to engage and design instruction for all learners, then these principles will be vital for use in our mentoring and for ensuring that we move toward attaining our Vision for Excellent Teaching. • Mentors must model in their mentoring the use of these principles. • Mentors must ensure that protégés consciously understand that it is these principles that make the mentoring effective and their own learning and growth so powerful. • Mentors must help protégés adopt these principles in their teaching practice and use them to design lessons. • Viewed from this perspective, we can now see that effective mentoring is practice at the adult level of exactly what we must do at the student level. • In conclusion, mentors can trust their intuition but also must consciously focus their mentoring to implement the Principles of Adult Learning. If mentors will do this, the Vision for Excellent Teaching will be realized in our work and gradually in our schools!
10:00 • The mentoring ideal	The leader presents: • Must mentors be perfect examples of effective practice? • This is neither necessary, nor desired. • An example of perfect practice is the "Sage on the stage," which is an outdated instructional model. Further, even our best teachers are still continually learning and *not* perfect. • What, then, is the "model" for what mentors must be? Mentors need to be examples of the professional commitment and continual struggle to *become* a model of best practice. Finally, this also means that mentors must continually struggle to be *visible* models of growing as mentors and teachers.

(Continued)

Time	Activity
10:05–10:20 • Fifteen-minute break	
10:20 • "Optical illusion" mentoring	*An Initial Glimpse of Our Mentoring Styles* *In advance*, choose two very different optical illusions which are obscure enough that they will take several moments to begin to understand. Create large posters or an overhead transparency of each. Do the following twice using a different illusion each time. Allow ten minutes for this activity. • Ask participants to quickly look at the illusion, trying to "get" what it shows. Caution them to not say anything about what they see. Tell them to raise their hand high when they "get" it. • Leave the illusion up until about half "get it" (usually about ten seconds) then remove it. • Ask those who get it to keep their hands up. These will be the "mentors." • The rest are the "protégés," and they must now go and stand near a "mentor." Caution again: "No talking." (Use these exact words.) "Mentors, your job is to help the protégés to 'get' the illusion." Tell protégés to raise their hand when they do get it. This usually takes forty-five to sixty seconds. • Repeat the above steps again, using the second illusion, identifying new mentors and protégés and asking the new mentors to help their new protégés get it. • (In the whole group) Ask anyone who was a protégé to reflect for a moment and then share with the group *how* their mentor helped them to get it. Summarize responses on a flip pad. You should get four or five different "mentoring strategies," including telling the protégé the "answer." • Point out the above and ask for discussion on which mentoring strategy might have been the most effective given the goal of "getting it." • Discuss the conclusions. A common answer is that there is no one clear "best" way. • Point out that, "We shall see a bit later if that is the case." Then say, "This was an insight into how you as individuals tend to mentor. Try to remember for later what you did if you were an illusion mentor. Now let's turn to see if we can gain further insight into our mentoring tendencies."
10:30 • The twenty-three ways mentors can help (one hour)	*Objective*: To demonstrate the need for mentors to learn specific ways of helping they tend not to use and thus to motivate their active engagement in the rest of the training. *In advance*, prepare two charts or transparencies of Figure 6.4 from the end of this chapter. Acquire two different colored markers that will write on this chart. Become familiar with each of the twenty-three ways mentors help so you can recognize and distinguish them while you observe mentoring. • Explain the activity objective. • Ask the group for two volunteers. Tell them they should be willing to share an educational, teaching, or (best) a mentoring challenge or problem they have, had, or are concerned they will face. Motivate the volunteering by telling the group that the person with the challenge will get the best experience and knowledge of the people in this room to guide their solution of the problem. Point out that, after you hear each problem, you will select the final one to use. For this activity to be as engaging and powerful as I have found it can be, it is absolutely vital that the problems and the volunteers be real, authentic, and not staged.

- Invite the two volunteers to join you and listen privately to each of their problems. Pick the one with which most participants in the training can identify. Thank the other and ask him or her to be seated.

- Divide the remaining group into two. The largest (about 60 percent) will sit in a semicircle around the volunteer and be "group mentors." The smaller group will sit outside the semicircle as "observers" during the activity and later will be mentors to the mentors. *Note:* if the training group is larger than thirty or so, divide into two and then use these directions for each of the two groups so they do their work at the same time. If you do this, you will need an extra set of the chart to complete and two volunteers for the second group (you cannot observe) to both listen for mentor statements and complete the chart.

- Privately tell the volunteer to be authentic and not to role play. Tell him or her, in stating challenges and responding to mentors, to give short answers so as to provide mentors with good practice in drawing out information from the volunteer.

- Tell the mentors they must act as one person, building on what earlier mentor comments or questions were offered and the responses. They should not seek to get their individual ideas or questions heard, but rather to allow each train of inquiry or thought to be developed. They should try to apply what they feel are excellent mentoring behaviors. They will have about forty to forty-five minutes to fully help the volunteer solve or plan to solve their problem.

- Tell the observers they will have two roles. First they will only observe and listen, writing out their own ideas and questions, but primarily recording things to use to mentor the mentors after the group mentoring activity is finished.

- Start the activity when all participants seem clear on the process and their roles.

- While the group mentoring proceeds, you are to listen for the specific mentoring methods used and fill in a box for that choice on the "Twenty-three ways . . ." chart. Use one color for the first fifteen minutes and the second color after that. This will reveal changes in the mentoring. Your objective is to create a visual representation of just the mentors' half of the conversation, primarily so they can see (again) their natural mentoring tendencies and their unused options. *Caution:* A mentor may start with one method and switch to a second one.

- *Observers' report:* When about forty-five minutes have passed or it is clear the volunteer's problem is solved or a plan to solve it is done, it is time for the mentors to listen and learn, and for observers to work.
  - First ask observers to use about two to three minutes to recognize the effective and valuable things they observed.
  - Then prompt the observers to use about five to ten minutes and their best mentoring skills to help the mentors *learn* (use that word) how they might improve their mentoring even further. (Observers do not have the "Twenty-three ways . . ." chart.) The choice of the word "learn" is so open-ended as to allow observers to use the best or the worst mentoring methods. This sets observers up for feedback and learning.

- *Mentors' response:* Finally, ask mentors to use about five minutes to give feedback to their observers, with the objective being to help observers improve their mentoring skills. That means mentors must use their best mentoring methods to help observers *discover* what was helpful and what was not.

11:30 • L: What do the data tell you about your mentoring tendencies?	Remind participants about the activity objective. Tell them (before showing it) what you did to collect the data. Display the completed "Twenty-three ways . . ." chart and ask them to review it, looking for patterns. Ask them to report and discuss the patterns they see. You may need to ask them questions such as – Did they change their mentoring after the first fifteen minutes? (two colors) – What were the predominant methods used during, before, and after the fifteen-minute point? – What methods of mentoring did they only do for a few times or not at all? – What goals do the unused methods serve that lack of use would leave unattained? – How might their mentoring have been even more effective?

(Continued)

(Continued)

	• Ask *individuals* to reflect on the last question and then briefly write out a goal for their own mentoring. Allow three to four minutes, then ask a few to share their goal. • Prompt with a question seeking mentor responses about the value for them in seeing a visual pattern of their behaviors. That should help mentors see that your strategy is a good one for them to use. • Quite frequently, *the biggest pattern* the "Twenty-three ways . . ." chart reveals is that "providing data" (your strategy) is an option which mentors do not use, yet it is so powerful! "Data" must be defined broadly to include offering description of any kind of patterns observed, not just numerical data. If this pattern happens, mentors must understand this. In fact, when you present your "Twenty-three ways . . ." chart to them you are modeling this very option for mentors. Point out both how helpful it is for them to see their own data presented in patterns and (if it's true) that this was an option they did not choose when they were mentoring. State that this is an option for which they will need to build their skill because the goal it accomplishes is so critical to new teacher professional growth.
11:40 • The problem with too much "telling" (Allow fifteen minutes)	*In advance:* Prepare copies of Gary Kilburg's case study in Figure 6.5 (see end of chapter) so that each participant has a copy. *Directions* • Use table groups with two or three participants reading the narrator's part to the rest, two or three reading the protégé's part and two or three reading the mentor's words. Allow about five to six minutes. • Ask each table group for discussion of the causes of the troubles described. • Ask several table reporters to share the conclusions or insights of their table group.
11:55 • Advice for when it's OK to "tell" (Allow five minutes)	*In advance:* Make enough copies of Figure 6.6 (see end of chapter) for each person to have one. *Directions* • Explain that, given the previous case study and its insights, there are obviously times when "telling" protégés what to do or offering advice is not helpful. Yet we choose the most experienced staff to be mentors so that experience is available to help protégés avoid trial and error learning. Clearly, we need some guidance on when it is OK to "tell" the protégé things and when it is best not to "tell." • Display the "Twenty-three ways . . ." chart again and say, "It's best not to 'tell' when the goal of the conversation is the development of the protégé's analytical and decision-making skills. Then, answering a question with an open-ended question or presenting data in a pattern is the better way to attain the goal." • Say, "However, when developing the protégé's critical thinking is *not the goal,* there are better options." Distribute Figure 6.6 to them. Read through and discuss it. • Briefly mention that, after lunch, they will gain some insight into their own *individual* tendencies regarding these issues.
12:00 • Lunch (Allow one hour)	
1:00 • Your individual mentoring style self-assessment	*Objective:* The assessment builds on previous work showing mentors their natural mentoring tendencies. It is designed to very reliably predict how an individual mentor will tend to behave across several protégés. The point of knowing this is to help mentors gain insights about their tendencies, and to consciously plan what they will do to remain appropriate in their work with a protégé, especially at times when their natural tendencies are otherwise.

In advance

- Reread first two parts of the section in this chapter on "Themes for a High Impact Mentor Training." Read through the part on the "Mentoring Process." *Caution:* you need to recall this information now but it should only be shared *after* the "Self-Assessment on Mentoring Styles" is completed.
- Prepare for each person a copy of the self-assessment in Figure 6.7, the "Mentoring Styles Tally Chart" in Figure 6.8 and the goal-setting page in Figure 6.9 (see end of chapter).

Directions

- Allow ten minutes to explain and complete this self-assessment.
- Be sure to read the directions aloud. They are critical for the validity of the assessment and for producing data that will predict individual mentoring styles.
- The assessment itself should take only about eight minutes, or less than a minute per item. If it is taking longer, push them to go faster as they are not giving their first impressions.
- Tell participants that, when part-way through the items, some items will begin to feel similar. They are. Tell them *not* to compare or play mind games with the items. Just take each one and record their first impression of what they think their tendency would be if they were the mentor in the scenario.
- Tell them *not* to look ahead, but do tell them now that *when done* with the twelve items, they will complete the chart at the end summarizing their responses.
- Walk around and observe to determine when all have finished the chart and are ready to move on.
Note: the data from the assessment will be used after the following section on the "process" is completed.

1:10 • The four phases of the mentoring process

Objective: This gives mentors a "bigger picture" and helps them understand that there is a knowledge base and typical process which they can use to be effective mentors. Help them see how their specific actions as mentors are steps in this process. *In advance:* Make one copy per person of Figure 6.10, "The Mentoring Process" (see end of chapter).

Directions

- Distribute Figure 6.10.
- Provide mentors with the information on the mentoring process from earlier in this chapter, referring to the figure to illustrate how this all fits together as a predictable sequence.
- Acknowledge that some protégés won't follow this sequence exactly or take the same amount of time. However, after mentoring several protégés, mentors see that this process is a great *general* description of what often happens. It's an excellent *guide* for *specific* practice with one protégé. Still, the needs of each individual protégé should dictate what mentors do, not this general process that is used when specific needs aren't known.
- Point out the balancing point between the focus on the work and the focus on the people must shift as they move in the process.
- Have mentors write their individual styles scores at each stage in the figure. Be sure the order is right and style titles match.
- This helps mentors see where in the process they will be fine using their intuition and where their natural tendencies may lead them astray. State the assumption that *all* mentors can do all they need to. The question is will they realize *when* to shift their approach to stay appropriate to protégé needs?
- Allow a few minutes for discussion, but know the next steps will clarify things further.

(Continued)

1:20 • Integrating the mentoring process and your mentoring style (thirty minutes)

Objective: Mentors must internalize previous information. This activity is the starting point for this process. Later training to ensure these goals and plans can be used in practice follows soon.

In advance

- Familiarize yourself with the mentoring styles information in this chapter, especially the section titled "Mentor Styles to Address When Planning Mentor Training."
- *Handout version:* Make your own new version of Figure 6.9, enlarging it to fill an 8.5 × 11-inch page and allow more writing space for mentors' goals. Their version is blank in columns 2 through 5, so mentors may write their own goals. Prepare one for each person.

Leader's version: Prepare another version of the new grid, adding the possible goals statements into each goal space as shown in Figure 6.9. To enable you to share only specific pieces of information at a time, make a transparency of your completed version. Cut it into *rows* using clear tape as a hinge to overlay each section on a transparency of the mentor version. Gradually reveal the information and keep the group focused on your words.

Activity

- Explain that this information is vital but it is not sufficient to internalize it at this time and put it to work in mentoring. Practice, setting individual mentoring growth goals, and planning implementation (the personal stage of the CBAM) are done to help each mentor become ready to use their strengths to advantage and to avoid problems where they are likely to arise.
- Distribute the mentors' copies of Figure 6.9.
- Use an overhead projector to project and gradually reveal each section of Figure 6.9. Working from top to bottom, have them fill in each row, adding mentor style data where appropriate.
- The "goal" rows at the bottom of the chart:
  - Figure 6.9 has *possible* goals. People can use their own words instead if they prefer.
  - Before anyone writes goals in the spaces, ask mentors to *darken the edge of only* those spaces where (in the first goal row) they scored a 0 or 1 and in the second row to darken the edges of spaces where they scored 5 or more. These are the only spaces where they need to set a goal since it is where they scored too high or low.
  - *Caution:* These possible goal statements *are* correct, but some will feel these possible goals don't make sense and may seem backwards. Check that they understand the following: scoring low (0–1) indicates a person may not feel comfortable or may not remember that they need to do something that is needed at a stage. Scoring a 0 or a 1 at a stage indicates that they need to do that behavior more or stay alert to when it might be appropriate. Living out this goal may require that a person write the goal into their calendar or planner, share the goal with someone else (the protégé?), or in some way ensure that they will check and remember that they may need to do it. Scoring high (5+) indicates that a person may tend to do something too often or too strongly and may take their strength to an extreme at some point. It can also indicate that they need to do that behavior less often, less assertively, or that they need to stay alert to that possibility. Living out this goal may require that a person write the goal into a calendar or planner, share the goal with someone else, and ask for feedback from the protégé as to whether or not the mentor is staying appropriate or going "overboard."
  - Mentors should finish writing their goals on their copies.
- At the top of the page, under the title, there are two blanks to fill in. The first is the one that says "teachers." My research shows that 70 percent of teachers and 98 percent of all mentors are strongest in the middle two styles.
- Ask mentors to raise their hand if they were strongest in the middle two styles and keep them up. This should produce an impact!

	• *Caution:* Be sure to notice which persons are *not* raising their hands. Some of these few persons may be very balanced in their styles. A few may have the very ineffective "tell" and "delegate" style. They must be carefully monitored and should receive individual attention during training and after. At some point, the trainer should receive from each mentor a copy of this page to use the goals when mentoring the mentors. At the end of training, there is a time when this is appropriate, but if a copier is handy, it's fine to make copies of each mentor's style goals page right now. If you do this, modify schedule times.
	Challenges of Mentoring New Teachers
1:50 • Poem: "I Don't Know," from an unknown new teacher (ten minutes)	*Objectives:* A brief activity to inject energy into the training and provide common vocabulary for the next activity. Finally, if you wish, you can follow up with a three- to four-minute discussion of how such a hierarchical relationship felt to participants.
	In advance: Make one copy of Figure 6.11, the poem (see end of chapter), for *half* of the people, those who role-play being a protégé.
	Directions
	• Ask trainees to find a new person for the next activity and to stand beside him or her.
	• Ask them to pick which of the pair will be the "mentor" and which the "protégé."
	• Have "protégés" raise their hands and give them the copy of the poem.
	• While protégés read the poem to themselves, ask mentors to use only nonverbals during the activity and to assume an "all-knowing" body position where they stand.
	• Tell protégés to either kneel or to sit on the floor in front of their "mentor." When they have done so, ask them to read the poem *slowly* out loud but with feeling to their mentor.
	• When all are finished reading, they can return to their seats.
	• When all participants are seated, you can ask for a general response to, "Anyone ever been there before?"
2:00 • Tom Gordon's model: why and when the "gate to change is locked" (25 minutes)	*Objective:* This activity builds on work done earlier. Its primary purpose is to help mentors understand when in the process protégés will be ready to learn from them, and when and why they may not always be so open.
	In advance
	• Make three copies of Figure 6.12 (see end of chapter) for yourself.
	— Version #1—block out the *four darker steps in the center* so only the text in the notes area on the two sides is showing. Make a transparency of that to use as the *top* layer of your final two-layer transparency.
	— Version #2—block out the text in the *notes* areas on both sides of the four darker steps so that all that is left are the four darker steps with empty space on the sides. That allows trainees to write notes. Make a transparency of that page for you and one *paper* copy for each person.
	— Version #3—make a transparency *sandwich* of version #2 on the bottom and version #1 on the top layer. Cut horizontal strips in the top layer so they are separate. Use clear tape to hinge these on one edge on top of the four dark steps transparency.
	Directions
	• Explain the objective. Point out that one of the hardest issues for mentors to understand is offering your experience and suggestions but finding the protégé does not use them.

(Continued)

175

(Continued)

	• Distribute the mentor copies (Version 2) of Figure 6.12 without side notes.
	• Display your transparency with the notes layers flipped back and only the black steps showing. Ask them to take notes in their own words as you work through the model and its implications for mentors.
	• Flip in the bottom horizontal "notes" strip and discuss the protégé side first, then mentor options.
	• Flip in the second strip up and discuss it. Emphasize that, at the lowest level, mentors' advice may be needed but not seen as of value by the protégé, but the second level shows protégés have discovered their need to learn something and how that creates the openness to mentor suggestions. The mentor's goal is to move protégés from unaware to aware.
	• *Skip to the top strip* of notes next and flip it in. Top *right* text tells how mentors behave when they are "on a roll" during their own teaching. They have so many routines established that it takes little conscious effort to do what is familiar. Working at this level is needed for the complex work of effective teaching. The challenge at this highest level is that mentors may struggle to explain to protégés what they are doing, how they do it, why, and when they do it. This happens because so much is going on at the *unconscious* level. Protégés can observe only what they see. For mentors to be able to unpack what they are *thinking* and make it accessible to protégés, mentors must move *down a step*.
	• Flip in place the last strip of notes. Explain that moving to this level occurs when mentors stop what they are doing, reflect on it, and then describe their hidden processes of decision making. When this happens, several great things will begin:
	  – Protégés gain insight into how expert teachers think.
	  – Mentors gain insights into their practice by consciously reflecting on it and their learning increases.
	  – Protégés see that expert teachers are so exactly because they are reflective practitioners.
	  – Protégés will gradually internalize and spontaneously start to use the questions the mentors ask.
	• Summarize by showing how protégés must move up the levels and mentors must move down to the protégé's level for there to be effective communication and learning. It is the mentor's responsibility to make this shift happen.
	• Ask for participants to share a time or two when they have seen this model in action.

2:25–2:40 • Break for fifteen minutes	
2:40 • CBAM—a system for assessing and addressing new teacher needs (forty-five minutes) 	*Objective:* To ensure that mentors learn and can apply the CBAM Stages of Concern model in their mentoring and treat individuals individually. *In advance* • Reread the earlier section in Chapter 1 that presents this model and its important uses. Make notes as you read because you will need to choose the ideas you will present to the trainees regarding this strategy. • Copy Figures 1.2 and 1.3 from that same section of this book, which you will use to teach the model. Copy the directions for using Figure 1.3 too. *Directions* • Use the Chapter 1 information to introduce your mentors to the CBAM and test their memory of the steps of the model. • Point to the big poster self-assessment that they completed at the start of the training. Read the column headings and ask them what was used to structure the assessment. If they don't "get it," show them how column headings are the CBAM stages. This shows you "practice what you preach," and it helps them internalize the model a bit more.

	• Ask them to use one minute to decide where on the CBAM they feel they are *right now* regarding their knowledge and use of the CBAM model. • Ask for a "show of hands" as you read each of the steps of the CBAM. If mentors are first timers, they are probably at the personal level by this point and ready to think about and plan how they could use the CBAM as mentors. – Take note of those who report being at a *lower* stage, so while you move to the next activity with the group, some other trainer can give those who need it more information and answer their questions to prepare them to move on too. Also note who raises their hands for being at a higher level than personal. They feel they are past needing the next activities with the whole group. Some way must be planned to help them with the challenges of *their* stage, usually problem solving specific uses. A second trainer here is a big help. However, these folks may not *really* be ready to move on past the group, but want to anyway. If you suspect this, keep them with the main group because they *will learn* from what comes next.
3:25 • Practicing the CBAM	*In advance* • Copy and read Resource II, "Practice in Identification of CBAM Stages of Concern." Read both the leader directions and the seven scenarios so you know them. • Make copies of the seven scenarios using the directions to decide the number of copies needed. *Directions* • Use these same directions during the training to guide mentors through each scenario, discussion of it, and deciding the level of the CBAM stages for each protégé. Allow eight to ten minutes per scenario. When all seven scenarios are done, use three to four minutes to discuss different groups' answers and see whether consensus can be reached. If not, don't take more time now as consensus is not as important as the practice.

Closing, Reflection, and Sharing

4:20 • Insights (ten minutes)	Allow two to three minutes for people to scan back over the day's materials and to reflect on their experiences. Ask for a few individuals to share with the group their individual insights or discoveries of things "to remember to use as a mentor."
4:30 • Adjourn for day	

Day 2

8:30 • *Review option* (Allow about ten minutes)	If any new participants have arrived, ask others who were here for Day 1 to share as a review what the key ideas were. If this option is used, adjust the times.

Strategies for Assessing New Teacher Needs

8:30 • Test of Memory—CBAM Stages of Concern: Use this in place of the above option, or after the option is done. (fifteen minutes.)	*Objectives* • To increase the number of mentors who have internalized and can apply the CBAM. • To identify mentoring peers who could serve as resources in the schools regarding the CBAM.

(Continued)

In advance

- Prepare a flip chart page titled "CBAM Stages." Divide the rest of the page into eight horizontal strips. On the bottom strip, write "0. Unaware."
- For fun, obtain a few buzzers, whistles, or other signal devices to use. The number should match the number of tables in the training. Make a sign to hold up that says "Applause."

Directions (10 minutes)

- Randomly pick seven people to go to the front. Number the people from one to seven. Each in turn writes with a marker what they think is the next Stage of Concern. Clap or correct if necessary to get the display right.
- *Critical distinctions:* Ask each table to take two minutes to select one person who knows the CBAM stages the best. It does not matter how many of these people there are.
- Ask these persons to bring chairs and *no* materials to the front of the room and sit there facing the group. Introduce these seven as the "CBAM All Stars."
- Ask each person to introduce him- or herself and to indicate where his or her table is. Cheering by that table is allowed.
- Provide each in the group with one of your signal devices if you choose to do so.
- Ask the All Stars the following questions one at a time, calling on the first to signal for an answer. Use the flip chart just created to help you with this activity. Affirm whether the answer (in parentheses) is right, but call on the next to signal whenever the first answer was incorrect.
  - "What is the essential work at the personal stage?" (planning how to implement)
  - "What is the essential work at the consequence stage?" (improving impact/results)
  - "What are the *three* essential activities of the mechanical management stage?" (implementing, skill building and problem solving)
  - "What is the difference between the mechanical and routine management stages?" (At the mechanical stage, the practice is not yet "routine." At the routine stage, the practice has become natural and comfortable.)
  - "What's another way of saying what protégés are at the *unaware* stage?" (They don't know what they don't know.)

Bonus round

  - "Why does the personal stage come *after* the information stage?" (People are not ready to start planning [personal] until they feel they know enough about a strategy.)
  - "Why does the collaboration stage come *after* the consequence stage?" (People improve as much as they can *on their own before* seeking further refinements from others.)
- Ask for applause for the group and return them to their tables. *Hint:* Don't push competition too far, collaboration is best. For example, the All Stars can help each other when "on the spot."

8:45 • Test: Gordon's steps from memory (ten minutes)

Objectives

- To increase the number of mentors who have internalized and can apply Gordon's model. *Note:* this is held until now because of what will follow and to provide morning review of yesterday.
- To identify mentoring peers who can serve in the future as resources in the schools.

In advance

- Locate a single die (from a game) to roll.
- Prepare six questions concerning Gordon's Model of Awareness, similar to what was done above for the CBAM.

	Directions • Without announcing why, pick six participants randomly from the group and bring them to the front as before. • Number these people from one to six. • Roll the die and use the number that's on top to select who answers the first question. Call for applause for the right answer and give correction *aimed at the whole group* for wrong or incomplete answers. • Repeat for all six of Gordon's questions. • Ask for applause for the group and return them to their tables.
8:55 • Compare and integrate Gordon's model and the CBAM (Allow 20 minutes)	*Objectives* • More practice using the CBAM and Gordon's model. • A single unified concept in mentors' minds about how protégé development proceeds. *Directions* • Give each table group three darker colored markers. Also give them two sheets from a flip chart, one to protect the table. • Tell them to orient the page vertically and title it "CBAM and Gordon." • Describe the task as comparing and integrating these models into one. Caution them to do a scratch copy first as sizes of the steps in one have to be adjusted to fit the other into it. They should label each step. Tell them they have fifteen minutes and show where they are to post their final versions. • As models are made and posted, you should review them in case a comment or correction is needed. • Once all posters are up, give the group three to four minutes to go up and look at others' ideas.
9:15 • Fifteen-minute break	
9:30 • What mentors do at each CBAM stage (Allow 30 minutes)	*Objective:* It is safe to assume that mentors know the two models, but this activity is done to ensure they can apply the models in practice. *Directions* • Have each table take back their integrated model from the wall. As they do this, give them another page of flip chart paper. • Then they tape the two pages side by side and extend a line for each step in their model across the second page to create space to write about that step. Allow two to three minutes. • Next they are to discuss, agree on, and write three things mentors could do at each step to address the needs of a protégé. • As these are done, review them all since a comment or correction will be needed. • While two from each group post their new posters, others should make an 8.5 × 11 inch page with the model but no mentor items. • Allow ten minutes and direct pairs to go with their note chart from poster to poster recording their favorite ideas. • Ask individuals to look at their mentoring styles score and goals and then consider which of the ideas they have just recorded might be ones they could forget to do (score 0–1). Next to those items they might write "Do more" or "Check if needed." • Next, each should consider their mentoring styles score, goals, and which of the ideas they have just recorded they might perhaps do too often or too assertively (score 5+). Next to these write "Do less" or "Check if needed."

(Continued)

(Continued)

	Directions
10:00 • A final CBAM refinement—make menus, not mandates (fifteen minutes)	Explain the following: • Novice teachers sometimes have enough insight to know what their problem is and *to discern the solution/help* they need from mentors. An example is, "How can I set up files to help me manage this paperwork?" This is at the mechanical management level of CBAM. A mentor would easily know what to do for such a specific request. • More often, inexperienced new teachers may *only know the problem* they have, but not the solution they need. An example is, "How can I manage this paperwork?" This is a less specific request, but mentors who realize this is at the mechanical management level would still know several options to offer. • Sometimes novices don't even know what their problem is, much less a possible solution (Bartell, 2005). An example is, "What should I do? I feel so disorganized!" This is so general that a mentor would not be sure of the protégé's CBAM level. Refer back to the earliest section of this chapter on mentoring styles for the details of an example to use for "Making Menus" and teach the strategy to mentors.
	Effective Communication and Questioning Strategies

10:15 • Trust-building strategies	*Objective*: Mentors are often trustworthy people, but mentors *also* need to proactively do specific things to create a trusting mentoring relationship as fast as possible. The following activity teaches mentors these strategies.
	
	Directions
	• Share the objective (10 minutes).
	• *Explain*: Early in a mentoring relationship, the mentor must make an extra effort to demonstrate all the same attributes we want to see in the protégé. By taking these steps first, the climate of trust is begun and the value of taking these risks in a safe relationship becomes evident to the protégé. Examples include:
	  – Demonstrate being trustworthy and predictable. Do what you say you will and don't do what you say you will not do.
	  – Be openly vulnerable for the sake of learning, growth, and improvement.
	  – "Make deposits" in the protégé's "emotional bank account" by showing and saying that you trust the protégé and appreciate their efforts at learning and growing. Acknowledge their professionalism and commitment to students and their colleagues.
	  – For the initial few months of the relationship, agree to 100 percent confidentiality, but define what is meant by that using the next activity. Point out that confidentiality is a two-way street since mentors take risks too.
	• Use wide masking tape and mark off a 2 foot square space on the floor. Label one side "Vulnerability Place" so it can be read by the group. Show it to mentors as you talk.
	• Every time during the training from here on that you model being vulnerable, obviously step or jump into that location. It seems silly but it allows you to talk about one thing and remind the mentors nonverbally what that requires without breaking the flow of the conversation.

10:25 • Confidentiality and the flow of information (thirty-five minutes)	*Objective*: We must define what being confidential means. Most problems arising in this area are due to partners having different understandings.

	In advance • Prepare a full page with three large circles on it, such as at the ends of a triangle. The circles should be only about 1–2 inches apart. • Between each pair of circles, draw a line as if to connect the circles, but not touching the circles. • Label inside one circle "The Protégé," in one "The Principal," and in one "The Mentor." • Prepare one copy for each mentor at the training. *Directions* • Pass out the prepared page to all. • Start with individuals doing the task alone. Each decides which ends of the lines should have an arrowhead on it pointing at a circle. The arrowhead means information about a specific mentoring relationship *ideally* should be able to flow to that person. A line may have an arrowhead on just one end or on both. If people have questions about a specific direction of flow, they should place a question mark at that end of the line (one to two minutes). • Give tables five minutes to seek consensus and make a diagram on chart paper. • Look for overall agreement by asking each table group to share their views by showing their diagram. If there is no strong agreement, allow five more minutes of general group discussion to see whether consensus can be reached. While this is happening, draw a similar diagram without arrowheads on the flip chart. • Again, seek general agreement in the room, but one arrowhead at a time. Point to the end of one line and ask for mentors who placed an arrowhead there to raise their hands. Write the number of hands at that place. Repeat until all arrowheads have been recorded. • Allow ten minutes for those with questions to raise their concerns. Discuss these and press for agreement one way or the other. • If agreement is generally possible, announce that this model should be followed for at least the first two to three months of the school year. If agreement is not possible, ask mentors in each school to meet (on their own time) and decide what their school will do. • Acknowledge that there are others, such as department chairs, who must also be considered for exclusion or inclusion in the flow of information about mentoring pair work, but this depends on whether or not they have input on novice teacher evaluations.
11:00 • Effective communication (30 minutes)	Do your own research and include advice for effective communication, such as how to give appropriate feedback, be an active listener, etc. Share with mentors that the potential for mentor-protégé problems is large in the area of flawed communication (Connor & Killmer, 1995; Guillaume & Rudney, 2002). I have found that most persons selected to mentor will know these strategies pretty well by the end of this training. Mentors and protégés "lump" many things into the category of "poor communications" but the problems are usually something else like lack of agreement as to what "confidentiality" means or a lack of following through to do the things they say they will. This training addresses each of these as they arise, not under "communication." *Note:* If you feel you must increase the time given this topic, consider using follow-up mentor meetings to do so. A good resource would be *Mentoring Matters* (Lipton & Wellman, 2001).

(Continued)

(Continued)

11:30 • Lunch	
12:30 • Capturing the potential of open-ended questions (thirty minutes)	*Objective:* Nearly everyone has a definition for "open-ended question" but this activity makes sure we are all "on the same page" on this topic. We can also expect that using this strategy is an unconscious choice a mentor may make because it seems the right kind of question to ask. The better alternative is to do it consciously because of what it achieves. *In advance* • Prepare a list of about ten questions, making about three of them "open" and the rest varying degrees of focused or closed questions. • At the top, provide the definition, "An open-ended question is one for which the mentor does not already know the answer. It is a question with several possible answers that cannot be specifically predicted, and it is likely that to answer it will require some critical thinking." • Along one margin next to the questions, provide a column for marking with the heading "Open?" • Allow a blank line under each question for rewriting it if needed. *Directions* • Explain the objective of the activity. • Ask the group to look back to the page "Twenty-three ways . . ." used on the first day and find where "open-ended question" is listed. Discuss the purpose this form of question serves (five minutes). • Ask each table group to share a verbal example of an open-ended question. Are these really open? Discuss a few and improve one or two (10 minutes). • Give everyone a copy of the prepared page on open-ended questions and explain, "Those that are open-ended mark 'Yes,' those that are not mark 'No,' and then rewrite them to make them more open." Ask pairs to work on this task and ask them to watch as they work for the hardest question to improve (five minutes). • After about five minutes, work through them all calling on some people to share their answers and improvements when needed (five minutes). • Ask for a show of hands to select the one that was hardest and discuss why it was hard and how it could be improved even more (five minutes).
1:00 • The problem-solving mentoring process—the power of questions (ten minutes)	*Objective* To help mentors understand the structure of the general process which "problem-solving mentoring" follows. *Directions* • Explain the objective and that the focus is on questions the mentor asks. • Project the results you collected for the earlier activity "Twenty-three ways . . ." Point out the change in colors for the data that took place after fifteen minutes. • Call on persons with insights to share about what pattern the color change reveals. In other words, what was the pattern of ways they helped early versus late in that activity? If there is quiet and your wait time does not produce volunteers, give pairs a minute or two to discuss it and then call on a few pairs.

	• Explain the following pattern and examples. Perhaps draw it on the flip chart pad.
	
	   – *Questions for the mentor's learning*—early in problem solving the mentor asks lots of quick, narrowly focused questions to try to discern what the real problem is and to gain some idea of what might need to be done about it. Examples are, "What did you do then?" and "How did that work?"
	
	   – *Questions for the protégé's learning*—when mentors understand the real problem, they switch to more open-ended questions and other less structured strategies to see whether they can get the protégé to figure out what the mentor has just figured out. Examples are, "Why did that happen?" and "What else could you do?"
	
	   – *Questions for the protégé's planning*—finally, more open-ended questions are used to guide the protégé to develop a plan of action. An example is, "How will you know if that is successful?"

1:10 • Pronoun power (fifteen minutes)	*Objective:* To help mentors understand the subtle but powerful changes possible by just switching the personal pronouns that the mentor uses.
	
	In advance
	
	• Use the above structure of the three kinds of questions to create a fairly complete one-page example of the mentoring half of a conversation. Design it so the conversation is centered on problem solving and so it uses about six questions for each of the three types of question.
	
	• Make two versions of this series of mentor questions. In one use inclusive personal pronouns such as "we," "us," or "our." The other should mostly use the exclusive pronoun "you" (excludes mentor).
	
	• Prepare enough copies so that half the group could have each version.
	
	Directions
	
	• State the objective.
	
	• Explain what a personal pronoun is, or ask the group.
	
	• Pair up the people and give each pair a set of the two versions. Ask them to compare them and consider what the impact of the changes are on the conversation. Allow three to four minutes.
	
	• When it is time, call on a few to share their conclusions.
	
	• Explain the difference between inclusive and exclusive as used in the two versions.
	
	• Ask them to look at the version with inclusive pronouns while you explain the following:
	
	   – *When mentors feel that protégés cannot solve a problem on their own,* mentors do not empower their protégés to fail. The mentors want to stay *"in a problem"* with the protégés, allowing the mentors' ideas and suggestions to be offered, if they so choose. That is when the inclusive pronouns of *"we," "us,"* or *"our"* should be used. An example is, "I wonder what *we* could do about that problem?" Such a question allows the protégé to respond but also lets the mentor step in if the protégé cannot figure it out.
	
	• Ask them to look at the version with exclusive pronouns while you explain:
	
	   – *When mentors feel protégés can solve a problem on their own,* mentors should empower the protégés to be responsible and independent. In this case, the mentor wants to stay *"out of the problem"* with the protégé analyzing and developing their own solutions. That is when the exclusive pronoun of *"you"* is used. An example is, "What could *you* do about that problem?" Such a question clarifies that the responsibility to figure it out rests with the protégé.
	
	• Point out that if one doesn't work, the mentor can immediately switch back to the other kind of pronoun again. Model an example of this.

(Continued)

(Continued)

1:25 • The three debriefing questions explained (ten minutes)	*Objective:* The mentoring experience must not just be a "great experience" for the protégé. The protégé's practice must be improved as a result, and this cannot be just a hope or left to chance. The three debriefing questions ensure that the protégé's learning is put to use to increase student success. That makes these questions the final link in our Chain of Causes and Effects.

	In advance
	
	• Prepare a handout with the title "Three Debriefing Questions."
	• In the *top half* of the page, write the following three questions:
	  – "What did you learn from our work today?"
	  – "Since I want to improve as a mentor, I need your feedback. What did I do today that helped you to learn that?"
	  – "I bet if what I did was important for your learning, that students would benefit from it too. How could you use what I did for you with your students?"
	• Draw a horizontal line at the center and in the *bottom half* use the following questions:
	  – "What did you learn from our work today?"
	  – "Since I want to improve as a mentor, I need your feedback. What did I do today that helped you to learn that?"
	  – "I bet if what I did was important for our learning that our students would benefit from it too. How could we use what I did with our students?"
	
	Directions
	
	• Explain the following:
	  – The activity objective
	  – That this activity will apply what we just learned (don't explain how)
	  – That this strategy should be used at the very end of almost every formal mentor-protégé meeting.
	• Pass out the handout. Ask pairs to compare the two versions for how they are different. Allow two to three minutes for this part.
	• Call on a few to share what they have found. Point out that this is an application of the previous activity's information.
	• Explain the goal for each question as follows:
	  – This asks the protégé to convert the experience into a tangible idea.
	  – This asks the protégé to shift from thinking about him- or herself to watching more carefully what the mentor is modeling. This may require a bit of "unpacking" together the first few times it is done. It also sets the stage for switching the protégé's frame of thinking from mentoring at the adult level to instruction at the student level.
	  – This asks the protégé to convert adult learning strategies into instructional strategies to be used with students.
	• Example: Let's say that when asked why the protégé learned something, the response was, "Because of the emotionally safe, accepting, and noncritical environment we have in our mentoring relationship. I'm not afraid to try new things and make mistakes." Then the third question would lead the mentor and protégé to discuss how safe and accepting their classrooms are. Do kids ridicule each other when mistakes are made? Does everyone understand that mistakes are a part of learning something? That could lead to planning for improvements in the classroom.

1:35 • Practice of the three debriefing questions (total time is one hour)	*Objective:* It is time to move to pair practice to ensure that each person individually understands and can apply this critical strategy. Use the directions and two scenarios in Resource III for this activity. *Be very sure to point out that, when finished, they should save their notes and scenarios for possible use later (during the Day 3 MoM Coaching Cycle #3 option).*

	In advance: Follow the "Leader Directions" of the scenarios in Resource III. *Activity directions:* Follow the information given in Part II of Resource III. *After the activity* • Follow the directions given for "After Each Practice." • Switch pair assignments and repeat the process so everyone gets to play each role and practice.
2:35 • Fifteen-minute break	

Experienced Mentor Panel Discussion

2:50 • Panel discussion (Allow a total of about one hour and forty minutes)	The trainer should review the earlier advice in Chapter 4 about collecting ideas during support groups for mentors to use in a panel discussion later. 2:50 Each panel member introduces self and tells the number of times each was a mentor (five minutes) 2:55 Training leader explanation of panel process (five minutes) 3:00 Structured questions for panel *from leader* (thirty-five minutes) 3:35 Open to questions *from new mentor trainees* (twenty-five minutes) 4:00 Advice *from each panelist* for new mentors (five minutes each for five panelists equals twenty-five minutes)
4:25 • End of the day insights (five minutes)	Insights or discoveries which mentors want to remember to use. A general sharing and review just as was done yesterday
4:30 • Adjourn for day	Reminder of focus for tomorrow

Day 3

High-Impact Coaching for Instructional Improvement

Rationale for Coaching	Research (Joyce & Showers, 2000) affirms the crucial value of coaching to ensure there is follow-up support for implementation of training in practice. As I have defined it, that is a key reason for mentoring. However, as recently as 2003, Kardos and Liu reported that, across one entire state, only 17 percent of protégés reported that their mentors ever observed them teach. There are many reasons for this, including the challenge of finding time for teachers to observe each other, which is why I have offered several solutions to the time problem. If we want mentoring to improve teaching, it must include observation of teaching.
Overview of day's activities	This day is almost totally practice. Practice "makes perfect" only if what is practiced is the best one can do. Be sure to tell mentors your expectation that they will practice *all day long, both* their effective mentoring strategies from the first two days *and* the new coaching strategies they will learn today. Remind mentors to also consider their mentoring styles goals and to try to live out these good intentions now as we begin practicing.

Pair Demonstration—An Example, Not a "Model"

	Leader note: Today has several options, each of which affects the time usage during the day in different ways. That's why few time markers are given after the day gets underway. To clarify the options and their time requirements, and help you choose the coaching activity options appropriate for your group, copy and review Figure 6.13, the "Day 3: Coaching Cycle Time Lines." Keep it handy as you read the following.
8:30 • Coaching Cycle #1 (time about one and a half hours)	Format: The trainer is the "teacher" and a volunteer is the "coach." The whole group collects data for the "teacher." The "teacher" is being himself or herself and not role-playing a new teacher. Trainer note: Different organizations use a variety of coaching models. I recommend the High Impact Coaching Model that I have developed, tested, and refined for almost twenty years. This model includes unique guidelines and strategies that make all the difference when it comes to improving instruction.
8:32 • Step 1: Choose a volunteer coach (Allow three minutes)	Trainer solicits a volunteer to be "coach." The volunteer needs no prior training or experience in coaching. The only focus for the coach is to understand the teacher's plan and learning need and a willingness to collect data to support the "teacher's" learning on the requested topic.
8:35 • Step 2: Pair pre conference (fifteen minutes)	The pair does a pre conference using the foci described just above. The trainer selects own actual goal for learning as basis for data collection.
8:50 • Step 3: Group observation of "teaching"	• Trainer "teaches" everyone the "High Impact Coaching Model." • Concurrently, the "coach" and the whole group collect data on the "teacher's" specific area for learning. (Keep the "lesson" to about twenty minutes.) • The "lesson" content is – Why we need coaching for professional growth? (need fresh eyes to see self better) – Definitions and a comparison of mentor coaching and evaluation using Figure 6.14. – The "High Impact Coaching Model," Figure 6.15 (see end of chapter).
9:10 • Step 4: Pair post conference (fifteen minutes)	• The pair does a post conference, using the model just presented. • Thank the volunteer.
9:25 • Step 5: Group coaching of the pair (Allow twenty minutes)	• Point out that the volunteer coach did not have the benefit of the High Impact Coaching process for a guide for the pre conference. • Invite all trainees to give the demonstration pair feedback on their coaching and, using the "High Impact Coaching Model," to discuss how knowing that process in advance might have changed the results.
9:45 • Step 6: Trainer Feedback (Allow fifteen minutes)	• The trainer leads the group in comparing their coaching of the demonstration pair to the High Impact Coaching Model post conference section. Did they use the model? • The trainer leads a whole-group discussion on the challenges, insights, and issues of effective coaching.
10:00 • 15-minute break	

Group Coaching Practice

	Format
Coaching Cycle #2 (Allow 1 hour and 15 minutes) Step 1: *Advance preparation*	*Format* The trainer plays the role of a "new teacher" being coached by a mentor. The whole group serves as the coach (similar to the "Twenty-three ways . . ." activity) The trainer needs to have prepared in advance a ten- to fifteen-minute "lesson" such as a new teacher might prepare—meaning not perfect. The "new teacher" believes that the goal is to follow the lesson plan closely. Some options include • A lesson plan for what teacher will do, but without considering or predicting how kids will react and what to do if plan fails • A lesson the new teacher experienced as a student during an undergrad methods course, but which is just being copied now without much understanding • A lesson for what the teacher wants the students to do, but without defining what the teacher will need to do to create that student reaction.
10:15 • Step 2: *Direction* (Allow five minutes)	• Explain the format for this activity. • Prompt the mentors to practice using the "High Impact Coaching Model" and to live out their individual mentoring styles goals. Allow a moment for them to get organized. • If at all possible, the trainer and mentors must try to stay in character until after the cycle is finished. If this is not possible, clarify when the trainer is in which role.
10:20 • Step 3: *Pre conference* (Allow fifteen minutes)	The trainer behaves as a novice teacher would; many long pauses, blank looks, one-word answers, etc. This forces the "mentors" to draw out the information they need to know how to help. Define that the pre conference will be over when mentors feel they know what data need collecting and have the "new teacher's" agreement on how the collected data will look.
10:35 • Step 4: *Lesson and observation* (Allow fifteen minutes)	The trainer teaches a ten- to fifteen-minute "lesson" to the group of mentors as if they are really students. The lesson has some flaws, such as options shown in Step 1. During the lesson, each of the mentors must collect the data requested.
10:50 • Step 5: *Post conference* (Allow fifteen minutes)	The trainer behaves as would a novice teacher, asking for feedback from the mentors first, expressing embarrassment or feelings that the lesson was great (whether it was or not), or showing surprise at comments by mentors and making the mentors work to get the novice teacher to analyze the data collected.
11:05 • Step 6 (Allow fifteen to twenty minutes)	*Debrief* the coaching with the trainer using the "High Impact Coaching Model" on the mentors *without saying so.* The trainer is acting as a mentor in this role, so may ask them: • How they felt their coaching went • Whether they followed the model. Where not? Why not? They might refer to a visual of the process as it is discussed, such as in their handout. • When they followed the model, what happened? The trainer may use mentoring strategies like "pronoun power" and open-ended questions to guide him or her to reach conclusions about areas for improvement and to set individual goals for improvement.

(Continued)

(Continued)

Be sure to end your own questions by using the three debriefing questions. Let them discuss applications as a group, but allow several minutes for each *individual* to write notes.

Group Assessment

Objective: To assess participant readiness for implementation that is planned for after lunch.

Do the following in advance:

- Arrange to have two lunches provided in the training room for two trainers at work.
- Ask another trainer to be available in the training room about 11:15 and for the rest of the afternoon. If Option #3 is chosen after the group assessment, that second trainer will be needed to lead it.
- Make two videotapes, each one of a different teacher actually teaching a lesson. If possible, make these new teachers—although, if necessary, any teacher is OK. The segments recorded should not be special events, but regular, some OK, some not OK, classes. It's usually best to
  – Make the video only about fifteen minutes long
  – Make one tape at elementary and one at secondary level if your schools are K–12.
  – Make the tapes at a neighboring school district, not your own. This keeps the focus during their use on the teaching, not the teachers.
  – Read ahead in the training information to where use of the videos occurs and plan the equipment you will need.
- If you have access to other teaching segment videos already, it is OK to use those instead.
- View the videos and write the needed scenarios for use in Cycle #4.
- Each person's scenario is a page or less that guides them in what to say, so their pre conference will "fit" with the video, which they will use for their observation.
- There should be a "teacher" and a "mentor" version for each scenario.
- The teacher version of the scenario needs enough detail so the role can be played well. For example
  – How old is the teacher and how much other experience has the teacher had?
  – The grade level and subject(s) the teacher teaches, and how that has been going
  – Whether the teacher has been open to prior offers of mentor help or not
  – The basics of the lesson plan (as seen in the video)
  – The problem which the teacher will share as the focus for mentor help
- The mentor version can be brief and just explain:
  – How long they have been in the formal relationship
  – When during the year it is
  – Whether the protégé has been using mentor ideas or trying to make it on their own
- Most information should be left out so the mentor has to use questioning and listening skills to figure out what is needed.
- The mentor's scenario can also state a goal suitable for your district, such as "Focus on assessing and addressing the protégé's needs," "Focus on helping the protégé to meet the state teaching standards," or "Your goal is to prepare the teacher for the principal's evaluation visits."
- Prepare a set of small posters (8.5 x 11 or bigger). Post these high on the wall at about 20-foot intervals, just before doing this step. Signs are for each of the CBAM stages, using short text on each such as

	– I need to know more before I try it. (info) – I understand it but need a plan before I try it. (personal) – I am doing it but am having problems. (mechanical management) – It's working pretty well. (routine management) – It's working OK but I want better results. (consequence) – It's getting good results, but I want to improve it more. (collaboration) – I could lead this workshop myself! (refocus)
11:25 • Step 7: *CBAM Connections* (five minutes)	Ask them to decide the CBAM Stages of Concern at which they each are right now "for using the High Impact Coaching Model." To indicate their choice (and generate some energy), ask them to stand under one of the signs that you have posted. Then ask one person in each group to count the number of people in the group and write that number (large) on the sign. Tell the groups at these signs to remember which one they are at for an activity after lunch. This gives them more practice in using the CBAM, as well as feedback about where they are compared to the rest of the mentors, and it tends to motivate any who have not actively participated. It also gives you some sense of whether they feel the need for more practice or are ready to implement their learning in independent pair work.
11:30 • Dismiss for lunch for one hour.	*Trainer choices to make during lunch:* Use the following information and Figure 6.13, "Day 3: Coaching Cycle Time Lines," to decide on your use of the CBAM data and to plan your next course of action. There are three options from which to choose. *Option #1* is used if virtually *all* participants are at the *mechanical management stage or below*. This indicates everyone is in need of more safe, group-level practice, trainer corrections, and advice and is not yet ready to independently implement. You will use both Cycle #3 and then Cycle #4 with the group. During Cycle #4, the group will see both videos A and B as their observations. That will take until about 4:00 P.M. You can end the training at that time, or use a shorter version of the closing activity, which is provided from 3:00–4:00 after the other options. *Option #2, Splitting the Group*, is used if a *significant number of trainees (six to eight or more?) are both at and below and* others are above the mechanical management stage. If this happens, you must be prepared in advance to accommodate their different needs. An option for this might be to use a second trainer and split the group to continue two trainings, each in a different room if possible. If splitting into two groups is needed, you must do so to model best practice, ensure their success as learners and give them the practice they need to eventually correctly implement the training in their individual practice. To *not* provide for this diversity is to break the "Chain of Causes and Effects" and risk no classroom level improvements. For the part of the group who are *at and below* mechanical management, one trainer will take them through Cycle #3 and then *both* of the two pairs practice with videos A and B in Cycle #4. That will take them to about 4:00 P.M. Then they could be dismissed, or do the shorter version of the closing activity until 4:30. For the part of the group who are *above* mechanical management, they will *skip* Cycle #3 and the second trainer will take them to a second room (if possible) where they will do both parts of Cycle #4, the pairs independent practice, using Videos A and B as their observations. That will take them to about 3:00 P.M. Follow that with the full one-hour version of the closing activity for them. In this case, you will need two VCRs and monitors or projectors to show at the same time the two different videos you made to each of the two groups who will each be on a different schedule.

(Continued)

(Continued)

	Option #3 is used if *all are at the mechanical management stage or above* when you check their CBAM level at the end of Cycle #2. These data indicate readiness to implement their learning in separate pair practice. In that case, the *whole group should skip* Cycle #3 and go directly to Cycle #4 next. They will finish Cycle #4 about 3:00 and will then do the full closing activity until 4:00 dismissal.

Small-Group Mentoring of Mentors Practice

After lunch	*Format*
Coaching Cycle #3—Optional (takes one hour)	• The training group is broken into small groups of five to ten.
	• One mentor will be coached by another mentor.
	• The rest of the small group fill the role of the Mentor of Mentors by observing the pair and collecting data for two specific things:
	– What effective mentoring strategies taught in this training did the mentor in the pair use?
	– What "High Impact Coaching" strategies from the training did the mentor use?
12:30	*Step 1: Decide the number of mentoring pairs and small groups to use in this activity.*
	We want no more than six persons in a group, but need two mentors as well. The intent is to ensure that every person is involved in this activity.
	An example: Presume you have a whole training group of 48 participants. Since 6 × 8 = 48, you will have eight small groups of six each. Since two of the six in each small group will serve as mentors, each small group will have four observers.
	Step 2: Set up the mentoring pairs (five minutes)
	The trainer in the example above needs six of the *same mentoring pairs and scenarios* used earlier at 1:40 P.M. on Day 2, under the topic "Practice of Three Debriefing Questions." The trainer explains what volunteers are needed and selects the needed number. Using the example above of a total group of forty-eight, the trainer needs six of these mentoring pairs. Have all the mentoring pairs stand to one side for a few minutes and locate their notes from that exercise. Tell them to pick *one* of their two scenarios for this activity.
	Step 3: Set up the mentoring small groups (allow five minutes)
	The trainer divides the *rest* of the training group into small groups and has each small group sit at a table. Using our example, each small group at this point will have four observers in it (two mentors to be added soon).
	Step 4: Directions for the activity
	Explain to all that
	• Each mentoring pair will talk to each other as the mentors they are, using one of the two scenarios from Resource III, the "Practice of Three Debriefing Questions" that they did earlier. In this case, the mentor from that original scenario will receive feedback and mentoring from the partner who was the protégé in that earlier scenario. In other words, the protégé from that earlier scenario is now mentoring the person who was their mentor.

- The rest of each small group will observe and collect data on the mentoring pairs' mentoring. Observers say nothing throughout the entire cycle. They observe, and collect data during their observation, looking for just the mentor's use of mentoring and coaching strategies taught in this training.

Step 5: Observer Groups and Mentoring Pairs Meet (allow ten minutes)

Each set of observers meets *separately from the pair* and discusses and then prepares a list of effective mentoring strategies from the training. Do *not* provide such a list to them, as recalling and deciding on these strategies is done to help internalize them. *Do* provide each observer with a copy of the handout page showing the "High Impact Coaching Model." Suggest that they use the right-hand margin to mark strategies they observed the mentor doing. (Allow ten minutes for them to organize while the trainer gives each a copy of the coaching model.)

While observers are doing their preparation task, mentoring pairs can review the scenario they selected so it is fresh in their mind. The one who was the protégé and is the mentor now should consider the effective mentoring and coaching strategies to use with the other mentor. The mentors' objective is to review their practice session and discuss as mentors how it could have been improved to better help the mentor improve. It's an authentic task!

Step 6: Activity—the Mentoring of Mentors (allow fifteen minutes)

- The trainer checks that each table group has three or four observers and a mentoring pair, and that each mentoring pair understands its task. Remind observers that they are to say nothing until the pair is done.
- Start the activity and allow about fifteen minutes for the mentoring pair.
- During the activity, the trainer should observe what the patterns of behavior are for the pairs and the observers, so the trainer can offer comments and suggestions or affirmations later.

Step 7: After the Pair Coaching Cycle (allow twenty minutes)

Remind the observers to use their own effective mentoring strategies and the "High Impact Coaching Model" to coach and mentor the *mentor* of the pair toward improved coaching and mentoring. Make an announcement about one minute before the observers should be finishing.

Step 8: After the Observer Mentoring (allow five minutes)

The trainer can describe the patterns of behavior observed for both the pairs and the observers. Then, *using the strategies from the training*, the trainer should ask the pairs and the observers questions to prompt their own analysis of their work. For example, the trainer could ask

- Which strategies were the hardest to actually do and why?
- Did your work in support of the other person's learning reflect your natural mentoring style, or were you able to implement the styles goals you set for your mentoring?

	Alternating Independent Pair Coaching Practice
Coaching Cycle #4	*Format* - The training group is broken into pairs, preferably a person they have never worked with before. - Each pair will do two complete coaching cycles. Partners will switch roles for the two cycles as follows:

(Continued)

191

(Continued)

   – Cycle A: Teacher to be coached = person A; mentor = person B
   – Cycle B: Teacher to be coached = person B; mentor = person A

- The focus of the pair conferences and observations will be the videos you have prepared in advance of normal teaching segments, each about fifteen minutes long.

- The trainer gives each pair their scenarios, which are prepared in advance and which have a "teacher" and a "mentor" version.

   – This written scenario is written by the trainer who knows the video content and has prepared the scenario so those who have not yet seen the video can still role play a pre conference that fits the video.

   – The "teacher" pretends to be the teacher in the video to come.

Step 1: Deciding the pairings (allow five minutes)

Partners can choose each other and, to the extent possible, you can ask for each pair to have an elementary and a secondary teacher (if that fits your district). They should bring their materials for reference during the activity and sit together.

Step 2: Which is the mentor? (allow one minute)

If you have an elementary and a secondary teacher in each pair, tell them the grade level of the first video and suggest that the person closest to that grade in the pair should be the "teacher" for that video. The other person will be the mentor this time.

Step 3: Activity Directions—Cycle 4A (allow ten minutes)

- Explain the whole activity using the "format" above. Clarify the role of the video as the "observation" step in the cycle.

- Explain how the trainer has seen the videos and written the scenarios to allow each person to understand what might be said so it will fit the video to be observed later.

- Prompt mentors to use the High Impact Mentoring and Coaching strategies from the training. That is the entire focus of the practice.

- Prompt "teachers" to be themselves if the videos are of experienced staff, or to be "new teachers" if the videos show new teachers. Your scenario should tell them that.

- Pass out the correct version of the first scenario to each person in the pairs and give them about four to five minutes to read their roles and prepare reference materials for the coaching cycle.

- Ask if there are questions on how to proceed.

- Tell them the time each of the three steps will have and the total time for the cycle. Then tell them to start.

- Pre conference takes about fifteen to twenty minutes, the observation about fifteen minutes and the post conference about fifteen to twenty minutes. The whole first cycle often needs about an hour.

- Your role during the practice is to listen in on as many pairs as you can, for long enough to hear the extent to which mentors use strategies for which they have been trained. The best way to do this is make several rounds early and then again later during their practice. Make notes for your debriefing comments.

| | • Consider a ten-minute break when cycle 4A is done. Since all finish at different times, wait until several have finished to determine when they should return and then announce it.

Step 4: Debriefing cycle 4A (allow about five minutes)

Ask for their questions and comments on the first cycle (4A) then, ask a few questions of your own, like

• Did any part of the activity surprise you?
• What did you learn from that practice activity?
• What will you do different in the next activity?
• Use your notes made while eavesdropping on the pairs, but I suggest that you do not use any specific names, whether your comments are positive or negative.

Step 5: Activity Directions—Cycle 4B

• Announce that it's time to switch roles: the teacher in the first cycle becomes the mentor in this next activity.
• Prompt mentors to use their High Impact Mentoring and Coaching strategies.
• Pass out the correct version of the second scenario to each person in the pairs and give them about four to five minutes to read their roles and prepare for the coaching cycle.
• Ask whether there are questions and tell them to start.
• Expect that this cycle may take a bit less time than the first—probably fifty minutes. |
| A Closing Activity

⊙ | What you use of the following is your choice. If time is short, I consider #12 to be optional, since it can be suggested at the training, but it can be done individually at home to save training time. The only question is, "Will they really do that?"

A Final Reflection on the Training

Participants can be prompted to think through the entire training and then to reflect on their new mentoring skills and mentoring goals. This is useful at this time, as the conclusions may have changed since they were first reached earlier in the training. Please read the next section and consider how these two sections will work together during the training.

• *Option 1*—One way to do this is to just say the statement given above.
• *Option 2*—A better way is to refer mentors back to the goals they wrote for their improvement as mentors (after mentoring styles) and ask them to update them now at the end of the training. Allow ten minutes for that step.
• *Option 3*—A very good, but more time-consuming, way (twenty to twenty-five minutes) is to
  – Refer them back to the agenda to mark those parts most helpful to them
  – Reflect on what from those key sections they need to remember and plan to use
  – Reread their own mentoring improvement goals and update them now, trying to integrate all three of these things |

(Continued)

(Continued)

Planning for Mentoring of Mentors

	Objective: To prepare trainees for an ongoing, formal support and accountability relationship with the program leader, who is the Mentor of Mentors (MoM). Detailed guidance for the MoM. is given earlier in this book and later at the end of this chapter. This section has two parts: Expectations for Mentors About Program Level Communication (30 minutes); and Sharing Mentoring Goals With the MoM (20 minutes).
Sharing Mentoring Goals With the MoM and a Final Needs Assessment	• The trainer should refer back to section #12 on "Reflections" to ensure that it integrates well with this and the above activity.
	• It is best if there are several MoMs to speed this up. If not, it is worth the time it takes.
	• All the following are best done during the mentor training time. A video with a mentoring sequence can be shown the group while waiting and this part is taking place. Good examples are
	– The "wax on, wax off" section of *The Karate Kid*, up to where Daniel realizes what he has learned.
	– A segment from *Finding Forrester*.
	• The trainer has selected a training location near a copying machine, or can provide a copying machine in the training room. If this cannot be arranged, mentors can hand copy their goals and "Communication Choices" so the MoM and the mentor will each have a copy. Another option, allowing mentors to do this work at home and send it in later, is usually a major pain and not recommended.
	• Mentors give their MoM a copy of their final mentor improvement goals and their "Communication Choices."
	• MoMs read the mentor improvement goals and "Communication Choices" on the spot so they can seek clarification or negotiate different terms right away. For example, if over half of the mentors choose to do a "dialogue journal" each quarter, that may be more work than a MoM can reasonably be expected to do. Staggering the dates when these will be submitted may help some, but the MoM may have to ask if some mentors can choose another written approach than the journal.
	• When the mentor and MoM agree on communication terms, that plan should be signed by both and a copy kept by both.
	• *Time:* The amount of time this takes depends on the number of mentors at the training. This factor can be addressed in one or more of several ways:
	– Have several program leaders or members of the design group available to check in and sign off on these pages.
	– Actually checking and accepting a mentor's form can take just a few seconds, if it is agreeable to the MoM. What creates a delay are those forms to which the MoM cannot agree, or which need further discussion for clarity. One option is to set these aside to deal with after the training is complete. Just collect and process them all, setting aside those needing more time and at dismissal, read the names of the mentors who need to "stick around for a few minutes."
	• Using the information in later MoM–mentor interactions means the MoM must be able to very quickly access the information whenever needed. The goal would be, in a phone call example, to have the information in front of you by the time the greeting has ended. That way the MoM can easily inquire as to progress on the mentor's goal, etc.
	• The very best way to manage this is a computer database with searchable fields and an interface for that search. Also add a few fields for dated notes made during or following each conversation to update the mentor's goal, write reminders for future discussion, etc. Of course, a paper-based system of mentor file folders could accomplish the same purposes.

At the same time: A final needs assessment	While all the above is happening, some are finished and some are waiting to see the MoM. Use this activity to keep trainees involved. Give each trainee table a different colored set of sticky dots than used at the start of the training. This gives you a great pre- and post-"test" of mentor growth as a result of the training, and it helps you demonstrate to mentors and others just what was accomplished. It also tells you what work remains to be done to support mentors.
A Big Send-Off 	I have two suggestions for ending the training. I recommend you do both. • *Hold a "graduation."* Prepare in advance a certificate for each participant. Also make an audio tape (from a video?) of the music "Pomp and Circumstance." Then, at the end of the training, play the music and call each mentor to the front to receive their certificate. End this with applause. • End the training with an inspirational "You can make a difference" message. Keep in mind that you have promised (as have I): that effective mentoring will increase teacher and student performance. That sounds (to some) a bit like changing the whole world! I like to use a quote from Margaret Mead, but with a younger crowd I sometimes have to explain who she was and why her words are significant. She said, "Never doubt the ability of a small group of thoughtful, committed people to change the world. Indeed, it is the only thing that ever has changed the world!" You might want to remember that statement as well. After all, "High Impact Mentoring and Induction" are all about changing the way we support each other, how we improve, and how we educate children. That sounds a lot like "changing the world"!

Mentor Expectations

(Provide in writing and then explain the following to mentors.)

- Mentors are *not* expected to be role models of perfect practice. However, each mentor is expected to be actively and continually seeking to become an even better mentor and teacher.
- The following is done because it dramatically increases the success of mentors at all levels of experience.
- The work of the mentor program coordinator includes a formal "Mentor of Mentors" (MoM) relationship with each mentor. That relationship is one of support and accountability for each mentor's growth as a mentor.
- As much as possible, Mentoring of Mentors should *not include discussion of specific protégés*, except when a critical situation warrants it.
- Mentors of Mentors establish the *same trust and confidentiality* with mentors as mentors do with their protégés.
- To facilitate MoM support, *mentors* are expected to *initiate* frequent communication with the MoM. Specifically, mentors are required to
  - Coordinate their work with the protégé's supervising administrator
  - Send the MoM an "action plan" including their final goals for mentor growth
  - Send the MoM a mentoring time log at the end of each quarter
  - Attend at least three of the four quarterly mentor peer support group meetings
  - Candidly contribute to program evaluation
  - Use *at least three* of the following communication choices, with *one choice to be done on a monthly basis*

Communication Choices

During the close of the initial mentor training, mentors will write out a proposed "Communication With MoM" page with their name, school, phone number, and e-mail on the bottom. That information is given to the MoM for consideration. If the MoM considers it adequate, the MoM and mentor will sign and date it and each will keep a copy. If not sufficient, the MoM will explain why and the mentor can redo it.

Mentors are to select and mark *at least three of the following, adding how often* each will be done. One of the three choices must be done *monthly:*

- Phone conversations with the MOM, initiated by the mentor
- Written letters, reflections, or e-mail interactions, initiated by the mentor
- Face-to-face conversations with the MOM, scheduled by the mentor
- Keeping a "Mentoring Dialogue Journal" and sending a *copy* of it to the MoM
- Observation by the MoM of the mentor and protégé at work, with conferences between the mentor and the MoM before and after the observation.

Please keep in mind the number of mentors overall with whom the MoM must work.

Thank you very much for your commitment to new teacher success and our profession.

POSSIBLE ELEMENTS TO ADD
TO THE MENTOR TRAINING MODEL

The components of the "High Impact Mentor Training Model" are designed to work across a number of kinds of organizations. Given this general purpose, the model is missing elements that would be unique to your specific organization, so you will need to add these items. Here are some suggestions of items to consider adding so that mentors in your specific program know all that is expected of them:

1. A description of your mentoring and induction program structures and the key program personnel

2. The district and teachers contract requirements of probationary teachers for participation in each of the components of the induction program, and/or state or provincial initial certification requirements

3. The resources provided to support novice and mentor teachers, such as
   – New Teacher Manual
   – A copy for each new teacher of *First Days of School* by H. Wong (1997)
   – Mentor Training Manual
   – Induction program section of the district website
   – The New Teacher "Hot Line" number, hours, a calendar of who is the mentor on call, etc.

4. The organization's expectations of mentors and protégés for
   • Time:
     – Amount and frequency of meetings spent working in mentoring generally (usually heaviest early in the school year)
     – Amount and frequency of time spent in coaching conferences and observation (usually includes the number of coaching "cycles")
     – Access to/budget for substitute teachers for released time to mentor (such as "eight days a year, may be taken in half-day increments")
     – Completion of a mentoring time "log," process, and frequency of submitting it, to whom, and by what due dates
   • Requirements and options for meeting attendance for mentors and protégés
     – Orientation meetings (all required)
     – Trainings (all required)
     – Quarterly peer support groups (three out of four required)
     – Optional mentor attendance at new teacher trainings for mentor familiarity, since mentors do required follow-up support for these
   • Other district forms and paper work required of mentors (caution—don't overdo this)
   • Mentor's professional growth goals and plan (for growth as a mentor)
   • Mentor's professional growth portfolio
   • End-of-year program evaluation survey

RESOURCES FOR THE MENTOR TRAINING

The following pages contain all the figures that were referred to during the previous "Directions" section, but which were reserved until here so as not to break the flow of the training details.

Figure 6.2 Your Knowledge and Skills in Mentoring: A Self-Assessment

Pick the ONE statement for each topic that best defines your current level of mentoring knowledge and skills and mark that level on each continuum.

I am not sure what is involved in this topic.	I know what this topic is but I need to know more.	What is expected of me and how can I plan to do it?	I am doing it but need to solve problems and build my skills.	How can I do this so it makes a difference and improves student learning?	I just want to share with and to learn from other mentors.	I know this so well that I could lead that part of the training.
			What my natural mentoring tendencies are			
			The roles, tasks, and expectations of effective mentors			
			How mentoring promotes novice teacher professional growth			
			Helping a novice teacher learn to think like an expert teacher			
			How to assess and address novice teacher needs			
			Strategies for effective communication in mentoring			
			Mentor questioning skills to prompt critical thinking			
			How to handle difficult mentoring situations			
			The best practice coaching process			
			Doing coaching that promotes reflective practice			
			How to be sure that coaching and mentoring do not become teacher evaluation			
			Conferencing, observation, and data collection strategies			

Figure 6.3   Principles of Adult Learning

ADULTS PREFER LEARNING SITUATIONS THAT

1. **ARE PRACTICAL AND PROBLEM-CENTERED, SO . . .**
    - Give overviews, summaries, examples, and use stories
    - Plan for direct application of the new information
    - Design in collaborative, problem-solving activities
    - Anticipate problems with applying the new ideas, offer suggested uses

    CAUTION: Guard against becoming too theoretical

2. **PROMOTE THEIR POSITIVE SELF-ESTEEM, SO . . .**
    - Provide low-risk activities in small-group settings
    - Plan for building success incrementally
    - Help them become more effective and competent

    CAUTION: Readiness to learn depends on self-esteem

3. **INTEGRATE NEW IDEAS WITH EXISTING KNOWLEDGE, SO . . .**
    - Help them recall what they already know that relates to the new ideas
    - Help them see how the new information is relevant to them
    - Plan ways they can share their experience with each other

    CAUTION: Find ways to assess participant knowledge before an event

4. **SHOW RESPECT FOR THE INDIVIDUAL LEARNER, SO . . .**
    - Provide for their needs through breaks, snacks, coffee, and comfort
    - Provide a quality, well-organized experience that uses time effectively
    - Avoid jargon and don't "talk down" to participants
    - Validate and affirm their knowledge, contributions, and successes
    - Ask for feedback on your work or ideas, provide input opportunities

    CAUTION: Watch your choice of words to avoid negative perceptions

5. **CAPITALIZE ON THEIR EXPERIENCE, SO . . .**
    - Don't ignore what they know—it's a resource for you
    - Plan alternate activities so you can adjust to fit their experience level
    - Create activities that use their experience and knowledge
    - Listen before, during, and after the event

    CAUTION: Provide for the possibility of a need to unlearn old habits

6. **ALLOW CHOICE AND SELF-DIRECTION, SO . . .**
    - Build your plans around their needs, compare goals and actual
    - Share your agenda and assumptions and ask for input on them
    - Ask what they know about the topic
    - Ask what they would like to know about the topic
    - Build in options within your plan so you can easily shift if needed
    - Suggest follow-up ideas and next steps for after the session

    CAUTION: Match the degree of choice to their level of development

Figure 6.4 Tally: The Twenty-Three Ways Mentors Help

	1	2	3	4	5	6	7	8	9	10	11	12	13	14	15	16	17	18	19	20
Outside the Relationship:																				
• Advocate for—sponsor																				
Within the Relationship: (Mentor does the thinking)																				
• Judgment—opinion																				
• Affirm and encourage																				
• Suggest an idea																				
• Tell																				
• Explain																				
• Infer—predict																				
• Focused question																				
• Share own experience																				
• Clarify																				
• Paraphrase																				
• Challenge																				
• Offer resources																				
• Guide																				
(Neutral)																				
• Empathize																				
• Wait																				
• Listen																				
• Observe																				
(Protégé must do thinking)																				
• Open-ended question																				
• Delegate																				
• Provide data																				
• Model																				
(Both do thinking)																				
• Collaborate																				

Leader's Directions:

1. Make a transparency or large poster of this chart.

2. Use one color marker to fill in boxes showing what the mentors do during the first fifteen minutes.

3. Use a different-colored marker to show mentor behaviors after fifteen minutes.

4. When the activity is done, display the data and ask mentors questions to get them to analyze the results.

Figure 6.5 Making Sense of Three Mentoring Team Relationships and the Obstacles They Encountered on a Recurring Basis

This is an excerpted case study from a research report by Dr. Gary Kilburg, George Fox University, posted November 28, 2005, at <www.mentoring-association.org>. Used with permission.

Laura (M) and Jennifer (P)

Laura was an especially gifted teacher in working with students. This was also her first experience as a *mentor*. She was a bit nervous about the experience but looking forward to the opportunity. One of the comments that Laura made at the beginning of the school year seemed to sum up how she felt about the initial mentoring experience.

> I have to admit that I'm a little nervous about being a mentor. I hope that I can provide the support and help that Jennifer needs. I worry, though, that I might not be able to provide her with everything she needs. But with that said, I still am looking forward to working with her this year.

Jennifer had just completed her fifth-year teacher education program and was looking forward to her new job. She had a lot of anxiety about the start of the new school year, with so little time to prepare, but she felt that with the mentor that the school district had assigned her, she would overcome any fears that she might have.

Laura and Jennifer met for the first time at the in-service and spent most of the day together in meetings. The following day was spent in a mentoring in-service which provided them with several opportunities to talk about questions that Jennifer had as well as just chatting about their personal lives.

Over the next few months, both Laura and Jennifer began to develop what seemed like a healthy relationship. On a number of occasions they had the opportunity to discuss their perspective about a variety of issues, including classroom management, parent conferences, grading, and working with some of the special needs students. At times they disagreed with one another about some of the issues, but nothing surfaced that negatively impacted their friendship.

When Laura began observing Jennifer in her classroom during the third month, something changed in the relationship. As Jennifer noted,

> I was surprised that Laura became much more authoritative and direct in her reflections of my teaching, particularly when I made a mistake. That seemed so odd to me because this just seemed like it came out of nowhere.

Laura didn't really seem to be interested in Jennifer's excuses or justification for what she was doing, she seemed more interested in results. It was not uncommon to hear Laura tell Jennifer, "Here is what you should do," or "Here is what you need to do." When Jennifer asked Laura about her method of mentoring, Laura replied that she felt Jennifer needed to know what to do so she wouldn't make the same mistake twice. According to Jennifer,

> I felt like I had no independence to make decisions on my own anymore. Laura's solutions always seemed to be my solutions. I felt very uneasy with the whole mentoring process. It was so opposite of what I was used to.

The harder Jennifer tried to work with Laura, the more frustrating it became. Jennifer's self-confidence was being affected and she began to feel uncomfortable any time she was around Laura. After a couple of months had passed, Jennifer decided that she needed to talk with the principal, who was also the mentoring coordinator, regarding the problem. After the meeting with the principal had concluded, Jennifer had this to say,

> The principal was very understanding of my situation, but was hesitant about intervening in this situation. He explained that he couldn't really assign another mentor because they already had been assigned and the other teachers were in their second and third years of teaching and were not considered to be mentors because of their lack of experience.

> The principal told me that I should just try to make the best of it and that he would support me as much as possible during the rest of the school year.

Although the principal was very helpful in providing Jennifer with guidance and support, he was not always available and that had a negative impact on the quality of the mentoring process and Jennifer's anxiety and self-confidence. As the school year and the mentoring experience came to a close, Laura had this to say about her experience as a mentor,

> I remember my first year of teaching, which didn't include having a mentor as a guide, and it felt like I was being thrown to the wolves on some occasions. In Jennifer's case I really felt that I needed to give her more direction because I didn't want her to repeat a lot of the mistakes that I made. There may have been times when I should have let her make the decision, but it just seemed much easier to tell her how to do it.

Jennifer, on the other hand, saw the new style of coaching by Laura in a different way:

> I felt like I was in high school or student teaching when the teacher would tell me what I needed to do. It would have been much more helpful to have discussed what needed to be done or to talk about the different options that might have been available. It would have been nice to have worked through some of the problems that I encountered, and to make the decisions about what to do by myself. But for some reason, that was not possible.

> I also have to say that I did appreciate what the principal was doing for me, but he just didn't have the time and he wasn't always available when I needed to talk with him. He also didn't have the subject matter expertise that I needed so I had to rely on some of the other second- and third-year teachers to help me out.

Figure 6.6   When Is It OK for Mentors to Give Advice?

If protégés always used their mentors' advice, mentors would never worry about giving it. The problem is when protégés do *not* use the advice mentors offer and the mentors feel they are becoming "nags" by "pushing" the protégé over and over to change, but without results. That's why this issue is critical. We need to know when we can feel safe offering our ideas and experience without fear of "burning a bridge."

It's OK if . . .	Why it's OK . . .
1. The protégé's area of interest or question has *one* right answer.	It reduces trial and error learning and time wasted for mentor and the protégé.
2. The protégé *asks* for the mentor's advice and suggestions, or for more information.	"The gate to change is *locked* on the *in*side." When the protégé asks for advice or information, we know the protégé is aware of the need to change, their "gate to change" is *un*locked, and there is readiness to learn.
3. Students' health, welfare, or safety is at-risk.	Protecting children is a teacher's primary responsibility.
4. All other approaches the mentor has used have failed *and* the protégé's ultimate success in the school district is at risk.	When it comes to their success in their career, protégé's deserve the truth. "Truth telling" in this situation is what good friends do. If the protégé fails, mentors must know they did *all* that they could to help.

Figure 6.7   Mentoring Styles Self-Assessment

Directions: Consider *all* of the following situations from the *same perspective*, that of mentoring for a beginning teacher. Circle the one letter that most nearly describes what your tendency would be to do in each situation.

1. ***The protege's performance is decreasing and is not responding to the friendly suggestions of the mentor or to the mentor's concerns for the situation. You recommend that the mentor should . . .***
   A. Emphasize following the district and school guidelines and objectives, and the importance of accomplishing all assigned tasks in a timely manner.
   B. Remain available for discussion and questions, but not push.
   C. Talk with the protégé and then set new goals based on what you both have agreed.
   D. Trust the protégé's judgment and be careful not to interfere too much.

2. ***The performance of the protégé is clearly improving. The mentor has made sure that the protégé understands the job to be done and both have agreed on what an excellent result would look like. The mentor should . . .***
   A. Engage in friendly conversation but continue to check that the protégé knows the job and standards.
   B. Take no specific action.
   C. Reinforce the importance of the quality of the protégé's work.
   D. Emphasize the importance of deadlines and task accomplishment.

3. ***The protégé seems unable to solve a problem alone. Usually the mentor has found the protégé can work out solutions independently. The protégé's past performance and mentor relationship have been good. The mentor should . . .***
   A. Sit down with the protégé and jointly develop some solutions to the problem.
   B. Let the protégé continue to work out the solutions individually.
   C. Act now to correct the problem and show the protégé what is needed in this situation.
   D. Encourage the protégé to keep after the problem and restate that he or she is available to help.

4. ***Recently the protégé's pace has been too slow and the class is behind on the curriculum. The mentor feels the need for a major change. The protégé has done very well until recently but has also stated recently that some kind of change is needed. The mentor should . . .***
   A. Not push for the change but work with the protégé to develop the changes.
   B. Decide what needs to be done and help the protégé understand and implement the changes.
   C. Allow the protégé to develop his own plans for improvement.
   D. Ask the protégé for his ideas, then develop an improvement plan to offer to the protégé.

5. ***The protégé's teaching performance has been dropping recently and she seems unconcerned about the problems. The mentor has had to remind her to follow the curriculum and to be more aware of the behavior of the whole class when working with individuals. In the past, redefining and clarifying her assignments has helped. Now the mentor should . . .***
   A. Let the protégé continue to decide on her own plans and challenge herself.
   B. State the concerns, ask the protégé for recommendations, and remind her of expectations.
   C. Restate the assignments and then monitor the situation closely.
   D. Express the concerns and jointly develop a plan, but do not push her.

6. ***A new mentor has been assigned because the original mentor has a long-term illness. The principal implied that the original mentor was too much of a perfectionist and "directed the situation too closely," but that the protégé was capable. This is the sixth week of school. The mentor has decided that, to help the protégé grow, a trusting relationship and decreased scrutiny are needed. The mentor should . . .***
   A. Try to make the protégé feel successful, involved in decisions, and self-confident.
   B. Emphasize the importance of deadlines and meeting district objectives and guidelines.
   C. Be careful not to intervene or supervise the situation or to offer suggestions at all.
   D. Get the protégé involved in assessing needs, developing ideas, and joint planning, and be careful to informally monitor tasks and plans.

(Continued)

7. *A vacation is approaching and student behavior will soon begin to challenge the protégé's new discipline system. A shift in the approach to classroom management is needed and in discussion the protégé has concurred. The protégé has been flexible and has adapted in other changes that were needed in the past. The mentor should . . .*
   A. Tell the protégé what adaptations are needed with "wiggly" kids and then monitor the changes.
   B. Explain some ideas for changes, gain agreement but then let the protégé plan implementation.
   C. Let the protégé develop the new approach but watch the situation and provide assistance.
   D. Do not confront the situation. Let the protégé decide what to do as kids' behavior changes.

8. *The class and students are doing well under the protégé and the mentoring relationship is a strong one, but the mentor feels the protégé is giving too little attention to teaching improvement goals which were agreed on earlier. The mentor should . . .*
   A. Let the protégé continue to set the pace and ask the mentor for help as needed.
   B. Discuss the situation with the protégé and suggest establishing some new goals.
   C. Develop suggestions based on the mentor's experience and ask the protégé to try these ideas.
   D. Be careful to protect the relationship and try not to be too directive or pushy.

9. *The mentor has a lot of fun with the protégé and they do many things together, but the protégé has not grown much recently. You have just realized that setting new goals and making new plans have been put off too long for lack of time and so changes are needed. You know the protégé has many abilities and strengths. The mentor should . . .*
   A. Let the protégé work out her own goals and develop her own solutions to any problems.
   B. Ask for suggestions of goals, set the goals himself, and set up a plan that will meet the goals.
   C. Redefine and suggest some new goals and plans. Monitor protégé performance closely.
   D. Jointly decide with the protégé what the goals and plans will be, but not push the mentor's goals.

10. *The protégé isn't responding as he usually does, even though you both just set some new goals for your work together. The mentor should . . .*
    A. Discuss the goals again, re-establish a commitment and the expectation for quality, but then allow the protégé to respond without pressure from the mentor.
    B. Confirm that the goals are understood and accepted, then watch for the protégé's next response.
    C. Avoid a confrontation by not pressuring the protégé. Give him more time to develop.
    D. Discuss and confirm the goals you both set and the expectations you have for following the plans, and then see that the expectations are met.

11. *You work in a school with very diverse students in every classroom. During the first six weeks the protégé has handled the initial responsibilities nicely and has shown some insight. The mentor and the protégé get along well. Now it is time to challenge the protégé to grow more. The mentor should . . .*
    A. Set a clear definition of goals and expectations for their work as a mentor-protégé pair.
    B. Give positive comments about past work and ask the protégé to help set goals and develop plans.
    C. Discuss the protégé's past performance and discuss any need for trying out new practices.
    D. Let the protégé continue to work independently and remain available to help out.

12. *The first semester is nearly over. The mentor has felt some distance forming in the mentoring relationship, even though it has been very good all along. The protégé has grown remarkably and has done very well on the job. The protégé knows what must be done for the remainder of the term. The mentor should . . .*
    A. Suggest any new ideas for the end-of-term activities. Ask to meet with the protégé and discuss the need to try new things.
    B. Allow the protégé to work out individual plans. Show interest and offer encouragement.
    C. Act right away to resolve any relationship problems and re-establish a closer relationship. Develop joint goals and plans.
    D. Let the protégé continue to work more independently. Suggest a few ideas for help and offer to assist at any time the protégé wants it.

Figure 6.8   Mentoring Styles Tally Chart

Directions: After all your choices have been circled above, move to the chart below. Circle the same choices listed after the item number. Then, at the bottom of each column, write the total number of answers you selected.

SITUATIONS	ALTERNATE ACTIONS			
1	A	C	B	D
2	D	A	C	B
3	C	A	D	B
4	B	D	A	C
5	C	B	D	A
6	B	D	A	C
7	A	C	B	D
8	C	B	D	A
9	C	B	D	A
10	B	D	A	C
11	A	C	B	D
12	C	A	D	B
COLUMN TOTALS ⟶				
STYLE STAGE NAME ➔	TELL (offer direction)	SELL (explain why)	SHARE (collaborate)	DELEGATE (step back)
Helpful Visual Symbols	Tr	TR	tR	tr

Figure 6.9   Goal Setting Based on Your Personal Mentoring Style

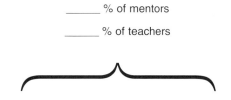

_____ % of mentors

_____ % of teachers

STYLE STAGE NAME →	The Mentor's Sense of Responsibility Shifts With Time			
	TELL (offer direction)	**SELL** (explain why)	**SHARE** (collaborate)	**DELEGATE** (step back)
Helpful Visual Symbols	Tr	TR	tR	tr
Enter your scores here				
GOAL: Need to *do more* or stay alert to do when needed if scored 0–1.	1. Listen for protégé questions which have "one right answer." If it is, share freely what you know and offer advice.	2. Think about the unwritten local rules, everyday processes, and traditions which your protégé won't know. Explain why these exist as they are.	3. Be more of a cheerleader, encouraging the protégé. Work on projects with the protégé, more as peers. Ask open-ended questions to check whether more information is needed.	4. If the protégé has shown adequate skill knowledge, and responsibility, encourage the protégé's independence. Don't hold on too long. Avoid creating a dependency.
GOAL: Need to *avoid* doing it *too much*, too forcefully or too often if the score is 5+.	1. If the protégé's questions do not have just one right answer, be a better listener. Ask more open-ended questions. Ask whether the protégé would like more ideas or information. Use "When is it OK to Tell" to guide you.	2. Be cautious not to over explain or explain when the protégé already knows the answer or information. Just ask the protégé, "Do you know why?"	3. Don't assume your protégé needs help. Ask whether the protégé would like some or more help to allow choices. Allow the protégé to show what they can already do or have learned previously.	4. Don't delegate responsibilities for the remembering of tasks or deadlines too soon. Ask the protégé what they need and whether they feel they are ready to do specific things by themselves.

Figure 6.10 The Required Shifts in Emphasis During the Developmental Mentoring Process

The questions for mentors are:

1. To what extent can you "read" that these shifts are happening for your protégé in each topic or skill area?
2. To what extent can you shift your mentoring approach to adjust to the protégé's developing professional maturity, so your mentoring remains appropriate across time?

As illustrated, the initial stage of the mentoring process is the "Tell" stage, where the tasks of starting school effectively must be more the focus of the mentor than building a relationship.

As the protégé begins to master everyday tasks, the questions often shift to deeper issues requiring explanation while the mentor's focus shifts to a more balanced attention to building their relationship while working.

When the protégé has assumed most task responsibilities, the mentor can treat the protégé more as a peer and can focus on the relationship even more.

Finally, as the protégé becomes mature professionally and is independent, the mentor withdraws from the formal relationship.

All these shifts are symbolized by the use of capital or lowercase first letters on the name of each stage.

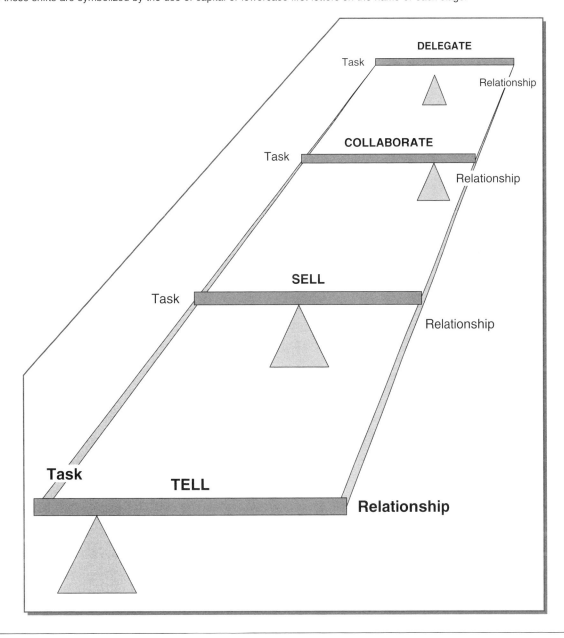

Figure 6.11 I Don't Know

I Don't Know

There is something I don't know that I am supposed to know.
I don't know what it is I don't know, and yet I am supposed to know.

And I feel I look stupid if I seem both to not to know it,
and not to know what it is I don't know.

Therefore, I pretend to know it.

This is nerve-wracking since I don't know what I am pretending to know.
Therefore I pretend to know everything.

By an unknown new teacher

Figure 6.12 Awareness and Learning Transitions

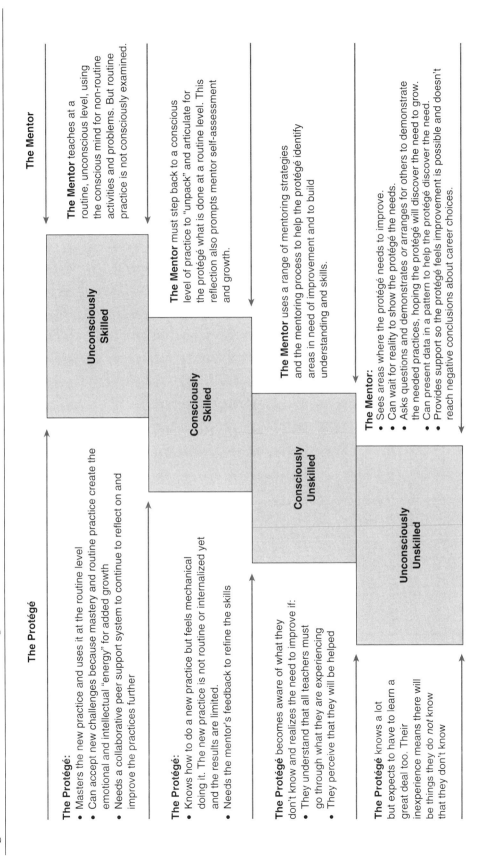

The Protégé

The Mentor

Unconsciously Skilled

The Protégé:
• Masters the new practice and uses it at the routine level
• Can accept new challenges because mastery and routine practice create the emotional and intellectual "energy" for added growth
• Needs a collaborative peer support system to continue to reflect on and improve the practices further

The Mentor teaches at a routine, unconscious level, using the conscious mind for non-routine activities and problems. But routine practice is not consciously examined.

Consciously Skilled

The Protégé:
• Knows how to do a new practice but feels mechanical doing it. The new practice is not routine or internalized yet and the results are limited.
• Needs the mentor's feedback to refine the skills

The Mentor must step back to a conscious level of practice to "unpack" and articulate for the protégé what is done at a routine level. This reflection also prompts mentor self-assessment and growth.

Consciously Unskilled

The Protégé becomes aware of what they don't know and realizes the need to improve if:
• They understand that all teachers must go through what they are experiencing
• They perceive that they will be helped

The Mentor uses a range of mentoring strategies and the mentoring process to help the protégé identify areas in need of improvement and to build understanding and skills.

Unconsciously Unskilled

The Protégé knows a lot but expects to have to learn a great deal too. Their inexperience means there will be things they do *not* know that they don't know

The Mentor:
• Sees areas where the protégé needs to improve.
• Can wait for reality to show the protégé the needs.
• Asks questions and demonstrates or arranges for others to demonstrate the needed practices, hoping the protégé will discover the need to grow.
• Can present data in a pattern to help the protégé discover the need.
• Provides support so the protégé feels improvement is possible and doesn't reach negative conclusions about career choices.

SOURCE: Adapted from Thomas Gordon's four-step model, *Parent Effectiveness Training: The Proven Program for Raising Responsible Children*, Three Rivers Press, 2000.

Figure 6.13   Day 3: Coaching Cycle Timelines

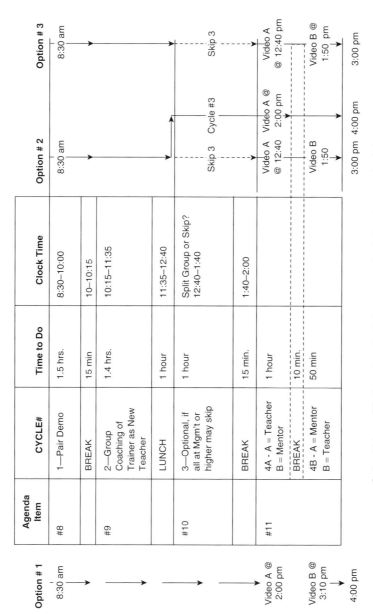

Agenda Item	CYCLE#	Time to Do	Clock Time
#8	1—Pair Demo	1.5 hrs.	8:30–10:00
	BREAK	15 min	10–10:15
#9	2—Group Coaching of Trainer as New Teacher	1.4 hrs.	10:15–11:35
	LUNCH	1 hour	11:35–12:40
#10	3—Optional, if all at Mgm't or higher may skip	1 hour	Split Group or Skip? 12:40–1:40
	BREAK	15 min.	1:40–2:00
#11	4A - A = Teacher B = Mentor	1 hour	
	BREAK	10 min.	
	4B - A = Mentor B = Teacher	50 min	

Option # 1   8:30 am

Video A @ 2:00 pm
Video B @ 3:10 pm
4:00 pm

Option # 2   8:30 am

Skip 3   Cycle #3
Video A @ 12:40   Video A @ 2:00 pm
Video B 1:50
3:00 pm   4:00 pm

Option # 3   8:30 am

Skip 3
Video A @ 12:40 pm
Video B @ 1:50 pm
3:00 pm

- Option #1 is used if *all are at mechanical management or below* when you check the CBAM level for coaching at the end of Cycle #2.
- Option #2 is used if *significant numbers are both at or below and above mechanical management* when you check their CBAM levels.
- Option #3 is used if *all are at mechanical management or above* when you check the CBAM level at the end of Cycle #2.

Figure 6.14 Comparison of Mentor Coaching and Evaluation

	Who Does Most of the Analysis and Decision?			
Assessment Processes	**High Impact Coaching**		**Teacher Evaluation**	
The Steps in Assessment	**Teacher**	**observer**	**teacher**	**Observer**
1. Decides the focus for data collection	X			X
2. Collection of data		X		X
3. Analysis of that data for meaningful patterns	X			X
4. Determination of the extent of a gap between what is desired and what was actually achieved	X			X
5. A conclusion about whether the gap is a concern or not	X			X
6. A decision about what needs to be done to improve the pattern in the data	X			X

(Evaluation spans steps 2–6 on the left side)

The person who does the analysis and reaches the conclusions:

- Discovers the need to change
- Becomes ready to change
- Feels the commitment to improve
- Does the learning
- Does the growing

So … if you want to ensure professional growth, you must promote:

- Collaborative support, and …
- SELF-assessment

Figure 6.15 The High Impact Coaching Model

Pre-Observation Planning Conference: *(Sequence does not matter)*
- The teacher's intentions for the lesson (objectives)
- The teacher's predictions for the lesson
- The teacher selects the focus for own learning and *growth*
- Agree on information to collect to support teacher's learning
- Agree on the format for collected information (tool)
- The coach's role, viewing place, post conference time and place, and other logistics

Observation:
- Data collection on selected topic using only agreed-on format

Post Conference: *(Sequence is crucial)*
- The teacher recalls own intentions and predictions
- The teacher describes own view of the actual teaching and learning experience
- The coach presents the data collected
- The coach's questions prompt teacher comparison of intentions, predictions and actual data, seeking a pattern
- The coach's questions guide teacher to drawing conclusions about
  - Mistakes or less than effective choices made by teacher
  - Results of lesson for students
  - Need for improvement in instruction
- The coach's questions guide teacher to design action plan for improvement
- Discussion on impact of coaching and ways to improve it
- The three debriefing questions

WHAT FOLLOW-UP SUPPORT IS NEEDED TO ENSURE MENTOR IMPLEMENTATION OF TRAINING?

There are two areas in which trained mentors must have ongoing support if they are to attain our goal of transforming teacher and student performance.

1. *Peer mentoring.* This is the support, encouragement, and challenging that comes from interaction with other practicing mentors. It should occur once a quarter and should involve every trained mentor whether they are currently assigned to a protégé or not. If the scale of the program is too large to make this practical, set up regional peer mentoring support groups. These might contain further training and problem solving, but the minimum activity is that which is outlined earlier under Mentor Peer Support Activities, knowledge building and peer support. Do not underestimate this strategy. It may be the most effective way for mentors to learn what works from each other.

2. *Mentoring of Mentors.* Mentoring of Mentors (MoM) is defined as supporting the mentors' professional growth and continual improvement as mentors. This is the support of the mentor trainer or some other mentoring and induction program leader. The Mentor of Mentors role is an essential strategy if there are program expectations that mentoring will actually improve employee performance and productivity.

Why So Important?

The focus of the support and challenge provided by the MoM is *gently but relentlessly* holding mentors accountable to live out the good intentions stated in their mentor professional growth goals, written during their mentor training. However, the ultimate application of the MoM process is facilitating the debriefing of the mentor's personal experience of *receiving* effective mentoring from the MoM. Herein lies the power of the Mentoring of Mentors strategy. Mentors know exactly what great mentoring is and, because the process is built on a mentor's personal experience, it is very compelling.

The MoM also has to teach mentors how to translate their personal experience as the MoM's protégé into practices they could do as mentors with their own protégés. That is why part of the MoM role is continually modeling for mentors what the desired mentoring practices look like and *then* asking mentors questions to get them to reflect on and plan their own application of those practices in their work as mentors and as employees.

The Structure of Mentoring of Mentors

The MoM conversation is a coaching session that is structured by the following steps to promote reflection, goal setting, planning, and accountability for professional development for the mentor.

1. Set some standard for quality mentoring practice. This is accomplished in the initial mentor training by defining the "ideal" mentor-protégé relationship and mentoring process.

2. Identify the current level of practice of the mentor relative to that standard. This was also done in the initial mentor training by giving the mentors a self-assessment for "mentoring styles" and in many of the other activities. This information should be updated each time there is a conversation between the MoM and the mentor.

3. Identify "areas for growth" to improve mentoring practice. This too was done in the initial mentor training, and the information should be updated each time there is a MoM conversation.

4. Set one or two goals for mentor development (also done in the initial mentor training). The goals should be updated each time there is a MoM conversation.

5. Create an action plan to implement activities to attain the goals. This would be the agenda for the first MoM conversation just after the initial mentor training. The progress on the plan should be checked at each MoM conversation and the plan revised as needed.

6. The mentor implements the action plan and collects data and artifacts of the process. The MoM dialogue promotes mentor reflection and allows monitoring of activities and growth.

7. Periodic meetings or conversations are held between the MoM and the mentor according to their plan.

The most critical steps of all are the last two:

8. Debrief the seven steps just described to promote the mentor's realization of learning from the Mentoring of Mentors experience and to prompt discussion of how the mentor can facilitate the use of those same seven steps to promote the protégé's growth.

9. Discuss how the mentor can use any of those same seven steps to promote the mentor's own growth and improvement in his or her own teaching.

One final step the leader should consider at this point is to return to Figure 2.8 in Chapter 2 and complete it by adding all that you plan to do. Now that the bulk of your program is designed, completing Figure 2.8 will help ensure that all of your activity plans support your program goals. The advice throughout this book has been offered with this target in mind.

7

Evaluating, Improving, and Sustaining the Program

Amazingly, program evaluation is the topic about which I get the fewest questions. Yet, when I talk individually with people, they *all* want to know how to make their program more effective. They *all* want their program's value to be evident to decision makers. Effective program evaluation is the answer, but it seems that many leaders skip this step.

Many leaders avoid program evaluation because they have not been taught how to do practical, useful evaluations. Even a doctoral degree does not guarantee that an administrator has the confidence to evaluate a program.

Effective, practical program evaluation does not require educators to be statisticians and should not be feared. Instead, evaluation is an important tool. In this chapter, I will explain how to design and conduct practical but powerful program evaluations. Program evaluations are essential, particularly if you ever find the value of your program being challenged. The following e-mails from an Induction Program Coordinator in Colorado show the importance of program evaluation.

26 Nov 2001
Hi Barry,

You stated in your book (my bible) that it was important to keep data since you never know when you may have to defend your program. I really took your advice to heart and have kept data on every aspect of the program including accomplishments.

Well, this past week the president of the school board questioned the value of funding for the mentoring program and I was able to quickly prepare a document illustrating the natural links to things the district values. I haven't heard a response yet as the document was just delivered today. However, I want you to know that it felt good to be prepared. I did not feel threatened by the question, I just felt ready to answer it with good solid factual information. I owe all that to you. I hope this finds you well.

—Mary Hasl

4 Apr 2003
Dear Barry,

I have some bad news . . . by restructuring the district the superintendent eliminated all curriculum and staff development programs on March 23. He wants to create a new vision that empowers school sites to have more control over budgets to meet their needs. Trust me, this was quite a shock to the entire district.

Since I am a part of staff development my Program Coordinator position is gone too. The principals are supposed to meet to figure out what the new structure will look like. I am, of course, very sad because I am very proud of the work I have done and will miss bringing the gift of mentoring to new and beginning teachers.

—Mary Hasl

18 May 2003
Hi Barry,

Wonderful news!!! As the principals worked to restructure the district they put mentoring and induction back on the district's plate and put me back in my role as mentor coordinator! Woo Hoo!! When teachers across the district were asked, "What do you need from central office in terms of support?" the overwhelming response was mentoring!! I am absolutely on cloud nine!! The vision *has* been internalized! The superintendent spoke with me personally and said how happy he was that I would be continuing as Mentoring Program Coordinator.

Your advice helped prepare me for the responsibility of representing a large program that is very important to hundreds of teachers and our district. I will never forget your warning, "Accountability is sustainability." Because of your insight my program is the only one to survive the cuts. Also, I am a clearer, more articulate voice for my fellow teachers and our profession. I am most grateful.

—Mary Hasl

Never doubt the ability of the vision we have been discussing and the models we have been using to transform the people and your organization. Why? People first become educators because they dream of making a positive difference in students' lives. If your program helps educators to better accomplish their dream, your program will be viewed as *essential* for teacher and student success.

Never doubt that *you* can attain this in your district. However, providing a highly effective program is only half the task. You must collect and analyze data and report about the resulting progress of participants toward high levels of practice.

> Don't wait for the questions to start. Hold *yourself* accountable before others do. Proactively demonstrate the value of your program to everyone. Remember, "accountability *is* sustainability."

Don't wait for the questions to start. Hold *yourself* accountable before others do. Proactively demonstrate the value of your program to everyone. Remember, "accountability *is* sustainability."

Notice in the e-mails from Mary that there was no mention of statistics or a process with a high level of angst. The focus is on written documentation of what is happening in order to be ready to answer questions that arise in the future. Doing this will not just answer the questions of the School Board, but *your own questions* about the program—questions you can predict today will need answering someday because of decisions you will need to make later.

We've already discussed the steps of providing an effective program. Once that is in place, a system of effective, practical program evaluation is needed to sustain and *keep* the program. The following is a plan for *learning how to evaluate* the program. Take it one step at a time and make it a collaborative process so you have help and build a wider leadership capacity.

The Program Evaluation Learning Agenda

1. Using the research showing induction's impact on results

2. Beginning evaluation knowledge

3. Designing an evaluation process and plan

4. Demonstrating compelling return on investment from induction

5. Other strategies for supporting and sustaining the program

USING THE RESEARCH SHOWING INDUCTION'S IMPACT ON RESULTS

> Over thirty years of research show the connection from effective mentoring and induction to student results.

A great *starting* place for defending the need for your program is the research literature on the impact of these programs. Over thirty years of research show the connection from *effective* mentoring and induction to *student results*. A selection of both the findings and the citations from this research follow. There are three things you *should* do with the following research findings.

First, you must provide this research to those whose support you need. You can use it to show teachers and district decision makers that the program is a significant way to improve teaching and student learning. Engaging others in dialogue about this research is much more effective than simply giving the research to people and hoping they will read it.

Second, you must collect your own program data, compare it with the research and try to locally replicate the results. Since you have advice the researched programs did not have, you can be confident of eventually *exceeding* these findings.

Third, you should write a document that shares your own baseline data and eventual results and the process for achieving them. At school board meetings and conferences, provide presentations that allow people to access your learning, models, insights, and results. Also submit articles to journals for publications. Be sure to close the articles with several bullets of structured findings and their implications for others' use.

THE EFFECTS OF NOT SUPPORTING BEGINNING TEACHERS

In many cases, (unmentored) beginning teachers have experienced personal and professional trauma and have lost self-confidence and questioned their own competence as teachers and as people (Hawk, 1984; Hidalgo, 1986; Huling-Austin & Murphy, 1987).

- "The report showed that beginning teachers have difficulty controlling students during classroom discussions and that their frequent response is to eliminate class discussion from their teaching repertoire" (Huling-Austin, Barnes, & Smith, 1985).

- "If beginning teachers are not provided with support and assistance during their early years, their coping strategies can crystallize into teaching styles that will be used throughout their careers" (McDonald, 1980).

- "Unassisted entry-level teachers often shift from a progressive teaching style practiced in preservice training to a traditional style" (Sandefur, 1982).

- "Unassisted beginning teachers can also develop negative teaching behaviors in which they are authoritarian, dominating, and custodial in their treatment of students" (McArthur, 1978).

- "The results indicate that nonsupported teachers may develop more slowly as teachers. Mentoring allows new teachers to move beyond a focus on disciplinary issues and the teacher's own survival and to begin to focus more on effective teaching and student needs" (Odell, 1986).

THE EVIDENCE THAT INDUCTION IMPROVES THE TEACHING OF BEGINNERS

- "As induction and mentoring were introduced into more and more schools . . . researchers reinforced what had already become evident to many practitioners: When these programs were well designed and implemented, novice teachers were not only staying longer; they were also developing into better teachers—and doing so at a faster rate—than had many before them" (Portner, 2005).
- "We have learned much about the benefits of high quality, standards-driven induction . . . from more than a decade of research in California. These benefits include
  - High retention of beginning teachers
  - Increased levels of professional efficacy and satisfaction
  - Improved teacher performance
  - More consistent use of instructional practices that lead to higher student achievement
  - Use of more varied and complex instructional practices
  - Improved ability of new teachers to engage in reflective practice and critical examination of their work" (Bartell, 2005)
- "Can you imagine it? The California Legislature has written into the new appropriations law that they have concluded, 'New teacher mentoring and induction is the most cost-effective school improvement strategy we know.' That didn't happen over night. We built the case and improved our results for a decade to earn that statement" (Olebe, 1998).
- "The Indiana study found that beginning teachers who were mentored had an increased awareness of curriculum, significant gain in the use of mastery teaching strategies, enhanced ability to communicate with parents and the public and an increased inclination to teach higher order thinking skills" (Summers, 1987).
- "Our study found evidence of improvement in beginning teachers for several critical teaching behaviors as a result of mentoring support" (California Department of Education, 1992).
- "The study found significant differences in how principals rated the teaching competency of experimental (mentored) and control (unmentored) teachers" (Blackburn, 1977).
- "The evaluation data indicated that the first-year teachers in the state (induction program) made much more significant progress in planning skills, handling class discussions, preparing teaching plans, managing discipline problems and their ability to teach" (Elsner, 1984).

EVIDENCE FOR INDUCTION AND STUDENT LEARNING IMPROVEMENT

- "With an organized, coherent and sustained induction . . . process, the Islip Schools on Long Island New York . . . saw an . . . improvement in student learning, which they view as resulting from improved teacher performance." "40% Regents diploma rate *before* induction program, 70% rate *after* induction was implemented . . . 50% advanced placement achievement at 3 or higher before induction, 73% achievement at 3 or higher with induction" (Wong, 2005).

> "It is noteworthy that as a teacher improves in effectiveness through training, the first groups of students to profit from improved learning are the lower ability students."

- "It is noteworthy that as a teacher improves in effectiveness through training, the first groups of students to profit from improved learning are the lower ability students" (Breax & Wong, 2003).
- "Average student gains in one year were 14% with ineffective teachers and more than triple that at 53% gain a year with effective teachers" (Sanders & Rivers, 1996).

While reviewing this research is exciting in and of itself, the next step is to gather specific data about the effectiveness of your program. The following section details this process.

BASIC EVALUATION KNOWLEDGE

There are a few definitions we need at the start. These will provide the background information required for you to successfully complete this task without taking a formal evaluation course.

The Five Kinds of Evaluation

In all likelihood, if you have an existing program in place, you do year-end surveys for "program evaluation." If your program is new, such a survey is a good starting point. An evaluation of reactions is the first of five types of evaluation. However, we must build and eventually implement all five types of program evaluation if we want a sustainable High Impact Mentoring and Induction Program.

Level	Indicators	What Each Level Measures
1	Reaction and planned action	• Participant and stakeholder feelings • Participants' planned implementation activities
2	Learning	• Skills, knowledge, and attitudes that have changed
3	The number of completed program activities	• The extent of implementation of new strategies in participants' practice • The kinds of barriers or unmet needs that are obstacles to on-the-job application of learning
4	Impact on district and program mission/vision	• Increases in student grades or assessment scores • Increases in teacher retention rate • Improved teacher and student attendance • Number of Initial Certificate teachers who gain their Standard Professional Certification
5	Return on investment (RoI)	• Benefit-to-cost ratio (savings) • The monetary value of the results attained • Non-financial benefits of results to district, program participants, and stakeholders.

The first four evaluation levels, defined by Kirkpatrick (1994), have found very diverse and popular use. The final level (RoI) was added by Phillips (1996).

If these five levels have a "ring of truth" to them, it is because the CBAM Stages of Concern mirror the first four levels of evaluation! We're already positioned for best practice.

- Evaluation Level 1 is participant reactions to learning about new practices (CBAM Awareness and Information Stages) and planning actions (CBAM's personal stage).
- Level 2 begins implementation and skill building (the mechanical management stage).
- Level 3 is full implementation (the routine management stage of CBAM).
- Evaluation Level 4 is the impact level (or the CBAM consequence stage).

Even our "Chain of Causes and Effects" fits these five evaluation levels, in that all the links, from the program design to the results (reactions, learning, plans, applications, and implementation), must be maintained and strong for your vision to be transferred down the chain and for the impact level to be improved. The fifth evaluation level of RoI fits neither the CBAM nor Chain of Causes and Effects models since our models are about attaining educational, not financial results. However, we all know how the "bottom line" of costs drives education, so we must evaluate at that level also to demonstrate our program's cost effectiveness.

DESIGNING AN EVALUATION PROCESS AND PLAN

As you work through this process, keep track of where you are by learning and recalling the three steps in designing effective program evaluation.

1. Plan evaluation to align with your program model.

2. Design the program evaluation process.

3. Plan the annual program evaluation process time line.

Plan Evaluation to Align With Your Program Model

If, when you started the design of your program, you did not use a model of educator development or the vision suggested, you probably based your program on whatever you could find from other programs that made sense. Leaders who have used this approach often feel a good program evaluation should assess the extent to which the planned activities of the original design are being completed. Using the "levels of evaluation" vocabulary, that "process" approach is a Level 3—application evaluation. Essentially, the basic question that evaluation level asks is, "What process is being used and does it conform to the design that was planned?" On the surface, that seems to accomplish what the title of this section asks us to do.

A very good example of such a "process" evaluation can be reviewed on the internet at <http://t2t.fms.k12.nm.us/data/t2tdata_year1.pdf> or at <http://t2t.fms.k12.nm.us/data/t2tdata_year2.pdf>, which shows the second-year report. This approach is often chosen because it answers a key question, it doesn't require a lot of wrestling with

> This approach by itself may not challenge the leader of the evaluation to learn very much that is new about doing evaluations, but neither does it provide much from which you or your program can learn. That is not its goal.

statistics, and most administrators with doctorates know well how to do it. However, here is an important insight.

This approach *by itself* may not challenge the leader of the evaluation to learn very much that is new about doing evaluations, but neither does it provide much from which you or your program *can* learn. That is not its goal. For our goal of increased teacher and student performance, this approach is only *one* of many questions we must answer.

When we started design of your program, we *did use a model* of educator development as the framework. The title of this section means a great deal more to us. For our evaluation to align with our program model (the chain and the vision), the program components and all the activities have to demonstrate the use of those models every day. Accomplishing that may sound like a year of work but it is really not. In fact, it's time for the "payoff' for all your hard work earlier!

Your Program Evaluation Should be Based on the Same Chain of Causes and Effects

Since that chain represents the transmission of the program's vision down through every level of implementation right into the classroom, identifying indicators that measure the extent and effectiveness of that transmission through each step in the chain is exactly what your evaluation process must do. Happily, this means that half of the necessary work has already been completed. All you need is to figure out what data to collect, and when and how to collect it, and you will have the information flowing in that can enable you to cause improvement, track progress, and demonstrate effects. It's that straightforward because from the very start you thought about program design, implementation, and evaluation as one integrated process built on the "logic" of that chain.

When You Have to Write a Grant Seeking Funding for a Program, You Often Are Asked to Include a "Logic Model"

Just think of your program's "logic model" as the "Chain of Causes and Effects" assumptions that research and expert practice support and that serve as the conceptual foundation of your program. In reality, you already have such a logic model. If you need to write a grant for funding your program start up or a proposal to request administrative support, you have a great deal of the work already done.

The Role of Our Program Evaluation Is to Provide You With a Series of "Windows" Into the Flow of the Vision at Every Link Down the Chain

If you know what was happening regarding each step before the program started, what should happen at each step, and you can collect data about what is happening at each step, you will know precisely the extent of implementation for the program.

You will also know the effectiveness or weakness of each link in the chain and exactly what is working and what needs improvement. You'll be able to track progress and even effectively predict when the vision should reach each step in the process. Eventually you will know when student achievement indicators—the last link in the chain—are about ready to improve.

Design the Program Evaluation Process

Designing the assessment system you need is a rather complex and challenging process, especially the first time. Program evaluation is not simple, but if you take it one step at a time, you will get where you need to go. To provide all the information you might need for some of the evaluation process steps would exceed the scope of this already rather long book. But the details I don't provide here are readily available at the sources given. What follows is an outline of what you will need to build. Remember to do so collaboratively.

The Program Evaluation Process

1. Develop parameters for program evaluation.
2. Define audiences for the evaluation data, conclusions, and recommendations.
3. Define the assumptions you have made that are inherent to your program model.
4. Determine the indicators that will measure the assumptions.
5. Define evaluation questions to assess the truth of each indicator.
6. Define the data needed to assess each indicator.
7. Identify target populations from which to collect data.
8. Identify or develop tools to collect data.
9. Decide on the need to validate the quality of the assessment tools.
10. Integrate needs assessment into program evaluation.
11. Define a time line for data collection, analysis, and reporting.
12. Select person(s) responsible for implementation of the evaluation plan.
13. Collect, organize, and analyze the data.
14. Develop targets for each indicator that needs to improve.
15. Write recommendations for program activities that are likely to improve the target data.
16. Analyze the adequacy, quality, and timeliness of the evaluation process.
17. Write recommendations for improvement of the evaluation process.

Details and Resources for the Steps of the Process

The above outline is not sufficient information for most of us to begin the process. You no doubt want something more specific. Here are some details for each step of the evaluation process and some resources for selected areas which are beyond the scope of this chapter.

Develop Parameters for Program Evaluation

Parameters are set to guide decision making so they define "What we will try to do" and "What we will not do." This step is taken to set boundaries around the work to be done so the scale of the project is manageable and your intentions are more likely to be implemented during and through the process. Parameters also determine the technical quality of a process, instruments, and the resulting data *and decisions.* The reliability, validity, and fairness of data and the conclusions are examples. The more "high stakes" the use of the evaluation, the more you need quality. Examples might include statements like

- We *will* limit the size of instruments and the time it takes to complete them.
- Therefore, we *will not* collect data *unless* we are sure that we will use it.
- Therefore, we *will* decide in advance how we will use all the data we plan to collect.
- We *will* provide data summaries and final conclusions with recommendations to all who provide us with data.
- To the highest extent possible, we *will* design assessments that also are educational for participants and don't just benefit the program.
- We *will* collect data from at least three diverse sources for each research question to allow comparison of viewpoints.
- We *will* always use a mix of both open-ended and fixed-choice items.
- We *will* field test all home-grown instruments.

It is best to make these choices based on whether they reflect the Vision for Excellent Teaching and Learning. In other words, *how you assess your program should reflect best practice in student assessment* and vice versa. Does the process honor individual differences and strengths, and support improvement for individuals, or does it demonstrate a "batch processing" mentality? Using parameters like these to design program assessment means that those assessments are more likely to give you the data you need for the program you are trying to build *and* to encourage good teaching practices and successful student learning.

Define the Audiences for Evaluation Data, Conclusions, and Recommendations

Would you write the same letter to your mother on Valentine's Day as you would to your sweetheart? Of course not. Audience makes a big difference in what and how we say things. That's why, when planning assessments, we need to consider to whom the data and conclusions will be shown. If you know that you will need to defend your program to a superintendent or business manager who is focused on saving money, you are sure to collect different data and present it differently than you would if that person is focused on customer satisfaction. Knowing this early in program evaluation design is like knowing your goals. Defining your data audience ensures that you collect no more than the data you need because you can focus your efforts and time on what is strategically critical to know and to say. There are usually multiple audiences.

Define the Assumptions You Have Made in Your Program Model

When we originally defined each link in the chain, we made a series of assumptions about what would cause a specific, desired effect. When we asked, "What must *mentors* do to teach protégés to teach according to the vision?" we assumed that if mentors modeled and taught novices the Vision for Excellence in Teaching and Learning and then gave them adequate support for implementation, then those novices would be able to use that vision in their work with students. Figure 7.1, "Assumptions in the Chain of Causes and

Figure 7.1   Assumptions in the Chain of Causes and Effects

Chain of Causes and Effects	Assumptions About the Causes and Effects
What must the mentoring and induction *program* do?	• Through their process and criteria, program components can communicate the Vision for Excellent Teaching and Learning.
What must the program *leaders* do?	• By their modeling and direct teaching of the program vision, leaders can communicate and facilitate adoption of that vision by program participants.
What must protégé and mentor *training* do?	• By providing great models of mentoring that demonstrate the program vision, clear and direct teaching to mentors of how to model that vision, practice and correction to mentors to improve their own modeling of the vision, and by teaching mentors how to teach protégés to be models of that vision, mentors will be able to teach that vision to new teachers.
What must *mentors* do?	• By mentor modeling and direct teaching, the protégés can become models of that vision in their instruction of students.
What must *novice teachers* do?	• By using strategies defined in the vision, teachers will meet individual students' needs, engage students in active learning, improve students' attitudes as learners, and improve students' success in learning.
What do we want *students* to do as learners?	• When students' individual needs are met and they are actively engaged in their learning, their attitudes about themselves as learners and their learning will improve. • When student learning improves, so will their performance (application) and their achievement (results).

3. Program Evaluation →

225

Effects," lists the series of assumptions we have made for each "link" in the chain. *Using the chain will produce* the effects we want, but to show that your *program has caused* this whole sequence of effects, you will need evidence for each of the assumptions.

Determine the Indicators That Will Measure the Assumptions

For each assumption, we discuss and select measurable indicators to check the assumption. We just assumed, for example, that the transfer of the vision from the mentor to the protégé would happen given training, support, etc. We believe it is a very probable assumption, but *we don't know the extent to which that will happen.* That's why we must specifically *define what it will look like* for mentors to teach protégés the district vision and for protégés to use that vision in their own teaching.

By defining an indicator for each assumption, we will know what to measure and how to develop the data collection tools and process. Use Figure 7.2 to guide you in adding your possible indicators on the right. Define what you will see happening if the assumptions are true.

Define Evaluation Questions to Assess the Truth of Each Indicator

Translate each indicator into a question to research and answer. In the case of mentoring the protégé, the indicator "Protégés learn how to teach using the vision because mentors directly teach them how to do so and support their implementation of that learning with students" might be translated into the question, "To what extent do protégés use the district vision in their own teaching?" However, since the vision contains several factors, the questions for this indicator need to be more specific. An even better version of that question is more specific because it defines one part of the vision to be assessed, "To what extent do protégés use the individualized differentiated teaching model with their students?"

That's a crucial evaluation question we'd need to answer so we can prove or disprove the original assumption. In other words, the evaluation questions we need to answer are shaped by the assumption we need to confirm. If we cannot confirm it in actual practice, our Chain of Cause and Effects did not work. Rest assured, I *know* that what we have developed works, but you have to demonstrate that it does in *your* local program to *your* local decision makers.

To define your questions, translate each of the indicators in Figure 7.2 into a specific, observable behavior that is stated as a question and that can feasibly be assessed. Figure 7.3 is an example of a format for that translation process, but of course more space would be needed and you could do it in a "table" on your computer. Also, be careful as you develop evaluation questions, since some indicators definitely need more than one question to be thoroughly assessed.

> Be careful as you develop evaluation questions, since some indicators definitely need more than one question to be thoroughly assessed.

The first indicator is a good example. "The program components and whole program are designed and function according to the best practices described in this book." Since there are numerous components and inter-component synergy is not simple, the questions for this one indicator alone will be numerous. Although this will be lots of work, remember that, since you are following best practice as you work, you will probably never have to change this work. This process is a bit tough right now but it gets much easier after the first time.

Figure 7.2 Evaluation Indicators to Assess the Assumptions in the Chain of Causes and Effects

Assumptions About the Causes and Effects	Evaluation Indicators to Assess the Truth of the Assumptions
• Through their process and criteria, program components can communicate their Vision for Excellent Teaching and Learning. • By their modeling and direct teaching of the program vision, leaders can communicate and facilitate adoption of that vision by program participants. • By providing great models of mentoring that demonstrate the program vision, clear and direct teaching to mentors of how to model that vision, practice and correction to mentors to improve their own modeling of the vision, and by teaching mentors how to teach protégés to be models of that vision, mentors will be able to teach that vision to new teachers. • By mentor modeling and direct teaching, the protégés can become models of that vision in their instruction of students. • By using strategies defined in the vision, teachers will meet individual students' needs, engage students in active learning, improve students' attitudes as learners, and improve students' success in learning. • When students' individual needs are met and they are actively engaged in their learning, their attitudes about themselves as learners and their learning will improve. • When student learning improves, so will their performance (application) and their achievement (results).	• The program components and whole program are designed and function according to the best practices described in this book. • Participants report that their individual needs are anticipated and met. • Participants can explain how the program uses the vision in processes. • Leaders model and direct teach the program Vision for Excellent Teaching and Learning. • Participants feel compelled to adopt the vision for their work in the program because leaders have done so and support them doing it. • Mentor training is designed to meet individual mentor needs, engage mentors in active learning and skill development, and give individual support for mentor implementation of the vision in their own mentoring. • Mentors use the training strategies, and model and teach the vision in their daily mentoring of protégés. • Protégés experience how compelling the vision is since they are learning to be better teachers every day using that model. • Protégés learn how to teach using the vision because mentors directly teach them how to do so and support their implementation of that learning in their work with students. • Protégés are motivated to increase use of the vision in their teaching as they observe increased student engagement and success. • Student engagement, persistence, creativity, and motivation in learning increase while discipline problems, incomplete and late work, and teachers' focus on their own survival decrease. • Student attendance and measures of learning increase. • Student application of learning, their products, and assessments improve.

Figure 7.3 Evaluation Questions That Assess the Evaluation Indicators

"Translate" each Indicator into a specific, observable question for data collection. Watch for indicators that may need more than one question.

Evaluation Indicators	Evaluation Questions
• The program components and whole program are designed and function according to the best practices described in this book. • Participants report their individual needs are anticipated and met. • Participants can explain how program uses the vision in processes. • Leaders model and direct teach the program Vision for Excellent Teaching and Learning. • Participants feel compelled to adopt the vision for their work in the program because leaders have done so and support them doing it. • Mentor training is designed to meet individual mentor needs, engage mentors in active learning and skill development, and give individual support for mentor implementation of the vision in their own mentoring. • Mentors use the training strategies and model and teach the vision in their daily mentoring of protégés. • Protégés experience how compelling the vision is since they are learning to be better teachers every day using that model. • Protégés learn how to teach using the vision because mentors directly teach them how to do so and support their implementation of that learning in their work with students. • Protégés are motivated to increase use of the vision in their teaching as they observe increased student engagement and success. • Student engagement, persistence, creativity, and motivation in learning increase while discipline problems, incomplete and late work, and teachers' focus on their own survival decrease. • Student attendance and measures of learning increase. • Student application of learning, products, and assessments improve.	• To what extent do protégés use the individualized differentiated teaching model? • To what extent do protégés actively engage students in learning?

Define the Data Needed to Assess Each Indicator

Generally, we need each link in the chain in place and functioning effectively, and we need data to show that to be the case. However, it is not that simple—as you may suspect from all your work with assumptions, indicators, and assessment questions. Program assessment must provide the *data we need, not just about the last link in the chain* (student learning), but about every assumption for every link in the chain. That means we need to know the *current* situation with each indicator we have defined and then we need to monitor the progress in the data year to year as those data move toward a match with the truth stated in the indicators. This requires rather specific survey items, lists of things to observe, and other such details. For example, what data could tell you the *amount of time* needed for mentoring to be effective for most protégés? How could you collect those data? Or what data would tell you the *optimal number of coaching cycles* needed for a mentoring pair to begin to positively impact teaching behaviors? How could you collect those data?

How will you do all of this? One step at a time!

Identify Target Populations From Which to Collect Data

Who has a viewpoint on each topic that warrants collecting it for comparison? To maintain the best quality in your conclusions, you need to have three data sources for comparison. (What is the truth when *two* sources don't agree?)

- *Mentors and protégés* have a perspective on almost everything that was done in the program, but that doesn't mean they should be asked about it. Would the data from them be used and for which evaluation questions?
- *Department chairs or lead teachers* can have a valuable viewpoint on a topic, but should you avoid them if they don't know much about something? Maybe finding out what they *don't know* is valuable. Ask them and see. The reverse is also true. These folks serve in in-between roles and sometimes see and know things few others can.
- *Site administrators*—the same issues apply here as to chairs, but you really must assess their views so they don't feel "out of the loop" with no input flowing either way. Their more unique role may shed light on a subject in ways that surprise you. Also, they can shut you down if they decide that mentoring isn't "worth it." Keep them involved so they can learn along with everyone else in the program. It may be that you invite them to a mentor training or other event and they don't come. Help them to *learn why* that time might be well spent.
- *Program leaders*—the same issues apply as above. Trainers may know a lot about one or two specific seminars but have little opportunity to have learned much about the wider program and its effects. Still, without at least initially assessing each of these groups' views, you do not really know what they know and don't know. Collect the data first and decide again later whether it is needed.

There could be other groups that should be kept informed and heard. Who are stakeholders in new teacher development? Help them learn through involvement what great things are happening and they can become advocates for your program.

Identify or Develop Tools to Collect Data

The objective for this section is to obtain the specific instruments and guiding processes that will be sent to the people you have identified and that will return to you the information you need to improve your program and results. Inherent in that statement is the fact that many such tools and processes will help you obtain that data and some will not serve your intentions. Each tool or process has purpose behind its creation, and so has both advantages to offer and built-in limitations. Picking what you need from among these must proceed very carefully if the process and tools will effectively *serve your* needs.

There is a vast range of evaluation methods and instruments available from which you might choose. The internet can provide many, businesses can provide many, and you could already have or develop your own as well. Here are the factors to consider.

- The problems with obtaining instruments from others are the financial cost and the need for their tools and your intent to reflect the same goal. Purchase of others' instruments or processes can be expensive. It is rather like software: you must buy an individual copy for each person to use or buy a license for all to use it every time you need to do an evaluation.

- The advantage of (mostly) using others' instruments is that they should have already confirmed the value and effectiveness of their tool for that goal. In other words, the instrument has been found in use to be a valid way to assess for that goal. That's great because, if yours is the same goal, you don't have to check the quality of the instrument to assure yourself that the data it will provide are worth using. However, remember that word "mostly" at the start of this point. Don't assume anything. The next section in this book gives more guidance on this issue.

- The problem with developing your own evaluation instruments is, first, that you have to do the work of designing them. If you are not sure how, that is a very telling issue, but you do have this book to guide you. A second problem is that you need to validate the quality and effectiveness of the tools before using them. Remember, the goal is not to collect data. The goal is to collect meaningful, credible data that will change people's minds and drive improvement. Don't just look for a mentor survey. Any old survey may not be worth using.

> You need to validate the quality and effectiveness of the tools before using them. Remember, the goal is not to collect data. The goal is to collect meaningful, credible data that will change people's minds and drive improvement.

- The advantage of using your own home-grown instruments is that you control the goal they serve. Also, you don't have to spend a lot of time finding the appropriate materials and you can get what you need without a financial cost.

There are entire books and graduate courses on how to develop effective, quality evaluation instruments and processes. This book is not one of them. I will give you enough hints to get you started, however.

First (and this is critical), use the same advice from "How to Develop an Evaluation Process" to develop individual evaluation tools. In other words, watch out that the individual parts of the evaluation system that you design align with the intentions and decisions already made for the system as a whole. Just check that the instrument you design is adhering to your existing parameters, designed to provide the data that you and the audience you serve will want, investigates your program assumptions about the chain, and so on.

> Watch out that the individual parts of your evaluation system that you design align with the intentions and decisions already made for the system as a whole.

Second, take reasonable steps to field test, and in a few other ways to assure yourself of, the quality of the assessment components, as described in the next section.

If you are starting the evaluation process and design of the components from "scratch," just take these steps later on as you can. Check quality after using the tool or during the next year. It is OK to use what you develop without checking their quality *if* you must collect baseline data right away and are running out of time, and *if* you are careful not to use the data of unknown quality to make major changes in your program. In checking the quality of self-designed evaluation instruments, your primary objective is not to prove their quality to others, although that will come later. It is to assure yourself that the data your instruments produce are worth the effort to collect and use to guide future program decisions.

Here are a few more suggestions to guide your work.

- "Customer satisfaction" surveys rarely provide the kind of diagnostic data we need to improve our programs. What surveys do provide is a sense of what may not be working, but usually they *cannot* clarify what we need to do to fix the problems and improve the progress toward your goals. Still, surveys are evaluation level 1, and do tell you whether or not the "campers are happy".
- A very common evaluation problem is that the task of collecting, organizing, and analyzing the data becomes too time and labor-consuming to be practical. The solution for this problem is to design backwards from data collection, organization, and analysis. Consider the form in which folks should return data to you that could speed the data processing of:
  – Handwritten observations or interviews of others
  – Handwritten narratives
  – Handwritten short answers
  – Penciled-in bubbles on a electronic answer sheet
- What will you do with data collected to facilitate your analysis? Will you store and manipulate data on paper, on cards, on charts, on a spreadsheet, or in a database?
- Understand that the basic process in data analysis is comparison of data: comparison of groups' diverse viewpoints on the same issue, of baseline data to this year's data, of the second year to the third year, or of what two different assessments— like surveys and interviews—tell you about the same issue. In all cases, you will attempt to find and understand patterns in the data. That will require you to take data from different people, places, times, or instruments and put them near each other so you can check for changes. That can be done on paper, in your mind, or on a computer. Plan what you will do now as you develop the instruments and processes so these work with data analysis later.
- When designing assessment tools, create a range of item types, including open-ended and forced-choice response methods. For example, at the end of a survey or set of interview questions (closed focus), ask an open question or two like, "What else might the program need to do to improve?" or "What else should we have asked you, but didn't?" Use of this range of item types ensures that your assumptions do not narrow what respondents can give you. It ensures that the data you get back prevent your assumptions from blinding you to the truth.
- Mentoring is an all-year-long activity, so why wait to the end to evaluate it and find out there were problems too late to do anything about it? Instead, use good instructional practice and assess the activity all year as well. Find out before it is too late what needs attention, and then fix it right away so the year can still be a "success." How could an all-year-long evaluation process be feasible and actually work? The article, "My Mentor, Myself" describes how one school district accomplishes this

goal. This overview, available at <www.nsdc.org/library/publications/jsd/kella her244.cfm>, explains how the district collects and analyzes data every month, the tools used, results, and lessons learned. The beginning sentence in the section titled "Collecting Data" should sound familiar to you.

- The following chart suggests possible assessment methods that match specific kinds of program evaluation questions. As you read these, ask yourself whether some of them are the "research questions" that your program needs to answer.

Sample Evaluation Methods for Program Evaluation Questions

1. *What?* Have the needs of new teachers and mentors been met?
   How—Needs assessment

2. *What?* Have new teachers and mentors grown professionally?
   How—Pre–post on a developmental scale like CBAM (Stages of Concern)

3. *What?* In what ways have mentors and protégés grown and not grown?
   How—Topic-specific scale or compare goals to pre- and post-learning or skills

4. *What?* Have mentors and protégés done all that the induction/mentoring program recommended?
   How—Log of time with check off for type of activity
   How—Protégé needs assessment

5. *What?* Has the kind of teaching desired become more the norm?
   How—Observations pre–post (by whom?), self-reports by protégé

6. *What?* Has student learning improved because of mentoring?
   How—Pre–post teacher reports for protégés and mentors
   How—Assessment scores?

7. *What?* Has there been *progress* toward the original goals of the program?
   How
   - A predetermined set of indicators or behaviors that can be monitored for progress
   - Observe or survey (or even better, both) for those behaviors

8. *What?* Have the original *goals* of the program been accomplished?
   How
   - Define indicators of "what success will look like."
   - Surveys, focus groups, or interviews that ask stakeholders' opinions on the question

9. *What?* Has the program provided sufficient support and training? (for whom?)
   How
   - Actual versus desired amount of mentoring time?
   - Mentor and protégé quarterly survey or support group discussion and vote
   - Questions asking mentors and protégés to identify specific parts of training and support that were sufficient or not on a 1–5 scale

---

10. *What?* What are the obstacles that prevent you from being the mentor or teacher you want to be?
    How
    - Mentor and protégé quarterly survey with some checklist items and an open response
    - Program leader and administrator observations
    - Interviews of representative sample of mentors and protégés
    - Mentor and protégé self-assessment on set of ideal skills

Decide on the Need to Validate the Quality of the Tools

The point of this section is avoiding mistakes that destroy the credibility and usefulness of data you collect (also see above). Helpful hints for increasing quality *after designing* evaluation tools include the following:

- *Triangulate.* Collect data from at least three different perspectives on the same topics. Compare these data against each other to reveal the meaning in data patterns and to confirm the credibility of your conclusions. The following box shows an item from an actual end-of-year survey displayed so the data patterns are revealed. Notice how significant the three viewpoints really are. Ask yourself, what else would you need to know to understand what these data are telling you.

> *Item 3: The program should hold mentors and protégés accountable for using the best mentoring process.*
>   Protégés = 84% agreement
>   Mentors = 0% agreement
>   Site administrators = 0% agreement

Which viewpoint is really true? Are there things some people are aware they don't know? How could this be made to reveal more so interpretation is easier and more confident? This shows that the effort required to "triangulate" three data sources really is worth it. There are important problems that are remaining unaddressed so far, but now *you know about them.* So what do you do next? What really needs fixing? Do you have all the information you need to answer these questions? How could the data collection tool be improved so you'd know what the problem is?

- *Check question validity.* "Validity" is the extent to which the tool really assesses what it is intended to assess. An example would be a question to determine ability to analyze information, but which is given to persons who do not know prerequisite information. They will be wrongly scored low for analysis when it is a knowledge-level fault. Why go to the trouble of designing an evaluation tool that yields data that may not be credible or could even steer you wrong in reaching conclusions? Each of your tools that has not been previously used and checked for validity needs to be checked by content experts such as those who teach a subject.

- *Examine reliability.* Especially check what is called "inter-rater" reliability. This means that persons observing similar events, hearing similar interviews, or scoring similar questions should be looking for and find very similar results and reach similar conclusions. This is rather easy to check and, if a problem is found, fairly easy to remedy.
- *Ensure fairness.* Fairness is a lack of bias and the presence of conditions that allow people being assessed the same reasonable opportunities to do the tasks.

Any good state or provincial Department of Education can provide you with guidelines for examining these factors—perhaps even on their websites. If not, there are other excellent sources you'll find with a Google search for those terms and the word "assessment."

Integrate Needs Assessment Into Program Evaluation

Conceptions of evaluation as only an "after event" process are simply untrue. "After" and "before" *exist together* because growth, learning, and improvement are a continual process. For example, an after-event evaluation can eventually evolve into needs assessment for the same participants at the next event. That is why, to be able to measure, monitor, document, and improve our progress, we must collect and monitor a *wide range* of the *same* data, *before, during, and after* events, and not just at the end of an event. This allows us to track what happens, step by step over time, and *that* allows us to find areas of strength or for improvement.

> Conceptions of evaluation as only an "after event" process are simply untrue. "After" and "before" exist together because growth, learning and improvement are a continual process.

Define the Time Line for Data Collection, Analysis, and Reporting

- *Establish baseline data.* Baseline data describe the conditions, knowledge, and skills levels, CBAM levels—whatever you will assess—that were in place *before* your program started and had the opportunity to make a difference. The baseline is the point against which all later data are compared to demonstrate progress, and that makes early collection of baseline data essential. This is why it is critical that you have designed evaluation at the same time as the program. Ideally, your assessments must be ready and *used before the program is implemented* because you *need baseline data for each evaluation question.*
  - If you did adequate needs assessments when designing the program, those needs can probably serve as most of the "baseline" data you will need.
  - If you already have parts of a program operating but you have not collected baseline data for some crucial indicators, you need to identify and remedy that flaw now.
  - The only exception to this is locating "found" data that already exist and that you can use for your purposes. The number of new teachers who have left is an example.
- *Establish an annual time line.* The school year already has its own pace, sequence, and crazy or quiet times. When you add your program calendar on top of that, it gets even more complex. As you plan adding an evaluation sequence on top of those, be very careful. *What is already going* on is important—for example, when you have evaluation conclusions to report to the board, you need to report before they decide

your next budget. Recommendations for program improvements also influence preparing the next budget request. You will want data showing you really do need a better training, more mentoring time, or other desired activity. Also, you don't want data collection from teachers just before the annual student assessment. Do yourself a favor and plan evaluation with such things in mind. *Consider what makes sense and is feasible in itself.*

- When will you have the time to do instrument design or revisions?
- When can you do the analysis?
- By when do you need final conclusions and recommendations?

Ideally, your assessments should help you, and also inform and educate folks who complete them. *When* they complete the assessment depends on what and when you want them to know or *not* to know something. Plan evaluation activities considering impact on other program events. Why do *two* activities if one can be used to collect needed information? Examples of this were provided earlier in the chapter on designing the Induction Program.

- *Establish a multiyear time line.* As you may expect, there are several things to consider in this area. Primarily, we need to plan multiyear assessment to monitor and document the changes that occur year to year because of experience, better training, or implementation stages.
  - You *need a schedule that spells out when* specific data should be collected at points during implementation. Once you have a baseline, predict the points and when you expect to see some earlier and later indicators change. Collect the data before the change, when it is expected, and after it is expected. Do this since you can't assume your prediction is right and you want data to tell you when changes actually start.
  - Identify and *collect data on early indicators* of progress, the earliest links in the chain. Early indicators are among the first things to change when program, leader and training strategies are established. For example, it may take a year or two to get best practices for recruitment, selection, matching, and training of mentors in place, and you should document the early indicators for development of and results produced by those components. However, changes in new teacher performance—a middle indicator—will not occur until those trained mentors have gained sufficient experience in the mentoring strategies and process. If we watch for improved student learning (a later indicator) early on in the process, we may wrongly conclude that "nothing is happening." Watch the early indicators early in the process and expect only the later indicators to change when the early and middle indicators are all strong.

Select Person(s) Responsible for Leading the Implementation of the Evaluation Plan

This is very straightforward. The key is to think beyond the specific person who can or should do it, to also consider what added benefits for the program can be captured. In other words, try to find or create as many reasons as possible for the final choice so you can obtain the most benefits from the process. For example, a graduate intern may be the perfect person this year, but then who will do it next year when the intern is gone?

Collect, Organize, and Analyze the Data

If you are a careful and sequential reader, you have already come across plenty of advice for this topic. If you missed those tidbits, they are worth finding. Just look to the "design" sections earlier in this process.

> Once you have collected data, determine what it can tell you. That process is essentially one of arranging the data to allow comparisons, searching for meaningful patterns in the data, and interpretation or assigning meaning to the patterns found.

Once you have collected data, determine what they can tell you. That process is essentially one of arranging the data to allow comparisons, searching for meaningful patterns in the data, and interpretation of or assigning meaning to the patterns found. This sounds clear, but there are a few tricks that make it work well.

- *Assemble all the data* that relate to the success of participants in the program. Use:
  - At least three to five years of trend data (at least work toward that)
  - Hard data (such as attendance, demographics, test scores, etc.)
  - Soft data (opinion data from surveys, observations, focus groups, or interviews)
  - Data that address program goals and objectives, participant growth, implementation of planned activities, etc.
  - Data that describe both mentor and protégé knowledge and behaviors.
- *Display these data so that any trends are apparent,* using one page per topic. This manipulation is best done by computer, so input your data into a spreadsheet or database that can sort many ways. Also, it is difficult to see a pattern when many numbers are displayed. Instead, simplify the numbers into symbols, such as a plus sign for indicators that have improved, etc.
- Data come in many different forms, such as percentiles, quartiles, lists of statements, and meets/exceeds/does not meet. *Convert each type of data into one common form.* This helps to reveal patterns better. I recommend using the "meets/exceeds/ does not meet" format. Here is how to do this conversion. Regardless of the original form of the data:
  - If the score or data level is "satisfactory," write a "M" for "meets our expectations."
  - If the score or data level is "not satisfactory," write a "DNM" for "does not meet" expectations.
  - If the score or data level is significantly better than satisfactory," use an "E" for "exceeds."
- *Write the translation results (M/E/DNM) into a data chart* listing indicators (factors) along one side and symbols of the results so far for each.
- *Make a "Hard and Soft Data Comparison Chart"* to collect the converted data (M/E/DNM) on a single page. Write a title at the top, topics along one side and data sources along the other axis. Enter the M/E/DNM in the right places.
- *Give a descriptive title* to each of the data summary charts and the written conclusions. *Link* the written conclusions and the data summary charts by placing them on the same page or at least creating a cross-reference so these two items are clearly related.
- *Look for patterns in the data displayed.* Arrange, sort, and rearrange data to allow comparisons of possible contributing factors and results. For example, does protégé rate of development increase as mentor experience increases, or as mentors change how they mentor? Data patterns must be found because data have no

inherent meaning by themselves. It is only when a pattern can be found that meaning can be assigned.

- *Assemble a collaborative "interpretation team."* The evaluation coordinator probably does all the comparison and data manipulation, but should seek help with interpreting what the patterns mean. Sometimes, only participants know what causes a pattern.
- *Write a narrative conclusion for each "topic,"* stating what the trends and other data are interpreted to mean. Consider factors that explain why the data look as they do, such as changes in staff training, instructional materials, media use, forms of assessment, or external factors that impact participants. The narrative conclusion should describe and explain the pattern observed.
- *Decide and write out recommendations for program improvement priorities.* Compare all these charts and conclusions with each other. Discuss whether all of these identified needs can be addressed effectively, or if a few should be selected as the priorities. I recommend no more than four improvement goals, and one or two is even better as that increases the focus for scarce time and resources. Bundle it all with a dated title, executive summary, table of contents, and numbered pages.

Develop Targets for Each Indicator That Needs to Improve

Improvement "targets" are the answer to the question, "How much is good enough?" Targets define the desired extent of improvement for a specific indicator within a specified time. If an indicator suggests a data pattern is not adequate, decide the "target" that must be reached to be acceptable. Do not use the term "standard," which has become overly linked with accountability.

Measurable targets themselves are valuable as motivators, but they are critical because of what happens in the process of defining and agreeing on them. The consensus-building process inherent to agreeing on targets ensures that targets *are* measurable since no one would agree to be held accountable to do something "fuzzy." Consensus on measurable goals also greatly increases the chances that you will actually attain the goals you set. Also, targets serve as hypotheses to test for what can be accomplished. The better you get at predicting accurately what you can and cannot achieve, the better your program planning will serve as a guide for implementation. Eventually you will be able to actually accomplish what you predicted you could and you will make commitments only for results you can attain.

> Improvement "targets" are the answer to the question, "How much is good enough?" Targets define the desired extent of improvement for a specific indicator within a specified time.

Make sure that each target

- Is observable and measurable
- Describes specifically *when* you expect to achieve the target
- Describes *what you expect the data to look like each year,* so you can measure progress toward the target

Use any of the following resource websites to help you define your desired targets:

- Outcome Measurement Resource Network, <http://national.unitedway.org/outcomes>
- Managing for Outcomes, <http://www.treasury.qld.gov.au/subsites/fmb/tier2/info.htm>

- Outcome Measurement: Showing Results, <http://national.unitedway.org>
- Outcomes Evaluation (includes basic forms, etc.), <http://www.gasbankscales.com>

Write up the list of targets with dates, etc. Use titles and cross-references to ensure that the appropriate data comparison and written conclusion are linked to each other and to each target for improvement. Make it clear why specific targets were chosen as priorities.

Write Recommendations for Program Activities to Improve the Targeted Data

After data analysis and writing conclusions, you will know—perhaps better than anyone—what is needed to fix problems, remove obstacles, and gain progress. Now

- In the left-hand column of a page, write a narrative paragraph or two describing the results of analysis and the priorities decided. Be sure to write about links to earlier data.
- In the right-hand column, across from each conclusion, write *possible activities* that would address the needs and deliver what is missing. Offer several options and, if sequence seems to matter, place them in order.
- Work with a collaborative group of three to five people who represent key stakeholder groups, who are experienced in the program, and whose decisions will mean something to others in and outside the program. Use this group to
  - Affirm, add, or adjust priorities and improvement targets reflecting the priorities
  - Review the possible improvement activity options you wrote and select those deemed of greatest importance or which are easiest to accomplish
  - Write "action plans" that describe what the program leaders, participants, or others must do to improve the data pattern and achieve the target
  - Help present the action plan and documentation to administration, school board, community, parents, teachers, and other stakeholders

Analyze the Adequacy, Quality, and Timeliness of the Evaluation Process

- Use the input from this representative group, your reactions, and those of other participants *plus* the data conclusions to identify areas of the evaluation model or any elements within the evaluation plan that did not function as intended or produce what was needed.
- Use these findings to design evaluation improvements and to plan a time line and responsibilities for implementing the improvements.
- If any evaluation tasks, quality checks, or other such tasks were previously left undone, schedule their completion and a person responsible.

Write "Recommendations for Improvement of the Evaluation Process"

- Write a report using this section title and including the time lines, assignments, activities, and reasons for the changes just described.
- Write a cover letter describing the contents and relating the program's commitment to thorough, candid, and transparent evaluation for improvement of the program, the evaluation system, and accountability for the results achieved by the program and participants.

- Write a one-page executive summary of the contents for just after the cover letter.
- Disseminate this written report to all involved persons and key decision makers.

DEMONSTRATING COMPELLING RETURN ON INVESTMENT FROM INDUCTION

Regardless of what your program accomplishes in the nonfinancial arena, there will be some key people and competitors for your funds who will question the cost effectiveness of your labor- and time-intensive program. Count on it and prepare for it.

Your *claim is* that induction is highly cost effective and more than pays for itself in both financial and nonfinancial ways. The *facts already exist to support your claim*—the research on improvements in new teacher and mentor performance *and* on student performance improvements, given at the start of this chapter, are powerful persuasion.

There is a clear connection between the mentoring and induction program and the improved teacher and student results due to the program models (chain) that place improvement of these factors at the heart of each program element. That makes your claim even stronger.

Now we also have overwhelming financial proof that your program not only achieves the very purpose of the school district, but also saves the district the money it is already wasting. That means that your program costs *nothing new* to run, even at a highly effective level, and actually earns money for the district by the cost savings it can provide!

RESEARCH ON RETURN ON INVESTMENT FOR INDUCTION AND MENTORING

The Alliance for Excellent Education research . . . shows that comprehensive induction cuts (new teacher) attrition rates in half and develops new teachers more rapidly into highly skilled, experienced professionals. It also found that induction . . . creates a payoff of $1.37 for every dollar invested in the program (Alliance for Excellent Education, 2004).

While this information is invaluable and exciting, these facts are often not enough to sway decision makers because they are someone else's, not your local district's, facts. Therein lies the most important strategy to put in place to assure the survival of your program, and through that the thriving of all new teachers and their students. You must collect and use your district's own local data to demonstrate the wonderful cost savings from increased new teacher retention and parallel *decreases in the cost of new teacher attrition due to your program.* Here are three useful strategies.

Strategy 1

Use local teacher attrition data to demonstrate that it costs less to provide adequate time for mentoring support than it does to provide inadequate mentoring time.

Basically, this strategy involves determining your local district's real cost of teacher attrition—a hidden, annual waste of money, and then providing proof that an adequately funded mentoring and induction program saves the largest part of that money by dramatically reducing teacher loss.

1. Start by working with your Personnel Director to chart the actual number of teachers who left the school district for whatever reason over at least the last three to five years. Build a chart that presents these numbers categorized by reason, such as retirement, spouse got a different job requiring a move, better salary elsewhere, difficulty with supervisor, left teaching career, etc.

2. Total up the people who left for reasons that the school district *cannot* control, such as retirement and spouse getting a new job.

3. Total up those who left for reasons the district might be able to influence.

4. Estimate the percentage for each of these groups from the total of all those who left.

5. Use the percentage from step 4 to estimate the remaining number in the "left for unknown reasons" group who probably left for reasons the district might be able to influence.

6. Add the total from step 5 to the total from step 3.

7. List all the costs to the district for recruiting, signing, orienting, and training a new employee for their first year of employment. Then do the same for those who stay two years.

8. Divide the costs to the district by the number of people leaving found in step 6 to arrive at the cost per teacher of attrition after the first year and after two years.

9. Estimate the current cost per novice teacher for your mentoring and induction program. Then estimate the cost of the programs if you were able to provide the time and other more effective elements you'd like to provide your new teachers.

Compare the costs of teacher attrition per person with the per person cost of effective mentoring and induction support. You may be surprised! Usually the cost of adequately supporting people (doing things right) is less than the cost of teacher attrition (doing it wrong).

Set up and document a few representative cases of what it takes to provide appropriate levels of new teacher support. Collect data on what happens to the levels of teacher retention each year in those cases. Keep in mind that 100 percent retention is not desirable, as not all persons who go into teaching should be teachers. A very attainable goal, however, is 95–96 percent retention.

> This research suggests that every district already has and spends the money on teacher attrition each year that it should invest in teacher retention through adequate mentoring and induction. Your district has all the money needed to provide the program your novice teachers deserve!

For an example of this strategy in action, read the Texas State Board of Educator Certification "Cost of Teacher Attrition" Research Study, which is posted on the SBEC website at <www.sbec.state.tx.us/SBECOnline/txbess/turnoverrpt.pdf>. Essentially, this study found Texas is spending millions of dollars more on replacing teachers than a good statewide mentoring and induction effort would have cost.

This research suggests that every district already spends the money on teacher *attrition* each year that it should invest in teacher *retention* through adequate mentoring and induction. *Your* district has all the money needed to provide the program your novice teachers deserve!

Strategy 2

Describe the nonfinancial costs of teacher attrition as well. Though it's hard to place a dollar value on them, there are a number of other "costs" of teachers leaving after one to three years that are very significant. You know this list yourself, but here are a few to get you started. Reasons include

- Wasted administrative supervision and evaluation time when the new teacher leaves and the principal has to start over again
- Lost momentum on school improvement and other initiatives. Start over again.
- Lost instructional consistency for students when novices replace staff who leave

Strategy 3

Use the wasted attrition money for more productive and cost-effective methods like enhancing the induction and mentoring program and its evaluation process. The "bottom line" here is that, as a district increases its expectations for improved results from mentoring, it must also increase its commitment of time and other resources for the support of mentors, the mentoring and induction program, and the novice teachers. In fact, it can be argued that only after such a commitment has been made would it be logical to expect increased results.

OTHER STRATEGIES FOR SUPPORTING AND SUSTAINING THE PROGRAM

Here is more information to help you locate the diverse kinds of support and resources needed to develop and sustain comprehensive, high impact teacher induction and mentoring.

Keep a "Changes Journal"

Capture the story of what has happened and when in a "changes" journal for the school district. So many things happen each year, but how many of them have real potential to impact teacher and student performances? That narrows the list considerably. Now narrow the list you keep even further by focusing especially on events that have potential to impact your program's process and results.

Just record the date and the event, plus possible ideas for how the event might change instruction, the professional climate or your program, and its results. Your goal is to capture this information so, several years later when data are available for analysis, you can refer to this journal for specifics and better interpret why changes in data patterns have happened.

Make Mentoring Visible

One of the reasons nonparticipants cannot value mentoring is that mentoring is invisible. Mentoring is a very special environment that is required for a beginning teacher to be able to develop rapidly as a professional. That environment requires a safe, low-risk, and positive support relationship with an experienced mentor. In order for such an environment to develop, the mentor-protégé relationship must be confidential, nonevaluative, and characterized by trust. These characteristics make the mentoring relationship a very special, unique but invisible situation. The mentor may be the only person who really sees the full extent of the professional growth and the impact on teaching that results, and mentors cannot tell others what they know.

Decision makers need to hear how successful the program is because they probably have no personal reason to value it. They need to see the difference mentoring can make in the lives of novice teachers, and they surely need to see the improvements in that novice's teaching and the results in terms of student learning. How could they value mentoring more? Try these ideas.

Mentoring Administrators and Other Decision Makers

Any new person deserves a mentor, whether they are a beginning teacher, a beginning principal, a beginning curriculum director, or a new member of the Board of Education.

> If you want the new administrators or other decision makers to value mentoring of new teachers, give those same leaders mentors too.

If you want the new administrators or other decision makers to value mentoring of new teachers, give those same leaders mentors too. Once decision makers personally experience the challenges and the benefits of mentoring, they usually become strong supporters of a mentoring program for beginning teachers.

Celebrate Success

The invisibility of mentoring is a problem, because program leaders cannot ask mentors about their protégés, nor should they ask protégés about their mentors, due to their confidential relationship. The trick is to access the great learning and growth that occur within a quality mentoring experience without breaking that confidentiality. The solution involves ten steps you can follow, which I call the "capture the success" strategies. These were presented in the sections for novice and mentor peer support group activities. After following those directions, find several ways to share the group conclusions, such as in

- A staff development department newsletter to administrators
- The induction and mentoring program section of the district website
- The year-end induction and mentoring program results report
- Comments delivered to the Board of Education about the induction program.

Prompt Decision Makers Toward Support

An even better use of these comments is to provide them in advance to decision makers whom you invite to speak at mentor training events, mentor recognition dinners, and beginning teacher orientation week events. These are circumstances in which decision makers want to affirm the value of mentoring, but they may have very little of substance to say on the subject. The strategy is to provide them with the concrete evidence that both meets their need for specifics they can affirm and educates them about results.

Seek and Use In-Kind Support

While there is a limit to the money some external sources can give you, these sources *can provide* other kinds of support that let you save your own dollars for other uses. This is an in-kind resource. For example, perhaps your mentors need mentor training and you can share the cost with a regional service center that provides such a training. If that training is focused on beginning teacher assessment and accountability measures related to certification, you may feel their training is insufficient. Still, that training probably covers classroom observation and data collection methods or training in how to conduct pre- and post-observation coaching conferences, topics you won't have to address in your training. You can add any missing topics to that external training at reduced cost and for less effort.

A LAST WORD

As this book comes to a close, I want to congratulate you on your commitment to developing a mentoring and induction program that positively impacts teachers and students! Throughout this book, I have presented proven strategies and specific guidelines to help you reach that goal. Now I offer one last caution. Keep in mind that you are *not* doing all this planning, work, and data collection only to show that desired changes have occurred. Your goals should not be limited to teacher instructional behaviors that better match the program's Vision for Excellent Teaching and Learning or increases in student learning. If you focus on these, you may not have the information you need to ensure lasting change.

Sustaining the improvements you create *is* your ultimate purpose. You need to understand when and what *caused* the changes. In other words, your goal is not just to improve student learning, but to *learn how* to conduct an induction and mentoring program that increases teaching effectiveness and student achievement. The process of evaluation is an essential final step toward sustainable, lasting improvement. Blessings on your journey as you work toward this higher goal!

RESOURCES

Resource I

Internet and Organization Resources for Mentoring

1. Best Practice Resources for Mentoring in Education

- At <http://www.teachermentors.com>
- Tons of resources and advice for more effective mentoring K–20
- Professional training and consulting services
- One of the author's own websites

2. The Business Mentor Center

- At <http://www.BusinessMentorCenter.com>
- Best practice resources for mentoring in noneducation organizations
- Advice for more effective mentoring and results
- Professional training and consulting services
- One of the author's own websites

3. The International Mentoring Association

- At <http://www.mentoring-association.org>
- Over fifty pages of public resources and 350 pages of "members only" resources
- Website originally designed by Barry Sweeny
- The premier professional association for resources, support, and professional development in mentoring
- Mentoring Base of Knowledge—annotated bibliography with almost 4,000 citations
- Dynamic annual conference each spring
- Supports mentoring in every setting and organization type
- Especially strong in support for Mentor Program Coordinators

4. The Mentoring Leadership and Resource Network (MLRN)

- At <http://www.mentors.net>
- The mentoring network of members of the Association for Supervision and Curriculum Development
- Primarily an education-based focus
- Access to most resources requires inexpensive lifetime membership
- Less active in recent years

5. Peer Resources

- At <http://www.mentors.ca>
- The website of Dr. Rey Carr, mentoring expert in Canada
- Many excellent resources and great professional development opportunities
- E-mail-based newsletter
- Primarily membership-based support

Resource II

Mentor Training Activity

Practice in Identification of CBAM Stages of Concern

Leader Directions

1. This activity consists of seven scenarios and a total of fifteen characters. Copy the pages with the scenarios and then cut them apart and assemble them so that only one scenario is on a page. Prepare the number of copies of each scenario needed, one per character, including one complete set for yourself so you can be the "narrator."

Prepare the number of copies of each scenario needed, one per character, including one complete set for yourself so you can be the "narrator."

- Consider the number being trained. Since there are seven scenarios, it's best if each group has about seven people in it. That would use each person at least twice. If there are not enough for two or more small groups (fourteen?), then just do the activity as a whole group.
- Also, remember that only a few are speaking in each scenario and the rest are listening, which is the skill being practiced.

   Example A: A training group of about fifteen people—make two small groups, and make only two or three copies of each scenario to distribute, one for each character, for each of the small groups.

   Example B: A training group of thirty people—divide the group into four small groups and make two or three copies of each scenario for each of the small groups.

2. Tell the whole group:
   A. "Now we're going to do some dialogues to practice listening for clues and assessing the CBAM Stage of Concern that a person is at."

B. "The dialogues are primarily between a mentor and a protégé, but sometimes, a friend of the protégé is involved."

3. *Divide the whole group* into the number of small groups you planned in step 1.

4. *Tell the group:*
   A. "There are seven scenarios we will use. Each of you will take turns being either a mentor, protégé, or friend in the dialogues."
   B. "When it's *not* your turn to speak, you will be listening for clues that indicate the CBAM Stage of Concern that the protégé is at. Don't offer your opinion until the dialogue is finished."
   C. Tell them the characters needed for the first scenario and ask the groups to decide who will read each character.

5. *Give each group* just the number of copies of the scenario for the characters involved, and for just one scenario at a time, to keep them focused.

6. Before you start each scenario, *ask them,* "Who is the mentor? Who is the protégé? to check that they are ready to start.

7. *Tell them,* "I will time each scenario. You will have about one minute for the readers to read their parts to your group, and only three minutes to discuss it and decide the CBAM Stage of Concern" for the protégé.

ACTIVITY FOR MENTOR TRAINING: PRACTICE IN IDENTIFICATION OF CBAM STAGES OF CONCERN

Scenario #1 (Parts include Protégé, Mentor, and Friend)

Scene 1

The protégé is reading a teacher's manual and has several other magazines stacked on his desk. Another new teacher enters the room, greets the protégé, and asks

Friend: "How's it going?"

Protégé: "OK, I guess. I have been reading this stuff for several hours trying to find helpful ideas and I feel exhausted. I need to try something else."

Friend: "I know. We have to start everything from scratch. Why not ask your Mentor for help"?

Protégé: "Thanks. I'll do just that. Thanks for the encouragement."

Protégé leaves.

Scene 2

Protégé enters the mentor's room.

Protégé: "Hi! You're looking well today. A few weeks ago you offered to help me with planning more engaging class activities. I think at that time I felt I had lots of good ideas for that and so, I didn't feel I needed your help."

Mentor:	"I understood that. So, how has it gone?"
Protégé:	"Pretty good in some cases and terribly in others. I really can't figure out *why* what I do works some days and not on others! It's like there's something I don't know."
Mentor:	"OK, so what are you doing to ensure that your activities are engaging for students?"
Protégé:	"Well, I feel that not lecturing all the time and just *doing* activities makes it more engaging. Right?"
Mentor:	"That would be a good start, of course, but that doesn't explain *why* the students would feel engaged. So what's different about the activities you've done when students are and are not engaged?"
Protégé:	"I'd only be guessing to answer that. That's why I came to see you."
Mentor:	"OK, let's try a couple of options. Did you use technology in any activity?"
Protégé:	"Yes, and that worked great, but I can't do that every day!"
Mentor:	"OK. Did you hold any class discussions?"
Protégé:	"Whoa! Yes I did, but I won't do that very often. It was like a lead balloon."
Mentor:	"So, what happened?"
Protégé:	"I asked a series of questions, and every time, only one or two students would respond, and even then their response was just a sentence or two."
Mentor:	"Do you think all the students really knew the answers?"
Protégé:	"Definitely. It was stuff we'd already covered."
Mentor:	"So, if that's true, why did you expect them to get more engaged than they did?"
Protégé:	"Hmmmm. Are you saying that if they already know the answers, why would they want to discuss it again?"
Mentor:	"Yes. So what's the solution then?"
Protégé:	"To have them discuss things for which the answers aren't already known?"
Mentor:	"I think that's a reasonable hypothesis. Why not just try it?"
Protégé:	"I will."
Mentor:	"OK, now, why do you think your students found the technology assignment so engaging?"
Protégé:	"Well . . . probably because the questions they were researching hadn't yet been answered."
Mentor:	"Probably true. So, how do you plan to use this idea to improve their learning?"
Protégé:	"I don't know, but . . . I will develop a lesson plan that we could discuss. OK?"
Mentor:	"Great. When do you want to meet again? Tomorrow morning?"

ACTIVITY FOR MENTOR TRAINING: PRACTICE IN IDENTIFICATION OF CBAM STAGES OF CONCERN

Scenario #2 (Parts include Protégé and Mentor)

The protégé is working in her room. Her mentor enters and greets her. This experienced teacher teaches the same level and content to other students as does the new teacher.

Mentor:	"Hi. I wanted to let you know that the lesson you developed and shared with the team at the last team meeting has been used by just about all of us now, and several of us like it. I think we'd all agree it works very well for what we needed."
Protégé:	"Cool! I'm glad it's worked as well as it has for folks. I like it too. But it seems like they found that 'several' do and some don't think it's effective."
Mentor:	"Well, we all wish it was not so time consuming."
Protégé:	"Hmmm. I agree with that."
Mentor:	"I hope you're not offended. You did ask."
Protégé:	"You are not the only person to feel that way. I've been thinking about that problem too."
Mentor:	"Good, I'm glad to hear that. I'd look forward to seeing any changes you make."
	Protégé looks frustrated.
Protégé:	"I said I was thinking about the problem, not that I have any solution in mind. I really think that lesson is about as good as I know how to make it."
Mentor:	"I know what you mean. Sometimes we can't see the forest for the trees. Why don't we put it on the team agenda for the next meeting and see what we can develop together?"
Protégé:	"Super, I am ready for that! The more brains, the better!"

ACTIVITY FOR MENTOR TRAINING: PRACTICE IN IDENTIFICATION OF CBAM STAGES OF CONCERN

Scenario #3 (Parts include Protégé and Mentor)

Scene 1

It's 4:30 p.m. and the protégé stops by her mentor's room.

Protégé:	"Hello. How are you today?"
Mentor:	"I'm beat, but I'm fine really. How are you doing?"
Protégé:	"Well, I'm pretty beat too, but I need some help. Got a few minutes?"
Mentor:	"For you, I always have time. What's up?"

Protégé: "Well, our beloved administrator stopped by to inform me she'd be visiting my classroom to observe my teaching in a few days."

Mentor: "She observes all of us, but especially new staff. So how do you feel about it?"

Protégé: "No problem generally, but she asked if at some point she could observe me doing a cooperative learning lesson."

Mentor: "OK, so I know you can do that. No problem, right?"

Protégé: "Well, when she said that, I told her I'd studied and taught a few cooperative learning lessons before. But then she said she'd want to know in advance what 'structure' I planned to use. That's what threw me. What in the world is a cooperative learning 'structure'?"

Mentor: "Oh . . . so you studied Johnson and Johnson's model, right?"

Protégé: "Right. So what?"

Mentor: "Well, what you don't already know is that she is trained in the Keagan Model. Ever hear of that?"

Protégé: "Nope. So do I have to learn the Keagan Model? Do I have to do it her way? And . . . is the Keagan Model a better one? What's the difference?"

Mentor: "Whoa! Those are great questions! Thanks for being so candid. That really helps me to know what you need to learn and where we need to start. Let's take those questions one at a time . . ."

ACTIVITY FOR MENTOR TRAINING: PRACTICE IN IDENTIFICATION OF CBAM STAGES OF CONCERN

Scenario #4 (Parts include Protégé and Mentor)

Scene 1

The scene opens with the protégé at work in his room. The protégé's mentor enters and greets the protégé by name and then says . . .

Mentor: "We have touched based a few times but haven't really talked in any depth recently, so I thought I'd check in with you. How do you feel about your growth as a teacher and your work recently?"

Protégé: "Well, I confess to feeling a bit restless to move on now because I have pretty much completed the unit you and I developed back in August."

Mentor: "I know it's been five weeks, but that seems a bit too quick. My students aren't that far along! Did you do the whole unit we planned?"

Protégé: "Our plans worked great. Yes, I've just about finished it all and I'm ready to tackle the next unit."

Mentor: "OK, so you're feeling restless and want a new challenge. Have your students learned all that this area has to offer? We just need to be sure that *they* feel ready to move on."

Protégé: "Well, they did well on the unit exam, and they are able to apply their learning in the class discussions we're having now when I probe for their depth of understanding. Maybe I could do more with the topics, but I do think I've accomplished and learned all that I need to by this point in my career."

Mentor: "I hear you, but I guess I should have been in observing you at least once. I just wonder if I'd agree that your students are ready to move on now. Anyway, it's probably too late for that now. So let's plan some time to meet to look at the next unit. That will help me prepare for it too."

Protégé: "Great. Thank you. How about tomorrow if we meet here after school, say at 4:30? I'll bring the pizza."

ACTIVITY FOR MENTOR TRAINING: PRACTICE IN IDENTIFICATION OF CBAM STAGES OF CONCERN

Scenario #5 (Parts include Protégé and Mentor)

The protégé enters his mentor's room, greets the mentor, and asks to sit down and talk. He is concerned about an upcoming student assignment and his lesson plans for it.

Mentor: "So, how is it going?"

Protégé: "Well, so far my assignments have worked pretty well, thanks to your ideas and my familiarity with the topics. However, I have a new assignment I'm developing and it's on a topic in which I don't have any experience. It's kept my head in the books the last few nights trying to get ready."

Mentor: "OK, what do you need to know about the assignment topic?"

Protégé: "That's not the issue. I *know* the topic but I want to make sure I have a good plan that will make students use higher level, critical thinking strategies in their work. I've been reading up on Bloom's Taxonomy again, just to refresh my mind on it, so that's OK."

Mentor: "So, what's *not* OK?"

Protégé: "I can't figure out how to be sure the students think at those higher levels."

Mentor: "OK, so I'll use those Bloom levels now and we can figure out a plan together, OK?"

Protégé: "What do you mean 'You'll use the Bloom levels'?"

Mentor: "I just think that I have to use the levels if you are going to learn to use them too. OK?"

Protégé: "Wait a minute! What you're telling me really is that, if I use the Bloom levels, the students will use them too. Is that it?"

Mentor: "Right. You got it! Now, you just pay attention to the *verbs* I use as we work on this, maybe take notes. Are you ready?"

Protégé: "Cool. OK, let's start."

Mentor: "Fine. Let's start by you *recalling* what the Bloom levels are."

Protégé: "Wait! Awesome! By your use of the verb 'recall,' I'm set up to think at the knowledge level."

Mentor: "Bingo!"

Protégé: "Wait a minute. I can really see what's got to happen. Wow, you are good! I'm going back to my room to see if I can plan this by myself now, OK?"

(Mentor smiles)

Mentor: "OK, you're sure?"

Protégé: "Yep, I get it. I'll let you know how it goes."

The protégé gets up to leave and thanks the mentor.

ACTIVITY FOR MENTOR TRAINING: PRACTICE IN IDENTIFICATION OF CBAM STAGES OF CONCERN

Scenario #6 (Parts include Protégé and Friend)

The protégé is working alone in her classroom, writing, checking other resources, and looking a bit frustrated. A new teacher peer of hers walks in and greets her.

Friend: "Hey, how's it going? Oops! Am I interrupting you?"

Protégé: "Well, yes you are, but it's a very welcome break."

Friend: "You look sort of intense. What are you into?"

Protégé: "Well, a few weeks ago I designed a lesson plan for my team on a topic to address a gap in the curriculum. First I used it, and then the whole team tried it out."

Friend: "So . . . how did it work out? Did they like it?"

Protégé: "It went pretty rough at first when I used it, so I made a few refinements to it that were a definite improvement. That's when I gave it to the others."

Friend: "And did they like it?"

Protégé: "Yeah, they all did."

Friend: "It seems like you should be happy, not frustrated."

Protégé: "Yeah, except when our team sat down to review the student results, we were all disappointed. They were just average and about 40 percent didn't pass. Since we all tried to carefully follow the lesson plan, we concluded that the lesson was the problem, not our teaching. So now I'm working on it again to improve it even more. Even though it works OK, the results are not as good as I want."

Friend: "So why don't you ask your mentor to help you? I'm sure she'd be glad to."

Protégé: "Oh, I agree she would help me, but I wanted to see how much I can accomplish on my own first. I'm sure I can figure out further improvements. I guess I just want to prove to myself that I can do it."

Friend: "Well, I wish you success. I gotta go. See you."

Protégé: "Thanks. Bye!"

ACTIVITY FOR MENTOR TRAINING: PRACTICE IN IDENTIFICATION OF CBAM STAGES OF CONCERN

Scenario #7 (Parts include Protégé and Mentor)

The protégé is in her mentor's room and they are talking.

Mentor: "OK, so it sounds like you feel you're getting the hang of it now. Am I right?"

Protégé: "Yes. This morning was the third time I tried the strategy with students and it's feeling a lot more comfortable now. Thank goodness!"

Mentor: "Why do you say 'Thank goodness'?"

Protégé: "Well, it was pretty stressful the first two times. I thought I knew what I was doing, but I discovered pretty quickly that it was going to take a while to develop the skills I needed to do it well. It took every ounce of brain power I had to get it right. And when other things went wrong, I couldn't handle it all."

Mentor: "I know. I was there, remember?"

Protégé: "Yeah, and I also remember being really embarrassed too! Thanks for not being critical at that point. I really needed your support to just get through it. I think I was struggling because there was just too much that I knew needed to be used, but I wasn't always sure when to do what. I'm sure glad you were there!"

Mentor: "That's interesting. If you were embarrassed and felt it wasn't going well, why were you glad I was there?"

Protégé: "Because every time I saw you, I knew you cared and wouldn't be negative. And, I remembered what you said about staying focused on the overall objective. That helped me to figure out which of my options would be best to choose at that moment."

Mentor: "OK, so this morning was the third time you used the strategy. Is it as stressful now?"

Protégé: "Not too bad. But, I still have to think carefully about what I'm doing. Now I know what to expect will happen, and I am just better at doing it than I was before."

Mentor: "So, are you ready for me to suggest a more complex version of this strategy?"

Protégé: "Whoa! Not yet. That could be a little overwhelming still! I think I want to do the process once more and see if I can do it completely without struggling. I just want to assure myself that I know what I'm doing."

Mentor: "That makes good sense and that's what I feel would be best too. But eventually we do need to add in a couple more variations before it'll be as powerful for students as I know you want it to be."

Protégé: "Well, I'm glad it's no more complex than it is right now. So far, it's just right for my skill level."

Mentor: "Good. That's exactly what we need. Well, let me know how it goes the next time you use the strategy, OK?"

MENTOR TRAINING ACTIVITY: PRACTICE IN IDENTIFICATION OF CBAM STAGES OF CONCERN

Leader's Answers

Scenario #1: Information

The protégé is trying to *do* things (trying to be at the management stage) that are not working. The mentor uncovers that the reason is the protégé does not really *know* what makes a lesson or activity engaging for students. The discussion shows the mentor helping the protégé to go back and get the missing *information.* After that, the mentor could help the protégé to *plan* (personal) how to implement it.

It could have also been "consequence" or "collaboration," but the protégé was not feeling successful yet, so it was not these stages.

Scenario #2: Collaboration

The protégé is implementing and has mastered a task to the point of establishing a routine that does not require full attention to execute it. Also, the desired results of the activity are acceptable. However, the results of the activity are not yet of as high a quality as is desired, and the protégé has done as much as she is capable of doing to improve those results. Therefore, the protégé seeks the advice of others to further improve results.

Scenario #3: Awareness

The protégé is unaware of what the Keagan Cooperative Learning Model is, and of what is needed to successfully do an activity using that model. To start with, the protégé asks a few questions. Pretty soon, though, the protégé's questions will stop because the protégé is not sure of all the questions that she might ask which would be appropriate for a discussion about the Keagan Model.

Scenario #4: Refocusing

The protégé has mastered an area and is easily capable of doing the tasks successfully and independently and of producing a high level of results. Therefore the protégé is seeking and ready for a new task or area of responsibility.

Scenario #5: Personal

The protégé has *sufficient information* and conceptual understanding of a task or skill and what should be done. However, the protégé has little or no experience in doing the activity and is reluctant to start. The protégé is concerned with the implications of the information for his own work. Therefore, he is focused on what is expected of him and then is ready to plan what needs to be done.

Scenario #6: Consequence

The protégé has gained sufficient skill to do the activity at a competent level with OK results. Now she has begun to shift attention to doing *what she can do by herself* to increase the effectiveness of the activity so it will achieve *better results.*

Scenario #7: Management

The protégé is past learning *about* a task and is understanding his own responsibilities for the activity. He has already developed a plan for using his knowledge to do the activity. Now the protégé is doing the activity and is focused on developing and mastering the skills needed to adequately do it. At first the protégé wants to just get the work done. As the protégé's skills at managing the task increase, the activity becomes more of a routine and the protégé becomes more comfortable and confident doing it.

Resource III

Mentor Practice Scenarios

Ending Your Conversations

Summary: There are two scenarios, which each pair role-plays one at a time. Each person in the pair fills the role of protégé and mentor once.

Leader Directions

Before the Practice Activity

Copy the pages with the scenarios so you can cut, separate, and assemble them. Protégés and mentors should receive the information intended for both of them, as well as their individual sections. Make sufficient individual copies of the scenarios so that eventually each person will get one of each of the two scenarios. For example, if there are 28 mentors to be trained, during Scenario #1 one half of these (fourteen) will need the protégé section and fourteen will need the mentor section. However, double these numbers as each person will play a role in two scenarios.

To Start the Practice Activity

1. Divide training participants into pairs. If there is a person with no partner, ask the less active of the mentor trainers to be the *protégé.*

2. Assign one participant to be a mentor and the other to role-play being a protégé.

3. Give half the protégés their copy of Scenario #1, and their mentors the mentor section for Scenario #1. Do the same for the other half of the group, giving them the appropriate protégé or mentor sections for Scenario #2.

4. Tell them they are to:
   A. Individually read their scenario. Allow two to three minutes.

B. Ask the trainer if there are any questions.

C. Roughly follow their personal "script" for the scenario.

D. Continue the conversation, role-playing an appropriate transition to the "three debriefing questions" that they will use to end their meeting. Mentors, it's OK to refer to the page on the "three debriefing questions."

E. Point out that the idea is for mentors to ensure that the protégé's learning from this meeting is applied in their classroom to benefit their students.

F. Tell them they have about eight more minutes to finish. Say "Go!"

After Each Practice Scenario

1. Ask protégés to stay seated and mentors to stand and give protégés their mentor section from the scenario they have just completed.

2. Have mentors stand along one of two opposite walls, one for those who did Scenario #1 and the other wall for those who did Scenario #2.

3. Ask mentors what CBAM stage they think the protégé was at in their scenario. Give each group five minutes to decide and elect a spokesperson to report their decision.

4. Meanwhile, with the protégés, tell them
   A. *Not* to trade protégé notes for the new scenario, because they will now become mentors for the scenario they have not yet practiced.
   B. Ask them to stand by their first scenario number on the remaining opposite walls.
   C. Ask them to move toward the center of the room and to meet someone from the other scenario, and exchange the *mentor* section of the scenario they already did for their next scenario. Then they can be seated again.

5. Tell them they will become a mentor and role-play the other scenario that they have not yet done. Also tell them they must select a new partner to be their protégé when the two previous "mentor" groups finish reporting. Ask them to read their new scenario now to prepare and to think about their task. They should identify and address the CBAM Stage, and end with the "three debriefing questions."

A note to the leader: This approach of having both scenarios going at the same time has several benefits, one of which is the moving around required at this time in the afternoon. If you wish, you can have all do one scenario, then the other later, but it's not so much fun.

MENTOR PRACTICE SCENARIO #1

Information for Both the Protégé and Mentor

- The date is October 2 of the protégé's first year.
- The protégé is twenty-one years old and just out of a five-year program with an MS in education. Except for some observing, lesson teaching, and student teaching as a preservice student, this is the protégé's first teaching job.
- The protégé teaches sixth grade social studies for four periods and one two-period section of an integrated class called "The Human Journey," a "humanities" class, with an art and a science teacher. These three teachers meet for a joint planning one period a day.

Protégé Section: Scenario #1

The protégé role-plays being at the mechanical management stage of the CBAM. Do not tell that stage to your mentor. Being at this stage means that the protégé

- Is at work implementing effective teaching as best as possible
- Is not very satisfied with several aspects of his or her teaching
- Has several problems to solve to get better at the assigned work
- Doesn't want more theory
- Is struggling to integrate what he or she already knows with what is being learned.

The basic issue for which you'd like the mentor's help is that you love teaching social studies and "Human Journey," but they are very different from each other and that difference makes you feel like two people instead of one.

"Human Journey" is tons of fun. You like working with the art and the science teacher. You like blending the history of culture, of humanity, and of science, and the kids love it too. You also feel that, even though you have a mentor, that the "Journey" team also mentors you. You really love the interaction with them and the project-oriented approach the three of you use to structure the class.

You feel very good about sixth grade social studies because you know the American colonial era content so well. However, you are aware the kids feel bored and uninterested. You have way too much to cover, but you wish you could figure out what's so cool about the "Journey" class and incorporate it into social studies to bring it to life.

Your assigned mentor is also a social studies teacher whom you've invited to talk. You have met four times before. When asked what you have learned from mentoring, state "the value of finding and then using your gifts to do your work."

Mentor Section: Scenario #1

After about five weeks of teaching, your protégé seems to be getting a solid handle on managing paperwork, time issues, and management of discipline. So think for a minute about what stage of CBAM that would be.

The protégé has invited you to stop in to talk, saying, "I need some help thinking about my teaching assignments and own teaching styles." On hearing this, you agree to meet after school to talk. This will be the fifth time you both meet. You have also realized the protégé said "styles" (plural).

On thinking ahead about the meeting, you recall that the protégé is teaching two very different classes: sixth grade social studies, which is mostly American History of the Colonial era; and a humanities class called "The Human Journey," which means working with the art and a science teacher. You have never taught such an integrated class.

You should remain alert to any clues the protégé might give to check the CBAM stage they are at and think about what you might best do at that stage.

Your goal is to get the protégé to clearly define the problem, discover his or her own gifts as a teacher and person, and to figure out how to use those as one person, but in two different classes. You believe this can be done if the protégé just understands his or her gifts and real problem well.

Finally, remember to end the conversation with the "three debriefing questions," getting the protégé to modify personal learning to the instructional level to find a way to improve student learning.

MENTOR PRACTICE SCENARIO #2

Information for Both Mentor and Protégé

- It is mid-February of the protégé's first year.
- The protégé is forty-two years old and teaching with an alternative license while working in the evening to earn a regular teaching certificate. Except for some observing, lesson teaching, and four weeks of student teaching last summer, this is the protégé's first teaching job.
- The protégé teaches seventh grade science for five periods and has two planning periods a day—which seems to be what helps this new teacher survive!
- It also helps that, before becoming a teacher, the protégé was a successful science lab technician for twenty years. Content knowledge is not this teacher's challenge.
- The principal's evaluations have been marginal, focusing especially on the need for expectations that are more flexible and appropriate to the students. At the last visit, the principal gave the protégé a written warning about this issue.

Protégé Section: Scenario #2

- You want to stay in teaching.
- You know you have lots to learn about being an effective teacher and really helping students to learn.
- You are struggling because you feel the principal has asked you to back away from high standards for science learning. You have no clue how to lower expectations and still feel good about your teaching.
- You know so much about science and feel that if kids could learn enough, they too would love science.
- You feel you are about to be fired and, right or wrong, you must disclose these concerns to your mentor (another science teacher), and hopefully get the insights you need to keep your job.
- Still, you realize that it is you, not the mentor, who must make the changes.
- When the mentor asks what you have learned so far, state, "As great as my science knowledge is, it is far from all that I need to be a good teacher."
- Add that you feel principals need to give new teachers the time they need to learn how to be good teachers.

Mentor Section: Scenario #2

After about twenty-four weeks of teaching, your protégé seems to have a solid handle on managing paperwork, time issues, and management of discipline. So think for a moment about what Stage of CBAM that would be, but be careful. The protégé's real problem may not be so evident at first.

The protégé has invited you to stop in for a talk, saying, "I need some help thinking about my teaching. The principal is thinking about firing me." On hearing this, you agree to meet after school to talk. This will be the third time you have both met for an extended visit. You have not been able to get the protégé to agree to let you observe and coach; nor has the protégé really ever shared deeply about what's going on in his heart and mind.

Earlier, you showed the protégé the seventh grade science curriculum, but the protégé seems to know a lot, or at least thinks he does. You have been asked for help pretty rarely.

The principal has told you the protégé needs to "get a life!" and "teach at a college." You are not sure what that really means, but can guess.

On thinking ahead, about the meeting, you recall that the protégé is teaching seventh grade science for five periods and has two planning periods a day.

You should remain alert to any clues the protégé might give to check the CBAM stage he is at and think about what you might best do at that stage.

Your goal is to get the protégé to clearly define the problem and develop a plan of action for improvement of the protégé's teaching.

Finally, remember to end the conversation with the "three debriefing questions," getting the protégé to

- Articulate his learning as a new teacher
- Modify that personal learning to fit the instructional level
- Spell out a way to use his insights to improve student learning

References

Alliance for Excellent Education. (2004). *Tapping the potential: Retaining and developing high-quality new teachers.* Washington, DC: Alliance for Excellent Education.

Auton, S., Berry, D., Mullen, S., & Cochran, R. (2002). Induction program for beginners benefits veteran teachers, too. *Journal of Staff Development, 23*(4). Retrieved from <www.nsdc.org/library/publications/isd/auton234.cfm>.

Bartell, C. A. (1995). Shaping teacher induction policy in California. *Teacher Education Quarterly, 22*(4), 27–43.

Bartell, C. A. (2005). *Cultivating high quality teaching through induction and mentoring.* Thousand Oaks, CA: Corwin Press.

Berlinger, D. C. (1998). Implications of studies of expertise in pedagogy for teacher education and evaluation. In *New directions for teacher assessment.* Proceedings of the 1988 ETS Invitational Conference (pp. 39–68). Princeton, NJ: ETS.

Bird, T. (1986). *The mentor's dilemma.* San Francisco: Far West Regional Laboratory for Educational Research and Development.

Blackburn, J. (1977). *The first-year teacher: Perceived needs, intervention strategies and results.* Paper presented to the American Educational Research Association.

Breax, A., & Wong, H. K. (2003). *New teacher induction: How to train, support and retain new teachers.* Mountain View, CA: Harry K. Wong.

Brewster, C., & Railsback, J. (2001). *Supporting beginning teachers: How administrators, teachers, and policy makers can help new teachers succeed.* Portland, OR: Northwest Regional Educational Laboratory.

Burden, P. R. (1990). Teacher development. In W. R. Houston (Ed.), *Handbook of research on teacher education* (pp. 311–328). New York: Macmillan.

Calderhead, J. (1992). The role of reflection in learning to teach. In V. L. Valli (Ed.), *Reflective teacher education: Causes and critiques.* Albany, NY: State University of New York Press.

California Department of Education (1992). Effects of new teacher support. *Teacher Connections, 1,* 6–7.

Connor, K., & Killmer, N. (1995). *Evaluation of cooperating teacher effectiveness.* Paper presented at the annual meeting of the Midwest Educational Research Association, Chicago, IL.

Coy, L. (2003a). *Advisory Board guidelines.* Retrieved August 2006 from <www.t2t.fms.k12.nm.us/ab>.

Coy, L. (2003b). *Farmington municipal schools mentor plan.* Retrieved August 2006 from <www.t2t.fms.k12.nm.us/instforms/forms/pdf/FMSMentorPlan.pdf>.

Coy, L. (2003c). *Transition to teaching: Consortium goals and objectives.* Retrieved August 2006 from <www.t2t.fms.k12.nm.us/data/t2tdata_year2.pdf>.

DuFour, R. (2003). "Collaboration lite" puts student achievement on a starvation diet. *Journal of Staff Development, 24*(4), 63–64.

Elsner, K. (1984). *First year evaluation results from Oklahoma's entry-year assistance committees.* Paper presented at the annual meeting of the Association of Teacher Educators, New Orleans.

Fendler, L. (2003). Teacher reflection in a hall of mirrors: Historical influences and political reverberations. *Educational Researcher, 32*(3), 16–25.

Fenstermacher, G. D. (1990). Some moral considerations on teaching as a profession. In J. Goodlad, R. Soder, & K. Sirotnik (Eds.), *Moral dimensions of teaching.* San Francisco: Jossey-Bass.

Fideler, E. F., & Haselkorn, D. (1999). *Learning the ropes: Urban teacher induction programs and practices in the United States.* Belmont, MA: Recruiting New Teachers.

Golden Teachers Program (2006). Golden Teachers Program goals. Retrieved April 16, 2006, at <http://goldenteachers.cps.k12.il.us/home/2goals.htm>.

Gordon, S. (1991). *How to help beginning teachers succeed.* Alexandria, VA: Association for Supervision and Curriculum Development.

Gordon, T. (2000). *Parent effectiveness training.* Solana Beach, CA: Gordon Training International.

Guillaume, A. M., & Rudney, G. L. (2002). *Faith, feedback and freedom: Student teachers' preferences for cooperating teachers' characteristics and behaviors.* Paper presented at the annual meeting of the American Educational Research Association, New Orleans.

Gusky, T. R., & Peterson, K. D. (1996). The road to classroom change. *Educational Leadership, 53*(4), 10–14.

Hall, J. L. (2003). *Title II: Impact on training mentors in a Utah school district.* Philadelphia, PA: Conference Proceedings of the International Mentoring Association Annual Conference.

Hawk, P. (1984). *Making a difference: Reflections and thoughts of first-year teachers.* Greenville, NC: East Carolina University.

Hidalgo, F. (1986). The evolving concerns of first-year junior high school teachers in difficult settings: Three case studies. *Action in Teacher Education*, *8*(4). 75–79.

Hord, S., Rutherford, W., Hulling-Austin, L., & Hall, G. (1987). *Taking charge of change.* Alexandria, VA: Association for Supervision and Curriculum Development.

Houston, R. W., Marshall, F., & McDavid, T. (1993). Problems of traditionally prepared and alternatively certified first-year teachers. *Education and Urban Society*, *26*(1), 78–89.

Huling, L., & Resta, V. (2001). *Teacher mentoring as professional development.* Washington, DC: ERIC Clearinghouse on Teaching and Teacher Education Digest.

Huling-Austin, L., Barnes, S., & Smith, J. (1985). *A research-based staff development program for beginning teachers.* Paper presented at the annual meeting of the American Educational Research Association, Chicago.

Huling-Austin, L., & Murphy, S. (1987). *Assessing the impact of teacher induction programs: Implications for program development.* Paper presented at the annual meeting of the American Educational Research Association, Washington, DC.

Johnson, S. M. (2004). *Finders and keepers: Helping new teachers survive and thrive in our schools.* San Francisco: Jossey-Bass.

Jonson, K. F. (2002). *Being an effective mentor: How to help beginning teachers succeed.* Thousand Oaks, CA: Corwin Press.

Joyce, B. R., Showers, B., & Fullan, M. (2002). *Student achievement through staff development* (3rd ed.). Alexandria, VA: Association for Supervision and Curriculum Development.

Kardos, S., & Liu, E. (2003). New research finds school hiring and support falls short. Retrieved April 18, 2006, at <www.researchmatters.harvard.edu/story.php?article_id+634>.

Kellaher, A., & Maher, J. (2003). My mentor, myself. *Journal of Staff Development, 24*(4). Retrieved from <www.nsdc.org/library/publications/jsd/kellaher244.cfm>.

Kilburg, G. M. (2005). *Making sense of three mentoring team relationships and the obstacles they encountered on a recurring basis: A research report.* Retrieved April 10, 2006, from the International Mentoring Association website, <www.mentoring-association.org>.

Kilburg, G. M., & Hancock, T. (2003). *Addressing sources of collateral damage in mentoring programs.* Paper presented at the Annual Meeting of the American Educational Research Association, Chicago, IL.

Killion, J. (2002). *Assessing impact: Evaluating staff development.* Oxford, OH: National Staff Development Council.

Kirkpatrick, D. L. (1994). *Evaluating training programs: The four levels.* San Francisco: Berrett-Koehler.

Knowles, M. S. (1980). *The modern practice of adult education: From pedagogy to androgogy* (2nd ed.). Chicago: Association/Follett.

Lipton, L., & Wellman, B. (2001). *Mentoring matters: A practical guide to learning-focused relationships.* Sherman, CT: Mira Via.

Magee, M. (1999). Curse of the trophy. *Journal of Stagg Development, 20*(4), 23–26.

Maslow, A. (1987). *Motivation and personality* (3rd ed.). New York: Addison Wesley.

McArthur, J. (1978). What does teaching do to teachers? *Educational Administration Quarterly, 14*(3), 89–103.

McDonald, F. (1980). *The problems of beginning teachers: A crisis in training: Vol. 1—Study of induction programs for beginning teachers.* Princeton, NJ: Educational Testing Service.

Moir, E. (2005). Launching the next generation of teachers: The New Teacher Center's model for quality induction and mentoring. In H. Portner (Ed.), *Teacher mentoring and induction: The state of the art and beyond.* Thousand Oaks, CA: Corwin Press.

Moir, E., & Glees, J. (2001). Quality induction: An investment in teachers. *Teacher Education Quarterly, 28*(1), 109–114.

Moir, E., Glees, J., & Baron, W. (1999). A support program with heart: The Santa Cruz project. In M. Scherer (Ed.), *A better beginning: Supporting and mentoring new teachers.* Alexandria, VA: Association for Supervision and Curriculum Development.

Moss, P. A., Schultz, A. M., & Collins, K. (1998). An interpretive approach to portfolio evaluation for teacher licensure. *Journal for Personnel Evaluation, 12*(2), 161–192.

Mutchler, S., Pan, D., Glover, R., & Shapley, K. (2002). *Mentoring beginning teachers: Lessons from the experience in Texas.* Southwest Educational Development Laboratory, Policy Research Report. Retrieved April 16, 2006, from <www.sedl.org/pubs/policy23>.

No Child Left Behind Act of 2001. (2004). Retrieved May 2, 2004, from <www.ed.gov/policy/elsec/leg/esea02>.

Odell, S. J. (1986). Developing support programs for beginning teachers. In L. Huling-Austin, S. J. Odell, P. Ishler, R. S. Kay, & R. A. Edelfelt (Eds.), *Assisting the beginning teacher.* Reston, VA: Association of Teacher Educators.

Olebe, M. G. (1998). Personal discussion with Barry Sweeny.

Olsen, K. D. (1999). The California mentor/teacher role: Owners' manual. Kent, WA: Books for Educators.

Parsad, B., Lewis, L., & Farris, E. (2000). Topic: Elementary and secondary education, teacher preparation and professional development, Retrieved from <http://nces.ed.gov/programs/quarterly/Vol_3_3/g3-3.asp>.

Peske, H. G., Liu, E., Johnson, S. M., Kauffman, D., & Kardos, S.M. (2001). The next generation of teachers: Changing conceptions of the career of teaching. *Phi Delta Kappan, 83*(40), 304–311.

Phillips, Jack J. (1996). Measuring ROI: The fifth level of evaluation. *Technical and Skills Training,* April, 10–13.

Portner, H. (Ed.) (2005). *Teacher mentoring and induction: The state of the art and beyond.* Thousand Oaks, CA: Corwin Press.

Richardson, J. (1997). Teachers can be leaders of change. *School Team Innovator,* March. Retrieved April 8, 2007, from <www.nsdc.org/library/publications/innovator/inn3-97rich.cfm>.

Romer, T. (1999). E-mail correspondence with author.

Rowley, J. (1999). *The good mentor: Educational leadership* (pp. 20–22). Alexandria, VA: Association for Supervision and Curriculum Development.

Rudney, G. L., & Guillaume, A. M. (2003). *Maximum mentoring: An action guide for teacher trainers and cooperating teachers.* Thousand Oaks, CA: Corwin Press.

Saffold, F. (2004). *Renewing experienced teachers through mentoring.* Paper presented to the annual conference of the International Mentoring Association, Tampa, FL.

Sandefur, J. (1982). What happens to the teacher during induction? In G. Hall (Ed.), *Beginning teacher induction: Five dilemmas* (pp. 41–46). Austin, TX: University of Texas at Austin, R&D Center for Teacher Education.

Sanders, W., & Rivers, J. (1996). Cumulative and residual effects of teachers on future student academic achievement. In National Council for Accreditation of Teacher Education (Ed.), *Summary of 1977–2002 data on teacher effectiveness, teacher quality and qualifications.* Washington, DC: National Council for Accreditation of Teacher Education.

Summers, J. (1987). *Summative evaluation report: Project CREDIT.* Terre Haute, IN: Indiana State University.

Sweeny, B. W. (1995). *Promoting the growth of new teachers: A mentor training manual.* Wheaton, IL: Resources for Staff and Organization Development.

Sweeny, B. W. (1996). *What to do and when to do it: Monthly mentor reminders.* Wheaton, IL: Best Practice Resources.

Sweeny, B. W. (2001). *Mentoring of mentors: How leaders ensure high impact mentoring.* Wheaton, IL: Best Practice Resources, Inc.

Sweeny, B. W. (2002a). *Administrative strategies for the challenges in new teacher support and success.* Wheaton, IL. Best Practice Resources.

Sweeny, B. W. (2002b). *Non financial costs of teacher attrition.* Wheaton, IL: Best Practice Resources.

Sweeny, B. W. (2003a). *The shifting balance of sources to which novice teachers turn.* Wheaton, IL: Best Practice Resources.

Sweeny, B. W. (2003b). *High impact strategies for mentor selection and mentor-protégé matching.* Wheaton, IL: Best Practice Resources.

Sweeny, B. W. (2005). Mentoring: A matter of time and timing. In H. Portner (Ed.), *Teacher mentoring and induction: The state of the art and beyond.* Thousand Oaks, CA: Corwin Press.

Sweeny, B., & Johnson, S. (1999). *Mentoring to improve schools.* Alexandria, VA: Association for Supervision and Curriculum Development. (Two-video set including Facilitator's Guide.)

Texas Center for Education Research (2000). *The cost of teacher turnover.* Prepared for the Texas State Board for Educator Certification, Austin, TX. Retrieved from <www.sbec.state.tx.us/SBECInline/txbes/turnoverrpt.pdf>.

Turk, R. L. (1999). Get on the team: An alternative mentoring model. *Classroom Leadership Online, 2*(8). Retrieved from <www.ascd,org/readingroom/classlead.html>.

Udelhofen, J., & Larson, K. (2003). *The mentoring year: A step-by-step program for professional development.* Thousand Oaks, CA: Corwin Press.

Veenman, S. (1984). Perceived problems of beginning teachers. *Review of Educational Research, 54*(2), 143–178.

Veenman, S. (1985). Perceived problems of beginning teachers: Review of research in teacher education. *Teachers College Record, 87*, 53–65.

Weeks, D. (1992). *The eight essential steps to conflict resolution.* Los Angeles: Jeremy P. Tarcher.

Wong, H. (1997). *The first days of school: How to be an effective teacher* (3rd ed.). Mountain View, CA: Harry K. Wong. (Includes a thirty-eight-minute CD video.)

Wong, H. (2001). Mentoring can't do it all. *Education Week, 22*(43), 46–50.

Wong, H. K. (2005). New teacher induction: The foundation for comprehensive, coherent and sustained professional development. In H. Portner (Ed.), *Teacher mentoring and induction: The state of the art and beyond.* Thousand Oaks, CA: Corwin Press.

Index

CORWIN
PRESS

The Corwin Press logo—a raven striding across an open book—represents the union of courage and learning. Corwin Press is committed to improving education for all learners by publishing books and other professional development resources for those serving the field of PreK–12 education. By providing practical, hands-on materials, Corwin Press continues to carry out the promise of its motto: **"Helping Educators Do Their Work Better."**

NATIONAL ASSOCIATION
OF SECONDARY SCHOOL
PRINCIPALS

Promoting Excellence in School Leadership

The National Association of Secondary School Principals—promoting excellence in school leadership since 1916—provides its members the professional resources to serve as visionary leaders. NASSP further promotes student leadership development through its sponsorship of the National Honor Society®, the National Junior Honor Society®, and the National Association of Student Councils®. For more information visit, www.principals.org.